Emperor of The World

A Novel
by Tom Scott

Dedicated to the men and women of the Armed Forces of the United States; especially those serving in harms way.

Acknowledgments

Thank you, Lord, for my many blessings; whatever abilities I have are given to me by You.

Thank you also to Dr. Claire Scott, Kristine Lay, Mike Perrotta, and Dick and Betty Bartlett, for their comments and suggestions.

My everlasting appreciation is given to Lynn, my wife of over 31 years, whose love for me, patience toward me, confidence in me, and understanding of me, helped accomplish one of my dreams.

Chapter 1

Sheila Rodriguez was a licensed Customs House Broker; a fact she was quick to point out to prospective clients of her company. She had already entered the required Customs shipping and classification information into her company's computer. The computer transmitted the information to the U.S. Customs and Border Protection computers. If Customs accepted the information, the cargo shipment would be released electronically, as the railroad car was rolling across the border.

Every commercial shipment that entered the United States required some type of release from Customs and Border Protection before it could be delivered. There was a classification number and a rate of duty for everything under the sun, from turnips to spacecraft. Figuring out the classification could be complicated and time consuming for importers, so Customs gave tests to prove that a Customs Broker knew his or her job. If you passed the test, Customs issued a license as proof to the importing public.

In the old days, all of the Customs releases were done with paper and ink. In the modern age of computers, the amount of paper was reduced, and cargo releases were mostly transmitted electronically.

Sometimes cargo shipments were delayed by the Border Patrol officers because they saw people hiding on top of the rail cars, and sometimes they just wanted to open a boxcar and do a spot check. Sheila hated the delays, but realized it was to be expected. It was international cargo, and those things happened. When delays did occur, the importers started calling her demanding that she do something. There were no delays this time.

This chemical shipment was identical to all the other ones for this importer. The invoice said it was a mixture of chemicals used in the production of anti-freeze. She used the same classification numbers she used on the other shipments, and Custom's computer programs accepted everything she had entered.

Sheila was no dummy. She had been in the brokerage business for over 20 years, and she knew what classification numbers would trigger a Custom's examination, and which numbers were safe and wouldn't. She didn't have to play with the classification numbers this time; the truth was good enough for a quick release. She was honest, most of the time, but not so honest she couldn't be persuaded to use safe numbers if a shipment was really important. Of course she expected something in return for the risk she was taking. Loyalty, an expensive dinner, or money; it depended on the customer and her mood at the time. That was how things worked on the border. Everybody wanted *something*, and *something* wasn't free for the asking.

She received the electronic release from Customs. If she had known the use these chemical shipments were being put to, she would have reported it to Customs immediately. This shipment, like the others she had processed, would add many thousands to the number of dead Americans the national news programs would soon be reporting about. There was no way to stop it.

Chapter 2

The air coming into the commuter car from the tunnel smelled of damp concrete and warm steel. The car rolled noisily along the rails of the D.C. Metro, swaying left and right, and bouncing up and down. Occasionally, when the car went around a curve, the brakes squealed like a scared pig. Every so often, one could catch the scent of someone's cologne or perfume, as well as whiffs of the gaseous emissions from yesterday's meals.

Security cameras were everywhere. Some were clearly visible, to dissuade trouble-makers who didn't want their pictures taken. Other cameras were nearly invisible, to record the acts of people who might be infamous in the future, after committing particularly shocking crimes.

What you could only guess at, were the locations of the dozens of radiation detectors and air sniffers. They were used to alert security officers to the presence of any dangerous materials or gases. Nobody knew where all the sensors were. The work of installing them had been done by several teams of government contractors. To be on the safe side, some of the detectors had been installed in one place, un-installed and re-installed in another location. Stafford was on a monitor somewhere at this very moment, being observed by an underpaid local government drone.

Benjamin A. Stafford, U. S. Army, Capt., Iraq... That was part of what would be on my U.S. Government issued grave marker if I was really messing this assignment up. Well, my marker would say those things even if I didn't mess this up, but I'm in no hurry to give the stone cutter another rush job.

I'm a super-bad-trained-killer. Yeah, sure. That might have been true years ago when I was in the Rangers, but now the description was only part right. Now I'm a trained, rusty, super-bad, paper pushing government bureaucrat.

The train made a stop. Stafford and the target got off and headed for the stairs leading to the street exit. He had been watching every move the target made, except for when he was distracted by a beautiful woman sitting across from where he was standing. While he looked the woman over, his real target moved out of his view.

Stafford knew that was a mistake, and he was paying closer attention now. City surveillance techniques were often difficult, and he hadn't used them much along the Mexican border. The surveillance instruction manual said there should have been another agent nearby as a backup, but Stafford was doing it alone this time. He glanced behind him.

Now I'm being followed. The target's about 50 feet back on the right, being very careful... staying close to the wall, protecting his weapon from being detected by anyone in the crowd.

How did he get out of my sight? Probably when I was looking that woman over. I didn't think it was possible to lose someone on a commuter train. I was wrong about that... I indulged myself looking at the woman, and lost him. I underestimated his abilities, and overestimated my own. This was becoming a lesson on how to get yourself killed. Okay, think, adapt, move! My best chance is to double back behind him as soon as I can find suitable terrain. Suitable terrain? I'm still thinking like a soldier. Well, it hadn't been so long ago.

I followed this guy twice before, and know where he's going. No need to circle around. I'll shake him off and pick him up later, closer to his destination. That might not be the best idea, since the target would know I was aware of his tail, but it's all I can do at the moment.

When Stafford reached the top of the exit stairs, he walked straight ahead for 15 feet, which was far enough for the top of the staircase to conceal his next move from anyone following him. He cut left through the crowd of people heading into the station. As he walked, he pulled off his jacket and purposely mussed his hair. He sat on a bench and picked up a nearby used newspaper. He opened the paper and looked over the top, scanning the people streaming out of the exit-way for the target following him.

He should have come out by now. In about ten seconds I'm going to go see if he's still down there.

Frank Hernandez had watched Stafford following him for the past two days. He judged Stafford as cocky, overly confident, and smart mouthed, which Hernandez was in the process of proving once again.

"Today's lesson is about to end badly for you," Hernandez whispered to himself as he approached Stafford from behind.

Chapter 3

S tafford was about to stand when he felt something hard press into the back of his neck.

"Don't you move a muscle!" a familiar voice snarled.

Stafford froze for a moment, and then jerked his head away; standing and spinning around to see what was being pressed into his neck... it was Hernandez' thumb.

"How did you do that? Where did you come from?" Stafford said.

"You got careless. I went up the other stairs, scanned the area, and spotted you sitting like a duck on this bench. It was too easy," the target said.

Stafford's "target" had been fellow Homeland Security Investigation (HSI) Special Agent Frank Hernandez, an employee of the Department of Homeland Security.

"I've told you before, Ben, you've got to be thinking and paying attention. Plan ahead. What would I do if the target did this or that? What would I do if I was in his place?"

"I know, I know. That's three times in a row you got the drop on me. Why don't you follow me next time?"

"No thanks. I like more of a challenge, and you need the practice. You also need to stop eyeballing the babes."

"You saw that, huh?"

"That was when I made my move, dummy," Hernandez chuckled.

"Every day I gain more respect for you, Frank."

"I wish I could return the compliment."

"Gee, thanks," Stafford said, grinning sheepishly. He stood and they began walking toward the Reagan Building, a few blocks away. They had not gotten off at their usual stop and so they had to walk a little farther than usual, but it was a sunny, cool, fall day. It was a nice day for a walk.

I wonder how Frank would have made out in my Army world of map reading, small unit tactics, and kill or be killed. He got me again though. He's right, I need more practice.

"Ben, if you don't mind me saying so, I don't think you're cut out for this job," Stafford looked to see if he was serious. Frank's expression told him he wasn't kidding.

"I'm no good at this cloak and dagger stuff…, you're right about that."

"Why did you leave the border for Washington D.C.?"

"You gotta be kidding… why did I leave the border? You worked the border… why did *you* leave the border?"

"Yeah, okay… it's not a nice place to work." Hernandez was searching for the right way to ask the next question. Stafford could see his mental wheels turning.

"Go ahead, man… just say it … I like straight talk," Stafford said.

"Okay. What motivates you? What do you hope to get accomplished here? I know it's none of my business."

"No, that's a fair question, although you're right…, it isn't any of your business. I'll tell you, but you're going to think my answer is corny." They stopped at a corner and waited for the traffic light to change

"Let's hear it," Hernandez said. Stafford cleared his throat.

"I think I see more of the big picture than most people. I see things in sort of a personal-historical perspective. When I consider the hundreds of thousands… even millions of Americans who served, fought, and gave their lives for this country, I'm humbled. Most of them were average enough guys like us. A few stand out in history because they did great things, but most aren't remembered outside of their family, and if it's been a hundred years, not even *in* their family."

"I remember them, Ben. Every Veterans Day, and Memorial Day, I think about the debt we owe. But you know, I've heard some veterans say they weren't trying to do anything heroic when they fought. They were fighting for each other, and trying to stay alive themselves."

"That's true, Frank. But they wouldn't have been in that position if they hadn't answered the call, or volunteered. Someone once said, "Some people *call* 9-1-1, and some people *are* 9-1-1." It had to be done, and they did it. I guess what I'm trying to say is that I want to serve and protect America to the best of my ability. That's all I want to do."

"Well, you were right, that's sounds corny..., but I like it," Hernandez said. He put his arm around Stafford's shoulder and gave him a squeeze.

"You're my kind of guy."

"Aw shucks, Frank..., thanks," Stafford said, as he feigned humility. He looked down and kicked an imaginary rock.

Hernandez lightened the conversation, and began talking about office politics. He added some comments about which cars were his favorites, and why. He especially liked BMW's.

"Isn't it amazing how short our collective memory is?" Stafford said.

"What do you mean?"

"I mean you say you really like BMW's. The streets are full of Japanese and German cars. During World War II, Toyota made vehicles for the Japanese Army. Mitsubishi made Japanese fighter planes, most notably the "Zero." BMW made engines for many German aircraft in both World Wars, as well as motorcycles used by the German Army. It seems the unconditional terms for surrender included our agreeing to buy all the cars Japan and Germany could produce." Hernandez looked at Stafford as if he had lost his mind.

"That's a strange observation, Ben. Do you suggest we hang on to old animosities forever?"

"No..., but somehow it seems like a slap in the face to all the people who died during the war, especially our servicemen and women who were captured and mistreated. Maybe we shouldn't be so forgiving."

"I think the Bible says something about forgiveness, like if you don't forgive, you will not be forgiven. Besides, most of the people who were mistreating our servicemen are long dead."

"I didn't know you were a Bible thumper, Frank."

"It also says judge not lest ye be judged," Hernandez said.

"I don't know about that... I'm a pretty good judge of people." There was an awkward silence after Stafford's last statement.

"Let's change the subject, Frank. How about we talk about something lighter..., like hegemony and world domination."

"No thanks..., that's way too heavy for me."

"Well, I've got an observation," Stafford said rubbing his hands together and grinning.

"I can hardly wait."

"Have you noticed how illogically things happen in the men's bathroom? When you're finished in the toilet stall, and you're tucking in your shirt, fastening your belt, and generally straightening up... just think... wouldn't it be better to have washed your hands before tucking in your shirt?"

"That's a good point, Ben, but isn't it impractical to have a sink in every toilet stall?"

"Yeah, probably. What you *should* be doing after you come out of the toilet, is washing your clothes."

"Ben, did your mother drop you on your head when you were a baby?"

"More than once probably. I'll ask her the next time I talk to her. I'll be quiet now."

Hernandez was glad for the quiet. Stafford made his head hurt sometimes. He was almost a body-double of Stafford. He was the same height and weight, six feet tall, and 190 pounds, although Stafford was more muscular than Hernandez, and worked out three times a week to stay that way. They both had military style haircuts, black hair, and were in their early forties. Stafford had gray hair in his temples, which was the reason he kept his hair short. Both were Caucasian, although according to the government, Stafford was a different brand of Caucasian than Hernandez. Hernandez was a Hispanic surname that meant something special to the various government personnel departments.

When Stafford had checked on his job application status with the FBI, which he had applied for at the same time he applied for the ICE Agent position, he was candidly told by a retiring FBI personnel specialist that, "Because of budget constraints, we couldn't hire you even if you were a disabled-veteran-black-female-lesbian-named-Lopez." He thought that was funny at the time.

Stafford was equal opportunity in the race department. He really didn't care what color a person was. He acquired that attitude in the Rangers. Getting the mission accomplished, and being able to count on each other when it really mattered, were more important than race.

He and Hernandez were similar, both men were in their forties, but Stafford thought that he was the better looking of the two. Hernandez had a "what's for supper honey" muffin-top around his waist. A man always ate better when he didn't have to cook it himself. Stafford never cooked, he microwaved.

Both men had trained at the Federal Law Enforcement Training Center, better known as FLETC, near Brunswick, Georgia. It was an acronym you could say; Fletcy. Hernandez graduated from FLETC seven years earlier and Stafford finished his training there five years ago. During the Second World War, before FLETC was created, the base was called Glynnco Naval Air Station, and housed blimps that hunted German U-boats operating in the Southern Atlantic. Parts of FLETC still looked like a Navy base.

Before starting the job with ICE, Stafford served as an officer in the U.S. Army for eight years. He completed tours of duty in Afghanistan and Iraq, and had seen more action than he wanted to remember.

Benjamin Stafford's step-father, Daniel Stafford, had spent over 30 years working for the U.S. Customs Service, later called U.S. Customs and Border Protection after the move from the Treasury Department to the Department of Homeland Security.

When Ben was a teenager, Dan Stafford married Ben's mother Marie. Ben's biological father was killed in a hunting accident when Ben was ten years old. Ben had witnessed the accident, and it had affected him deeply. Dan Stafford had taken to the teenager immediately, formally adopting him and legally giving him the Stafford name. His step-dad told him often, "Don't forget *who* you are, or *whose* you are."

Dan Stafford had been Ben's motivation to join the U.S. Army, as well as applying for a job with ICE after he left the military. The elder Stafford had served five years in the Army in the early 70's, and been stationed in Vietnam, Georgia, and West Germany. Ben's step-dad told him stories about his Army and Customs experiences. Most of the stories were funny, some were sad, and all were interesting to a young boy.

The Mexican border was Ben Stafford's first assignment after graduating from FLETC. It had been an eye opener for him, as well as his second trial by fire. Stafford was fond of saying "been there…done that… didn't like it," about bad assignments.

Stafford applied for a headquarters transfer because he was fed up with the heavy workload of cases, as well as the violence, and corruption. He thought the level of violence was lower in the Army. He remembered reading an article about the murder rate in D.C. being higher than the U.S. casualty rate in Iraq. Truth was often stranger than fiction.

Before joining ICE, Frank Hernandez had been a police officer in New Mexico. While he was working as a cop, he heard that Federal jobs were safer and had a better salary. He applied for the ICE Agent's job and got it. His wife liked his new job better than his job as a police officer, and she didn't worry as much.

After FLETC, Hernandez was assigned to Detroit, Michigan. He didn't like Detroit, and his wife hated it. When his probation period was over, he tried to transfer back to the southwest. He knew the Mexican border was a tough place to work, but figured at least he would be out of Detroit and closer to his extended family in New Mexico. There were always openings along the border, and his transfer was quickly approved.

After he worked for a few years out of the El Paso ICE office, he grew tired of the work situation. He always did more than his fair share of the work because he was bilingual. "Hey man, can you ask this guy"… was how most Anglo agents began a conversation with him.

Although Hernandez and Stafford worked out of the same ICE office, they didn't know each other well.

Since Stafford's arrival at headquarters, Hernandez had taken the time to be nice to him, but they still didn't move in the same circles. Stafford was single, which excluded Hernandez from Stafford's after hour's woman chasing episodes. It wouldn't have helped if Hernandez had been single, because Stafford liked working alone when it came to chasing the ladies.

Hernandez' transfer to headquarters was a way off the Mexican border, with promotion potential as a bonus. Spending a few years in headquarters was a good idea if you wanted to climb the career ladder, which Hernandez wanted to do. He could always transfer back to the field at a higher pay grade. He planned to go back to the field as a supervisor someday.

At the Reagan Building, Hernandez and Stafford were screened by civilian contract security guards, showing them their credentials and building passes. After security, they walked to elevators that would take them to the Federal office levels. The first three floors of the building housed many other government and commercial offices. The HSI offices were above the third floor.

HSI was redundantly named. It was a division of ICE, and ICE was part of the Department of Homeland Security. So organizationally, it was DHS/ICE/HSI. Washington loved acronyms, especially ones that could be made into words, like NASA. But DHS had been cobbled together quickly, and nobody had the luxury of spending time creating the wordy acronyms. ICE was a good as they got.

When they reached the elevator security station, they showed their passes again to the guards. No one complained. After Oklahoma City and 9-11, good security was a necessity.

Two weeks earlier, Hernandez offered to give Stafford some pointers on surveillance techniques. The two had been doing surveillance this morning on the Metro, when Stafford had been surprised from behind. In return for Hernandez tutelage, Stafford agreed to show Hernandez a few Ranger fighting moves that weren't taught in FLETC.

"Are you going to be in the gym later today?" Hernandez said, as the doors of the elevator shut.

"Probably... the good Lord willing and the creek don't rise." Stafford grinned.

"If the creek don't rise? You really *are* a country boy, aren't you?" Hernandez said.

"You betcha. Who do you think made America great?" Stafford grinned again.

"Spanish pioneers, African slaves, Chinese laborers and boatloads of European immigrants. It was also fortunate that Native Americans died by the millions as white settlers spread disease among them and stole their land," Hernandez said. The look on his face told Stafford he wasn't trying to be funny.

"Sorry, man, I didn't mean to step on any toes," Stafford said, as the elevator stopped.

"See ya later," Stafford said. He wasn't in the mood for that kind of comment. Even when he knew he was wrong, he didn't like being corrected, and never had. He didn't like making mistakes.

"Sure. Okay, later," Hernandez said. The elevator doors closed.

Stafford walked into his office. He jokingly referred to his office as 'the orifice.' He enjoyed the puzzled looks on people's faces as they wondered if they had heard him correctly.

Even with a floor map, he couldn't find his office on his first day in headquarters. Stafford couldn't understand the layout of the offices. The room numbers were confusing. Room 113.34K was followed by room 113.36B. It must have made sense to *somebody*. If he was asked to go to an unfamiliar part of the building, he would stop someone on the way and ask for directions.

Stafford's office was not far from the elevator, so he didn't have any trouble getting up or down. Calling the room an office was stretching the meaning of the word. Most of the work areas on his floor were crammed with people, desks, and office machines. Rank and file desks were small, had one drawer for file storage, and were placed touching each other. Work papers were piled high on everyone's desk. Having a private phone conversation was impossible.

The overcrowding in the Reagan Building resulted from the Department of Homeland Security mergers. There had been an influx of new people, and jobs, after 9-11. Since then, headquarters struggled with the lack of space. Next year's budget would have more money for office space. That was the rumor every year. In other words, get on with it and do the best you can. The HSI offices on 12th Street had more room, but this was where the powers that be wanted him to work for now.

Having HSI officers, who organizationally were not under the authority of Customs and Border Protection, working in CBP's offices was not so strange. Before the birth of the Department of Homeland Security, Customs was part of the Treasury Department, and Immigration was part of the Justice Department. Before the merger, Customs and Immigration had their own investigative agents. DHS merged the investigative branches of both agencies into one unit, thereby muddying the investigative waters for the foreseeable future. Old dogs can be taught new tricks, but it takes a much longer time to teach a lawyer how to be a doctor.

HSI agents in the field investigated a variety of crimes involving human trafficking, cybercrime, export violations, money laundering and weapons trafficking. The HSI agents working at CBP headquarters had been assigned there because ICE headquarters wanted agents to be available to Customs management personnel. The agents were supposed to provide intelligence, information, and insight, which CBP managers could use to make more informed decisions, at least that's what the policy goal stated. In reality, the HSI agents shared almost no intelligence information with anyone, and kept to themselves, unless there was an office birthday or retirement party where there would be free food.

"Good morning ladies and germs," Stafford said cheerfully, as he walked to his desk. He received a muttering of replies; some profane. Most of the agents looked, saw who it was, and ignored him.

The job of all the agents in his office was intelligence, more or less. The real work was report reading. The agents read hundreds of reports and tried to determine patterns in various classifications of crimes the field offices investigated.

There had been some successes resulting from their report reading. One agent noticed an increase in the number of seizures of false alien resident cards from Charlotte, North Carolina. When the Agent called to follow up on the seizures, it led him to a CBP field officer who had a special knack for spotting false alien resident cards. Using the field officer's tips for detecting false cards, intelligence bulletins were sent to other field offices. The bulletins led to an increase in seizures and arrests nationwide. If only all the agents in the intelligence office could be so successful.

Stafford arrived 15 minutes early for work. He had to be careful when he came in early. A few of the Customs supervisors thought coming in early was a violation of workplace rules. They didn't mind if you came in late and then went to breakfast, but they better not catch you coming in an hour before your shift and trying to work. Go figure.

Some agents were already busy at their desks. There was more work to do than there were hours in the day. Many agents risked the reprimands, and sneaked in early to keep up with the workload.

Well, good for them, Stafford thought. He worked to live, not lived to work. He had a life away from the office. He worked hard, was organized, smart, and his assignments were always completed on time. Stafford sat down at his desk, leaned back in his chair for a few seconds, and then got up and headed for the coffee pot.

He put his 50 cents in the honor system coffee can. Fifty cents was forty cents too much. The first person to arrive was supposed to make the coffee. No one wants to admit to arriving first, so they just heated the coffee left over from yesterday. Extra sugar always helped.

Returning to his desk with his cup of muddy water, he sat down and pulled the seizure reports in front of him. He was still on his own time, but figured he would do a little work anyway. For Stafford, work and personal time had a way of averaging out. He gave a little here, and got a little there. He had known a few agents who purposely arranged to do all their bowel movements at work, on the clock, so not to waste their personal time at home.

Stafford's assignment was to review the reports of arrests, seizures and investigations from ICE offices along the Southern border for accuracy. He had checked the monthly investigative summaries for more than a year, and was beginning to tire from the task. The investigations resulted primarily from drug, money and vehicle seizures. There were a few seizures that originated from commercial importation violations, such as fraudulent invoices or shipping documents. It was boring stuff.

There were no large mistakes in the seizures he studied. There were no cases that the U.S. Attorney had declined to prosecute because the statute of limitations had run out. Letting a case expire was a big no-no. There would be angry phone calls if that happened, by one of the Headquarters Directors, to the Special Agent in Charge of the offending ICE office. Sometimes, heads rolled.

There were so many ICE and CBP directors, he couldn't keep them straight. There were also Assistant Directors, Deputy Directors, and Deputy Assistant Directors. The title wasn't important. What *was* important was for everyone to remember to feed their egos at the appropriate time. Ego-feeding was usually done by people with higher pay grades than his. He never fed egos. There were exceptions, but that was away from work, and on his own time.

When Stafford's step-dad worked for Customs, the mission was protecting the revenue and stopping the importation of illegal drugs. Since the terror attacks of 9-11, the new, more important goal, was stopping terrorists from entering the United States. If you were searching a person to determine if he was a terrorist and found drugs instead, then you took what dropped into your lap.

Every CBP employee knew that not finding 100 pounds of cocaine in a car's gas tank, or in someones suitcase, didn't have the potential to bring down a skyscraper. As diligent as the Officers at the ports of entry were, it wasn't often a terrorist was discovered and dealt with appropriately. Stafford was certain there were terrorists in the country who had simply walked into the U.S. across the Rio Grande River, like hundreds of thousands of others had done. Who was kidding whom?

The reports Stafford was reviewing contained no terrorism related arrests, so he concentrated on the other statistics.

Over the past several months, Stafford noticed a steady decline in the total amount of cocaine seized along the Mexican border. By itself, that fact wasn't noteworthy. Drug seizures would normally increase somewhere else, using a different smuggling technique. There were only so many ways something could be smuggled, and the Customs officers working the border saw them all. Stafford made a mental note to go back and look at reports from earlier in the year, to see how long the decline had been going on.

The more organized and experienced smugglers rotated their concealment methods by hiding the contraband in car gas tanks, fake pick-up truck beds, camper shells, vehicle spare tires and anything else they could think of, to prevent customs officers from finding their product. Sometimes the smugglers were so confident they didn't bother to hide the drugs at all. When you opened a car trunk or suitcase, there the stuff was in plain view.

There was always the possibility that some of the Customs officers were being bribed. There were always some officers who thought they were so smart they weren't going to be caught. In reality, an arrestee was always trying to reduce their prison time by informing on someone, and so the smart ones got caught eventually.

Customs officers never stop searching, and smugglers never give up trying to get a load through. Declines in cocaine seizures and arrests. No increases in other locations. We weren't that good at scaring the traffickers off. Something's going on, but what?

Chapter 4

S tafford had been studying the arrest and seizure reports for almost four hours without a break. He looked at the wall clock. His eyes hurt, and it was time for lunch.

Stafford's phone rang. He answered and began his official recitation of the headquarters mandated phone greeting, which he embellished on the chance he'd say it to the headquarters yo-yo who thought it up.

"Good morning sir or ma'am. You have reached the United States Department of Homeland Security, Immigration and Customs Enforcement, Homeland Security Investigations, Special Agent Benjamin Stafford speaking, how may I..."

"All right, all right, enough already. This is Beth..., do you say it that way just to annoy people?"

"Of course."

"Well, it works."

"I'm glad to hear it. So, Miss Supervisor Beth..., how's it going in Container Security Initiative land today? Have you any interesting happenings to tell me about?"

"None I can talk about, other than the usual false radiation alarms. I'll tell you something interesting though. Did you know that in every country where we have CSI teams pre-screening outbound containerized ocean freight, the foreign Customs authorities have already recouped the multimillion dollar cost of the container x-raying equipment?"

"No kidding. How'd they do that?"

"Because when they aren't looking at the containers we ask them to examine, which is most of the time, they x-ray other high risk containers they were not able to look at before. They find drugs, weapons, and all manner of contraband in those ocean containers. It's amazing!"

"Do you think I could get a CSI Special Agent position in the south of France?"

"What do *you* think?"

"I think somebody's Uncle Harry is already there enjoying a bottle of wine and a piece of cheese."

"Since you brought up the subject of food..., I'm eating lunch downstairs today, Ben. Would you like to join me?"

"I certainly would."

"I'll be on my way down in five minutes. See you there."

"Just so you know, Beth, I want to talk to you about some drug seizure reports. Something doesn't add up."

"If you want to talk shop, I'll come by your office later. See you downstairs." She hung up.

Beth thought about Ben.

Good looking, often charming, interesting to talk to. But one minute he was a smarty pants, the next minute a worker bee. He did have a good sense of humor. I think I'd like to know him better. I wonder how he'll act toward me when he finds out I'm a Christian.

Stafford was different than other men she had known. He was overconfident, by her standard, and was a braggart. But the overconfidence made him somewhat appealing. Some men would have looked foolish, but Stafford looked strong. She couldn't explain it. She thought she knew what all the posturing and bragging was about; the same thing it was always about with men; sex.

The basic motivation of men was so primitive. Why couldn't they be more caring? Did they think it made them look weak? They were always trying to impress somebody, anybody.

Beth guessed that when a man was watching the weather forecast on TV, he was wondering what the weather girl would look like in a bikini. She couldn't know how right she was. The accidental honesty of men calling each other "dog" in everyday conversation did not escape her.

As Beth St. James was thinking about Ben Stafford, he was thinking about her.

I like just about everything Elizabeth St. James has to offer. I like the rhythm of her name. She is a straightforward woman... I definitely like that. I also like the fact that she's beautiful and enjoys my company. What beautiful woman wouldn't enjoy my company? You dog you. I'm no ordinary man after all, and she's just a woman and can't help herself.

Stafford smiled and stood up, rubbing his rear end with both hands. His back was stiff from sitting for so long. He started for the door.

Pete Nelson saw him out of the corner of his eye, standing there rubbing his butt. Stafford usually had something cute to say, Nelson thought. Most of the time when someone spoke, a reasonably intelligent statement followed, but not with Stafford. It was always a wise crack. He was a joker, and the joke was always at our expense.

"Going to lunch early ya'll. Hold my calls," Stafford said loudly, true to form. Nelson had heard enough.

"Okay Stafford, we'll hold your calls, and you can…" Nelson released a string of profanity and crude gestures.

"You really should remember to take your medications, Nelson. I'll check in on you later."

"Drop dead, wise guy."

Stafford walked into the hallway, and headed for the elevator. He jabbed the down button and started whistling a hymn.

What a pain in the neck. A great bunch of guys I work with. No sense of humor. Let Nelson have the last word. I know his type. If you really annoyed him, he took it personally. Then the practical jokes would start. Not the kind of jokes that make you laugh. His would be the kind that made you want to punch someone in the nose.

Stafford's thoughts of Nelson dissipated when he saw Beth. She was waiting for him at the entrance to the food court. She was a beauty. She was tall, had long auburn hair, weighed about 135 pounds, and had a fine figure. She was everything a man could want, and she was smiling at him.

"How's it going, handsome?"

"It's going fine now." His heart was beating faster. She made him feel like a school boy again. He had a few indecent thoughts.

Beth looked at the lunch menu behind the fast food counter, studying their lunch choices.

"Beth, shouldn't we have this menu memorized by now?"

"I think the pizza is less fattening and healthier for us both."

"You always say that. If you were any healthier I wouldn't be able to stand it." Beth laughed uneasily.

He ordered the pizza. Beth left him hanging, by changing her mind, and ordered a salad at the last second.

"Women... I never met one who didn't think she should lose ten pounds."

"That's probably true, Ben."

After he and Beth picked their table and sat down, she waved at a man and woman who were carrying their trays, looking for a place to sit down. They acknowledged her, and she motioned them to come and sit at the next table. Stafford felt disappointed he wasn't going to have Beth to himself.

The new arrivals set their trays down. Stafford stood up to shake hands. They introduced themselves as Sam Person, and Anne Dawson. Sam Person pronounced his last name in the Scandinavian style, making it sound like *Pears-Sewn*. Stafford had a habit of providing more information than one really needed to know, and in that spirit, he began explaining about the new arrivals last names.

"Did you know you both have son's names? I think last names are really interesting. A woman's maiden name was her father's family name. To show their independence, some women keep their maiden name when they get married, which is actually their father's name. So where is the independence from men? Legally, a husband becomes the bride's next of kin. Why differentiate yourself from your husband and not your father? A woman had no choice in the first case, and her father loves her more. A husband may be a passing fancy. I'm glad I figured that out. I wonder if women think like I do. I hope not." Stafford took a bite of food. The group ignored what he said and began their own conversation.

"Did you know Beth and I live in the same building? That's how we know each other," Anne said. "Sometimes we bump into each other here at the food court."

Stafford saw Anne, like most women, was having a salad. Sam was having a hamburger, French fries, and a chocolate milk shake. The man had no fear of cholesterol at all.

"That's neat. I wish I was renting a condo. Maybe I'll check into that," Stafford said.

They made polite conversation. Sam talked with his mouth full. Through his food, he managed to say he worked for the FBI, but didn't say in what capacity. Stafford was mesmerized by the way Person could talk and chew at the same time. He was waiting for a big chunk of burger to fly out of Person's mouth. It didn't happen. When he wasn't trying to talk with his mouth full, Person had an air of superiority. Stafford estimated he was a mid-level manager in the bureaucratic food chain.

Maybe he's a food taster.

Stafford never had much use for the FBI. He sometimes worked with them in the El Paso office, when their official jurisdictions overlapped. His impression then was they were prima donnas who would rather practice giving a press conference than do real work. Person was FBI, so in Stafford's book, he had one strike against him already, fearless carnivore or not.

Anne Dawson, who Stafford noted was nearly as pretty as Beth, said she worked for the Department of Health and Human Services. When she and Sam had time, they met at different lunch spots in the area.

Sam and Anne are obviously fond of each other. I wonder what she looks like in a bikini. I've got a good start on being a dirty old man. Maybe I'm a dirty old man already, and fast approaching perverthood. Is perverthood a word? I think I'll look that up in the dictionary.

"Sam and I better be running along or we'll be late getting back to work. Beth, maybe we can all get together on some weekend after Sam and I finish our bike ride. I'll call you later."

"Okay, Anne, call me and we'll talk about it."

Anne and Sam stood up. "Nice meeting you, Benjamin," Anne and Sam said simultaneously. They giggled.

"You can call me Ben."

"Nice meeting you, Ben," they echoed each other again. Sam and Anne walked off, still giggling.

"Aren't they a cute couple?" Beth asked.

"Yes, they are a really cute couple. I don't know when I've seen a cuter couple. They make me think of children, puppy dogs, and cotton candy. I feel all warm inside."

"Oh, stop it," she frowned. "They're a really nice couple. They're obviously good for each other." Her frown turned into a smile as she watched them walk out of sight arm in arm.

"Do you have a bicycle, Ben?"

"No, I've been driving my car a little, using the Metro mostly, and walking."

"Can you get a bike?"

"Maybe..., do you know some good places we can bike to?"

"Certainly. In fact, if you go biking with me, I'll show you some things you probably wouldn't have seen otherwise." Beth had a serious look on her face. Stafford's engine began to race.

"I can see by the expression on your face that I better rephrase my last sentence. I can show you around town if you'd like, Ben."

"I'd like. I haven't ridden in a long time, but like they say, once you learn, you never forget." It was Beth's turn to smirk.

They got up and walked to the elevators, dropping their lunch trash dutifully into the garbage can as they passed. As they walked side by side, Stafford felt pleased they were going to see each other away from work.

A few hours together on a bike might be just what I need to see if she deserves more of my attention.

"So, we have a date then?" he said smiling.

"It looks that way, Ben. We just need to pick the day."

"Would my lady care to lunch with me on foam plates on the morrow? We can discuss it then," he said in a mock British accent.

"But of course darling..., do call me," she said in her best Hollywood has-been celebrity style.

"Okay..., and by the way, are there any condos for rent in your building?" She let his words sink in before answering.

"I think there are some rental notices posted on the building's bulletin board. Why don't you come by and take a look sometime?"

"I'll do that," Stafford said happily, as he searched his jacket pocket. He found what he was looking for, and handed her a piece of paper and a pen.

"Would you write down your address and phone number for me? I'll give you a call before I come by."

Beth took the pen and paper and did as he requested. As she handed the pen and paper back to him, she said, "I don't give my address and phone number to anybody who asks, you know."

"I imagine not, but then I'm not just anybody, am I?" Stafford looked directly into her eyes with a confidence she liked, and also found a little annoying. Beth looked unflinchingly back at him. They broke their gaze, and continued walking. Beth spoke quietly and slowly.

"So far, you've played your hand pretty well, but whether you are just anybody, I have yet to determine."

"I think there may still be a hint of winter in the air," was all he could think to say as they stepped into the elevator. He had her phone number and thought he might be able to make a good impression if he could get her alone. He felt guilty about the thoughts he had been having about her and her friend. He dismissed the feeling as the elevator stopped at his floor.

"Talk to you tomorrow," he said, as he left the elevator.

"Looking forward to it," she said with a smile. The elevator doors shut. Beth shook her head.

Men are so predictable, it's all about sex. I read somewhere that men give love to get sex, and women give sex to get love. Well..., some women.

Chapter 5

Aminute after Stafford left for lunch, Ron Boyer, the HSI Intelligence Section Supervisory Agent, came out of the office copy room. As Boyer passed Nelson's desk, he asked him to come with him into his office. Nelson then received a chewing out from Boyer for using vulgar behavior and language in the office. Such misbehavior might have been ignored or even encouraged in the field, but in headquarters there was zero tolerance for it. This was probably because of the high concentration of lawyers, women in leadership positions, and also because congress didn't like competition.

Stafford returned from lunch and sat at his desk. He pulled the printout of the seizure reports in front of him and tapped it with his fingers, thinking. As much as he disliked the thought of asking Nelson for advice, he had been there longer than Stafford, and might have an idea about why the seizure totals weren't following past patterns. Stafford swiveled around in his chair so he could talk to Nelson, who had his back turned to him.

"Hey, Pete..., mind if I ask you a question?"

"I've got nothing to say to you, pal. You're on my short list," Nelson said without turning around.

"Oh..., well..., now you've hurt my feelings," Stafford said.

Nelson was fed up. He stood quickly, pushing his chair backward with the back of his legs. He was facing Stafford, who was still sitting down.

"Stafford, why don't you come and help me get a case of copy paper off the top shelf in the supply room?"

"Sure. Anything for a friend."

Nelson glared at Stafford, and then headed for the supply room in the rear of the office. Nelson looked behind him a couple of times to make sure Stafford was following. Stafford followed, with a pretty good idea about what was going to happen in the supply room after they got inside.

As soon as the supply room door shut behind Stafford, Nelson thrust his face into Stafford's. Their noses touched as Nelson shouted "I'M NOT TAKING…"

That was all he was able to say before Stafford's fist slammed into his stomach, just below the rib cage. The punch knocked the wind out of Nelson, forcing him to bend over and take a couple of steps backward. Stafford hadn't used his full strength, which could have caused serious injury to Nelson.

"You shouldn't have done that," Stafford said calmly. Nelson had one hand on his stomach and the other hand on his thigh. He was still bent over, gasping for breath. He twisted his head to one side, and looked at Stafford, expecting another punch.

"Take it easy, Pete. Calm down and relax. Take slow breaths. Take your time."

It took Nelson three breaths for Nelson to say "This… isn't… over."

Stafford crossed his arms in front of his chest. "You wanna continue this dance? I can wait until you get your wind back."

"You… you… lousy..."

"What *is* your problem, Nelson? You've been riding me since I got here. Is this office too small for the both of us?" Nelson regained enough breath to stand and speak more normally. His fists were clenched tight at his sides.

"I ought to… I HATE guys like you! You think you're so smart. You think you're the only person that was in the Army? The only one that was in a war? I've been there and done that. You haven't done anything. You were probably some rear echelon paper-pusher who opened doors for the General. That's all you were."

"You sure you're not describing yourself?"

"I ought to break you in half."

"So what's stopping you? Coming to the supply room was your idea."

"I only wanted to talk. You hit me first!"

"You shouldn't have jumped in my face like you did."

"Let's meet in the gym after work. We'll settle this then."

"So after we settle this, are we gonna be able to play nice again? I don't think so. I'll meet you in the gym, but when we're finished, the loser is leaving headquarters..., and by the way..., that would be you."

Stafford left the supply room and went to his desk. Nelson came out, and walked into the hall, heading for the men's room. Stafford watched Nelson leave, and then looked at the ceiling and took a deep breath, grateful for the time Nelson would be away.

Maybe I shouldn't have punched him. Maybe he shouldn't have jumped in my face like that. Maybe if frogs had wings, they wouldn't bump their butts when they hopped. Woulda-coulda-shoulda.

Stafford re-read the reports he was working on, recalculating the numbers. Maybe there was a simple math mistake, he thought. The report was computerized. The decimals were all in the correct places and the units of measure were all correct. He needed more information. He decided to call a friend in El Paso who might provide some insight.

He called the El Paso ICE office phone number from memory. ICE Special Agent James Dupree answered, and Stafford listened to the required DHS phone greeting. Stafford let him recite the entire thing.

"Jimmy boy, how's it going?"

Dupree recognized Stafford's voice immediately. "Hey Ben, what's cooking? Why did you let me recite the whole greeting?"

"I just wanted to hear your voice again. I need to pick your brain, Jimmy. Have you got a minute?"

"Sure, buddy, what's on your mind?"

"About twelve thousand kilos of missing cocaine."

Stafford's office grew quiet. Every ear in the office was straining to hear what he was going to say next. There was silence on the phone line. Stafford wondered if Dupree had heard him.

"Jimmy? Did you hear me?"

"How did you find out about that, Ben?"

Stafford didn't know what to say. Obviously, there was something going on that Dupree felt was supposed to be secret, and it involved tons of cocaine. He thought fast, and decided to stall the conversation until later.

"Jimmy, maybe we shouldn't discuss this on the government line."

"Good idea. We need to talk. Call me on my personal cell after you get off work." Dupree hung up without allowing a reply from Stafford.

Stafford's mind was racing. The other agents in the office glanced at Stafford, and then went back to work. There would be more than one phone call made about missing cocaine, and Stafford's strange conversation.

What has Dupree gotten himself into? Forget Dupree, what have I gotten into?

Chapter 6

The American border agents relied on informants, dumb luck, and electronic gadgets to find his drug shipments. Dumb luck wouldn't help the Americans. His scientists assured him that there was no way an x-ray or physical inspection of his shipments could reveal there was cocaine present. Claudio Reynaldo Roja was pleased with the new smuggling method. In the last six months, none of his drug shipments entering the United States had been discovered.

Although Roja was convinced his current shipments were undetectable, he was also a realist. He knew it was only a matter of time before one of his men was arrested and told the police or Customs what they knew in exchange for less prison time.

He always found out when there was an informer in his organization. He always made them regret they had cooperated, even if he had to wait years until they were released from prison. They would pay for their disloyalty, and if they went into hiding, then one of their family members would pay in their place.

Roja's penalty for those who talked to the authorities was to have their tongue cut out and nailed to their forehead. Of course this was fatal. All his men knew this was the punishment for being a rat. He found it unbelievable that as terrible as the punishment was, someone always talked to the police. They feared jail more than death. They feared the police more than him. It was beyond his understanding.

When Roja was arrested, as he sometimes was, his lawyer filed the proper "motions" with the presiding judge. If the judge was smart, he took the money. If the judge was stupid and refused, Roja would offer less money with a promise to kill the judge's mother, father, wife, son, daughter, or whoever was most dear to the judge. Proper motivation was all the key. It was so simple. Fear and greed made Roja untouchable.

Roja liked to quote from the Bible. One of his favorite quotes was one he considered quite prophetic in regard to his drug dealings.

"There is a time for every purpose under heaven."

Roja considered *now* to be his time, and *drug dealing* to be his purpose. He believed God would help him become very rich. He was living proof that Satan could quote from the Bible.

The bribes for the crooked police and customs officers, the expense of the various methods for smuggling, and losses to the police and Customs of some of his drug shipments, were simply a cost of doing business. Drug smuggling was a business, and he was simply a businessman.

If a smuggling method was discovered, Roja would stop using it for two or three years. They could not look at every such shipment forever. His government informants would tell him when it was safe to try it again. All he had to do was be patient.

However, he was not so patient when dealing with people he thought had cheated him. He was informed that many of his drug shipments were being tampered with after passing through U.S. Customs. The drugs had been contaminated by some chemical, which made it hard to process into crack. The street dealers were complaining to their local suppliers, and their complaints had gotten back to Roja. He suspected the shipments were being skimmed by one of his people for personal profit.

He knew who the thief was. He had eliminated all the possibilities and was left with one answer. There was no other person with the knowledge of the shipments, except his drivers on the other side, and they were watched very closely.

The man responsible was on the Mexican side of the border. He was the man who had arranged all of the shipments that had been tampered with. As soon as Roja figured it out, he asked his trusted old friend, Silvio Nuñez, to come to his house for a meeting. Silvio was now lying at Roja's feet, broken and bleeding.

"That's enough," Roja said. Roja's bodyguards stepped away and threw the metal rods used for the beating into the trunk of their car. Roja looked down at the condemned man.

"Look at me." The man slowly turned his head. Blood had run into his eyes and it was difficult to see his old friend. He finally saw Roja in front of the car, standing near the men who had beaten him.

"So..., you thought you could steal from me? You thought I wouldn't find out?"

Silvio tried to answer, but the pain was too much for him. His jaw and teeth were broken. He knew he was going to die. It would make no difference now, but he had to try. He spoke slowly, holding his jaw with one hand, as he leaned on his other arm to support himself.

"Claudio..., I never stole from you. I swear it... on my mother's grave. You are making a mistake."

"You made the mistake, Silvio. You can tell your mother hello for me." Roja slapped his favorite bodyguard on the chest with the back of his hand.

"Jose'..., finish it."

Roja walked to his car. The driver opened the door for him and he slid inside across the cool leather seat. The driver shut the door behind him, and Roja made himself comfortable.

"Unpleasant business isn't it, General Miner?" he said without turning his head toward his guest.

The general was wearing civilian clothes, but he looked every inch a military officer. He was retired now, but his physique was still slim and muscular. His gray hair was cut close to his head. He was clean shaven. He could command men with a look.

"Indeed it is, Señor Roja, but violence is often required to protect one's interests."

"Precisely," Roja said, nodding his head. Roja crossed his legs, picked up his glass of brandy, sniffed, and took a sip.

"This is excellent brandy…, don't you think?" Miner took a sniff, and sipped from his own glass, and rolled the brandy around his mouth, savoring the taste.

"Yes, it's quite good."

"I can have a few cases sent to you if you like."

"Please do. Thank you very much."

"Drive back to the house, and turn up the air conditioning," Roja said to the driver.

As the limo departed, Jose' stepped closer to the condemned man. He had already inserted his earplugs, having anticipated his need for his shotgun. He checked his earplugs by snapping his fingers next to each ear. Next, he squeezed the pistol grip of the shotgun tightly with his right hand and braced his right forearm against his side, just under his ribcage. The other guards walked away, putting their fingers in their ears.

He pressed the safety off, and turned his left hand palm down over the barrel to keep it from hitting him in the face when he fired. The muzzle was pointed at the face of the man sitting in the dirt. There was no need to use the sights at this distance. Jose' saw the man stiffen, and close his eyes, knowing what was next.

Jose waited a few seconds, trying to judge by the wind on his face whether he was standing in the right place. There was no need to make a mess of ones clothing by being too quick on the trigger. He decided he was positioned properly.

He pulled the trigger. The gun kicked. The ear-plugs worked like the pharmacist said. The gun sounded like a loud clap. The man's face disappeared, and he dropped to the ground, as a mixture of bloody mist, gun-smoke, and dust drifted away. There was no need for a second shot. In the limousine, Roja and Miner didn't hear the shotgun blast. They were already far away, heading to Roja's ranch.

"You know, General, I find it difficult to understand you. You spent thirty-five years in the Army of the United States. You took an oath, did you not, to defend the United States from all enemies?"

"Yes, I did. Every American soldier swears to support and defend the Constitution. Why does that make me hard to understand?"

"One could hardly believe that directing a drug and gun smuggling organization would follow that oath. Some might consider you unpatriotic. What made you change your mind about defending your country, General?"

"I haven't changed my mind about defending America, I've only changed my methods. The oath of allegiance says I will defend the constitution from all enemies…, foreign and domestic. The United States has been taken over by politicians and judges who don't believe what the Constitution says. They are the domestic enemies I swore to defend America from. They think the constitution is made of clay, and they twist its meaning to suit their political and social agendas. They think the people are too stupid to know when they're being lied to and used. All that is about to change, Señor Roja. I can say no more than that."

Chapter 7

G ood morning, Sol, Lewis, Rennie, how ya'll been?" Will said, as he
shook hands all around the restaurant table and sat down.

"We're just fine now, we've been waiting for you," Solomon said.

"Sorry I'm late, boys. I needed to stop for gas," he chuckled. "I'm here
now, so no more waiting." Nobody spoke for the next minute. They
watched the overweight waitresses clearing dishes and wiping dirty tables.

"You know, there's somebody missing from this get together... Ben
Stafford. Is he still in the Army, Will?" Lewis said.

"Nope. He got out and got a job with Homeland Security. The last I
heard, he was transferring from Texas to Washington D.C... that was about
a year ago."

"Do you have his number? We could call and say hello." Lewis said.

"I have his cellphone number at home somewhere. I'll call and tell him
we all miss him."

"I'm starved," Sol said. "Let's order breakfast and get things going."

They ordered the breakfast buffet and went to the hot bar. Even though
the breakfast buffet was all you could eat, they loaded their plates to
overflowing, thereby conserving their energy for other things, like having
heart attacks.

This was not the place that he, William Robert Williams, would have
picked for regular breakfasts, but the other guys had talked about "Rancho
Deluxe" as *the* place for breakfast.

It was more "Rauncho Deluxe," and had been built about 50 years ago.
Its better days were long gone, but it still passed for Spanish chic in this
part of Alabama. The floor was covered by the original dark red carpet,
and from the ceiling hung fake wrought-iron lanterns. The lantern light

competed with the morning sunshine, strained though it was through the haze of years of kitchen grease that had settled on the large windows. The windows gave patrons a scenic view of the parking lot, and the Gas and Bait store just across County Road 265.

The windows had several small, round, conical, depressions, where glass was missing. The dimples were lasting evidence that someone had fired a BB gun at the place; no doubt trying to settle a grievance with Ozzie and Harriet when they had eaten here.

Wallpaper murals depicted skinny bullfighters holding spiked sticks over bleeding bulls. Red Naugahyde tablecloths covered every table.

How many Nauga's do you have to skin to make a naugahyde tablecloth? He smiled at his dad's tired joke.

Will had better taste than this. He liked the restaurant at the Whole Way Inn because they used real table cloths, and had a live band on Saturday night. The waitresses were pretty there too. He looked around at the waitresses here. They all looked like they had had too many beers, babies and free trips to the breakfast bar.

They finished eating, leaned on their elbows, and slurped their coffee. Lewis Poindexter brought the meeting to order, of a sort. It had been Lewis' idea to start meeting one day a week for breakfast, to talk about anything that came up.

"What are we going to talk about today boys? Politics? Religion? Women? Maybe we could solve some of the world's problems."

Lewis always did have big ideas. Like most ideas that would later be considered mistakes, such as sleeping with your wife's sister, it sounded like a good idea at the time. Actually, it *was* a pretty good idea... the meeting for breakfast, that is.

They had been close friends in high school, but the years since then had separated them by more than time. Some had joined the service, gotten married, become fathers, and divorced. Their life experiences had reformed most of them in adulthood, but not all of them.

"I wanna talk about space aliens," Rennie Gordon said.

Sol Mooney smacked the table with his hand, wincing at Rennie's suggestion as much as from the pain he felt from hitting the table too hard.

"Not that again!" He rubbed his smarting palm.

"You've been carrying on about aliens since you were a kid. Just because your daddy named you after some alien doesn't mean you have to act like one you know."

They all knew that Rennie's father had named his son after Michael Rennie, the 1950's actor who played the alien "Klaatu" in the movie "The Day the Earth Stood Still." Rennie Gordon's middle initial was supposedly F for Fitzgerald but some people thought that the F might really stand for Flash. Rennie Flash Gordon. That wasn't so hard to believe.

"You said we could talk about anything, and I wanna talk about aliens."

"Okay, Rennie, say what you gotta say."

"Thanks, Billy Bob."

"Don't call me Billy Bob unless you want me to call you Flash. You know I don't like being called Billy Bob. While we're at it, don't call me Double-Bill either."

"Okay, I won't. I forgot Will, sorry. But just listen to this, you guys. I heard a fella on TV say that the movie *E.T. The Extra Terrestrial* was really about Jesus!"

"Say what?"

"No, really. No offense, Lewis. I know you're a born-again Christian and all that, but it was really interesting to hear what this guy was saying"

"I'm not offended, Rennie. Not yet. Tell us how this guy figured it out. This ought to be good."

"Well, he said that this Steven Spielberg guy was really making a movie about Jesus. Did ya see the movie? You remember that little E.T. alien guy healed people by just touching them with his big ole fat finger? At the end of the movie, E.T. died and came back to life after three days, just like Jesus. Then he went back into heaven, just like Jesus."

"Jesus didn't zip off in a space ship, Rennie."

"I know that, Will, but they said it was all symbolic you know? Somebody asked Spielberg about it later and he denied it. He's a Jew ya know, so he'd have to deny it, or all of his Jewish friends would disown him." Lewis's face turned red.

"Oh, for crying out loud, Rennie! What's being a Jew got to do with it? Jesus was a Jew, too. So what? Can we talk about something else now?" Lewis said.

"Rennie, you ain't right boy," Sol said.

"Well thanks..., coming from you that's a compliment."

"Shut your mouth, Rennie!" Sol said.

"Now girls, let's settle down. I've heard that talking about religion or politics can cause problems... Looks like it's true. Let's change the subject."

"Will's right," Lewis said. "Let's change the subject. Has anybody here seen any other movies lately?"

"I saw a pretty good one the other day. I got the movie from the library. It's free that way, ya know. It starred Nicholas Cage and some good-looking woman."

Will knew Sol was a ladies man. As much as Sol liked to eat, and liked beautiful women, the ultimate party for Sol would be to date a beauty contestant who owned a restaurant. Sol wouldn't know where to begin.

"Just how good-looking was she, Sol?" Will asked.

"She'd make a train jump the tracks and follow her down a dirt road, blowing the horn all the way," Sol answered solemnly.

"That pretty, huh?" Will snickered. The others were laughing at Sol, but he figured they were laughing at Will.

"Well anyway, it was a pretty good movie. Nicholas Cage had ESP or something, you know... extra... sensory... perception...," he said slowly and carefully. "He could look into the future for a few days and see what was gonna happen next. The cops were after him, but he always knew when they were coming and what they'd do. They could never catch him."

They all nodded and uh-huh'd they understood.

"Well, look here boys..., the morning is getting kinda long. It's time for me to get. I think I'm gonna drive into Dothan and see an early movie. Anybody want to come along?"

"No, but thanks anyway, Rennie. I believe we got other things to do," Lewis said.

The others nodded as they got up, sucking air through their teeth in attempts to loosen stuck food particles. They reached for their wallets, and ambled to the gum-chewing cashier. After paying, they walked into the parking lot.

"Will, how about calling Ben Stafford. See where he is and what he's been doing," Lewis said.

"Okay, and I'll let ya'll know something next time I see you."

"Sounds good. See ya'll next week then. Same time?" Lewis said, looking around at everyone. Nobody answered.

"Next week it'll be then," Will spoke for all of them.

*   *   *   *

Rennie wanted to ask his daughter Carrie if she would go see the new science fiction movie with him. She didn't like that kind of movie. She liked books and movies about vampires. He thought that was just a bunch of baloney. How could there be romantic vampires?

Once, he tried reading one of her vampire books to see what she was getting into. He didn't like what he read, but figured it was just a phase she was going through. She was only 19 years old. He smiled as he remembered how she used to play with toy trucks. She grew out of that. "It'll pass," he had told himself again and again.

After the movie, which he liked, Rennie decided to go by Carrie's apartment to see how she was doing, and find out why she wasn't answering his phone calls. She had just moved to Dothan, and gotten a part-time job to help with the expenses of going to school, and living on her own. He thought she was mature enough to handle the work and school, but life and boys were another matter.

He and Carrie had argued many times over his treatment of her boyfriends. That was one of the reasons he figured she wanted to move out and be on her on, so he couldn't see what she was doing. She was almost grown, but she was still his daughter. He had only been trying to protect her from over-anxious young men. He knew what the game was with them, because he had been an over-anxious, over-sexed, young man once himself.

He tried calling her cellphone again, but still didn't get an answer. Now he was worried. There was no other number he could call. She didn't have another phone.

He arrived at her apartment complex about 3pm. He knew she should be home from work by then. He saw her car parked in the spot below her apartment. She hadn't started classes yet because she missed the registration. She gave him an excuse about being too busy, but he had an idea she had been partying too much after moving there. He expected better of her, and told her so.

"Well, that's a relief, she's home," he said to himself.

He climbed the stairs to her apartment and knocked on her door. He started to smile as he prepared himself to see the love of his life. He and his wife had not agreed on much, but one thing they did agree on was how well their daughter had turned out. He waited for her to open the door. He knocked again, harder this time. He waited.

"Carrie! It's Dad. Open the door." Nothing.

He decided to take a look around the complex and see if he could find her, or the apartment complex manager. The door to the apartment next door opened, and a young woman stepped into the hallway. She recognized him from two months ago when he helped Carrie move into the apartment.

"Mr. Gordon?"

"Hello. I'm Carrie's father. Do you know where she is?"

"She should be home, but I haven't seen her since she came in yesterday afternoon. She was supposed to take me grocery shopping this morning. I knocked on her door, but she didn't answer. Some of her friends came by this morning, too. She didn't answer when they knocked either, and they left."

"Where does the apartment manager live?"

She told him. He started jogging in the direction she pointed him in, cursing himself for not insisting on a key to Carrie's apartment when he left her there. He had a sick feeling in his stomach. As he ran, he prayed aloud. "Please, God, let her be okay. Please, God, let her be okay."

He found the manager and explained the situation to him as quickly as he could. The manager agreed to open Carrie's door, but told Rennie he had to wait outside while he checked the apartment. They hurried to Carrie's apartment. The manager opened the door and stepped inside.

"IS ANYBODY HERE?" the manager yelled.

He took another step and stopped. He put his hands to his face.

"Oh no," he said. Rennie looked past him and saw Carrie lying on the floor. Her face was a purplish-gray color.

"NO! NO! NO!" he cried.

Rennie's knees began to buckle. He took a couple of steps toward where she lay on her back, and then fell to his hands and knees. He crawled the last foot to her. A low moan came from deep in his chest. It was a moan of anguish; a plea for God to bring her back to life, and stop his heart instead. His tears fell as he touched her arm. It was cold.

His little girl was gone.

Chapter 8

The Gadsden Council liked to conference call at least once a week. The phone meetings were chaired by the group's founder, Major General Andrew Jackson Miner, U. S. Army, Retired. At today's meeting, the members learned their covert plan, codenamed Operation Plow, had begun.

Years of planning and positioning people was beginning to pay off. This week's numbers were impressive; 1153 dead in Pennsylvania and Maryland alone. The general public, health departments, and law enforcement authorities were unaware of what was causing the deaths.

The meeting's participants did not know the identities of the other group members. They had been warned not to try and find out. Miner knew everyone's identities because he had recruited them, one by one. The recruiting took five years, but he had to be sure they could be trusted with America's future.

It had been six years since the death of General Miner's wife, and three years since the death of his only son, who was an infantry Captain. His son was shot from behind, by an Iraqi soldier who had been under his tutelage. The death of his son began Miner's and America's downward spiral. America was in trouble, and he was going to save her.

Everyone in the council was willing to give their life for America. They were also willing to risk their fortunes for their country's sake. Secrecy helped protect them and all they had acquired during their many years of faithful service. Death was still a possibility, but instead of death at the hands of America's enemies, death might be the sentence of a Federal court for the treason and murder they were committing.

Over an encrypted internet line, General Miner announced the success of Operation Plow, giving the figures gathered from public and confidential sources.

"Sir, if these numbers are correct, the mortality rate is nearly 40 per cent."

"The rate is closer to 100 percent, Number Three, if you factor in the repetitive nature of drug abuse, and the fact that not all the deaths have been attributed to drugs."

"How soon before we have the nationwide figures, sir?"

"We should have those figures in the next two weeks. I will not have any updates for the next scheduled meeting. Continue Operation Plow implementation as per your standing orders. Would someone make a motion that we cancel our next meeting, and schedule to reconvene in two weeks?"

"I make the motion."

"I second."

"Thank you Number Four and Five. All in favor, say aye."

"Seven ayes noted. The motion is carried. We meet again in two weeks. Congratulations, and God's blessings to all of you, gentlemen. This meeting is adjourned. Connection terminates in three seconds." The connection indicator light went out.

"An appropriate word... terminates... very appropriate indeed."

Chapter 9

S tafford tried to concentrate on his reports, but couldn't. His heart was beating faster than normal. After his confrontation with Nelson in the supply room, his adrenaline level was high. If he hadn't been at work, he would have tried doing push-ups, or jumping-jacks to get rid of the extra adrenaline. He took a couple of deep breaths instead.

He had too much on my mind. Beth, fighting, work, and the missing cocaine. His friend Dupree had stepped in something smelly in El Paso. He wondered what he was going to hear when he called Dupree back.

"Hurmmph," Stafford mumbled and rubbed his face with both hands.

Nelson swiveled around in his chair. "Are you talking to me?" Stafford thought about saying what came first to his mind, but decided not to make things worse.

"No, I was just talking to myself."

"Oh, really?" Nelson said doubtfully, looking him in the eyes.

My dad's advice when I was a teenager... "If you can walk away from a fight, do it. If you're forced to fight, don't get mad, never throw the first punch, but fight to win." That was still good advice. I didn't follow it. I threw the first punch.

Stafford took a long, deep breath and said, "Nelson..., I owe you an apology. I overreacted in the supply room. I shouldn't have hit you. I'm sorry."

Nelson's eyes went wide, and his mouth opened a little, as if he was about to say something, but he didn't.

"I'll understand if you can't accept my apology, but I wish you would, and forgive me for hitting you."

Nelson considered not accepting the apology, but he decided Stafford would be more open with him if he considered him a friend. Nelson's look of disbelief faded. Stafford could see he was thinking, weighing all his options.

"Oh, that's okay. We all make mistakes. I accept your apology." Nelson extended his hand. Stafford smiled, and shook it gladly.

At least Nelson was one less thing he had to think about. They let go of each other at the right moment, avoiding the feeling a man gets when you hold another man's hand too long. Stafford leaned back in his chair, folded his hands together in his lap, and tapped his thumbs together.

"Since we're on talking terms again, I'd like your opinion on some quantity discrepancies I've found in my seizure printouts. Have you got the time for me to tell you about them?"

"Sure. Is that the missing cocaine you were talking about on the phone earlier?"

"It is. I guess I got everybody's attention with that phone call. I didn't realize what it would sound like until after I said it."

"All of our ears really perked up," Nelson laughed. "Show me what you have, and I'll try to figure out if the coke is really missing."

Nelson took the reports and was reviewing them, when his cellphone vibrated. He looked down to see who was calling, and recognized the number as Dupree's.

"Excuse me, I'll be back in a few... I have some personal business to attend to," Nelson said.

"Okay..., I need to stretch my legs too."

They got up from their desks and walked out of the office. Stafford went to the break room, a few doors down the hall. Nelson walked to the elevator and pushed the up button.

Stafford looked around the break room. The room was empty. He thought this was as good a time as any to call Dupree and see what his story was on the missing cocaine. It had been obvious something strange was going on, but he wanted to give Dupree a chance to explain what he said. Stafford was not going to wait until after he finished work.

Stafford pulled out his government cellphone and pushed the one touch button for Dupree's personal cellphone. Dupree answered on the second ring, the caller I.D. on Dupree's phone only showed "unknown caller."

"Department of Homeland..." Dupree started to say from habit.

"Whoa, Jimmy..., personal phone. This is Ben Stafford, can we talk now?"

"Uh... sure, Ben. Now is fine."

"Let's continue our conversation about the missing cocaine. What happened to it?"

"Um... I'm glad you called to let me explain about that," he laughed. "We had a little screw-up here in the destruction of some coke we had seized. The coke was supposed to go to the local incinerator, but someone got sloppy and lost a few of the bundles. The whole thing is under OPR investigation right now. The investigation isn't common knowledge outside of the office, so I was wondering how you heard about it. That's why I asked you how you knew about it. Are you working with the Office of Professional Responsibility now?"

That was a plausible explanation, and may have had some truth in it, but he sounded like he didn't believe it himself, so why should I?

"That's a lie Jimmy, and you know it. What really happened to all that coke?"

"N-n-nothing," Dupree stammered.

"I asked you about several thousand pounds and now you say it was a few lost bundles. There's something you're hiding. What is it?"

"Nothing."

"What have you gotten yourself into?"

"Nothing, I said."

"No..., don't lie to me, Jimmy! You've gotten yourself into *something*."

"I don't know what you're talking about. I haven't gotten myself involved in anything..., and I don't appreciate you making accusations."

"Jimmy, I'm going to have to report this..., if for no other reason... to protect myself."

"Go ahead and report it... you'll look like a fool if you do. Now if that was all you wanted to talk about, I have to get back to work." Dupree hung up. Stafford flipped his phone shut.

From his field interrogation experience, Stafford knew he could usually tell when someone was lying. You didn't need a lie detector machine. People gave themselves away with other visual clues when they lied. Lies were not easy to detect over the phone, but Stafford had known Dupree for some time, and was familiar with the way he talked, and fidgeted when he was nervous. He heard the hesitation in his voice. He heard the click-click...click-click of him working the button on his ball point pen; a habit of Dupree's whenever he was under pressure. Stafford was sure Dupree was lying. The hardest part was figuring out *why* he was lying.

The answer might come with some digging. Well..., I'll just have to dig then.

Stafford returned to his office. Nelson wasn't back from his break yet. He picked up his desk phone and dialed the number to OPR, 1-800-RAT ME OUT, he used to joke. It wasn't funny now. He hung up before the number rang. He needed more time to think about what he was going to say.

Nelson was on the outdoor smoking area on the 7th floor. There was a cool breeze there. He opened his personal cellphone, located the call from Dupree, and listened to the voice-mail. By the tone of his voice, Dupree was in a panic about Stafford calling him about missing cocaine.

"I don't know why I recruited you," Nelson said softly to himself.

Nelson had met Dupree at an advanced investigation techniques class at FLETC three years earlier. Nelson saw an opportunity to recruit Dupree into the organization, because he was a simpleton. He had a college degree, and had passed all the job tests and interviews. He had the knowledge, but lacked good judgment. Dupree was a perfect target. In retrospect, he provided almost no useful information, and frequently put his group contacts at risk.

Nelson tried to call Dupree and found his line was "busy or out of the calling area." On a hunch, Nelson dialed Stafford's government cellphone. Stafford's number was "busy or out of the calling area." Nelson didn't think that was a coincidence. He wondered what Dupree was telling Stafford. He tried Dupree's number again, and this time he answered.

"Hello?"

"This is Nelson. Why did you call me? What did you tell Stafford?"

"Nelson! I'm glad you called. I just got off the phone with Stafford. He asked me about the cocaine! How could he know about that?"

Nelson wanted to reach through the phone and choke the life out of Dupree. He was barely able to control his voice to keep the anger from coming through.

"Well, if he knows anything, it will be because YOU told him! What did Stafford ask you, and what did you tell him?"

"He just wanted to know about the missing cocaine. I made a mistake the first time he called... when I asked him how he knew about it. I told him why I said that."

"Great. And how did you explain asking how he knew about the missing cocaine?"

"I told him we were doing a seized dope burn at the local incinerator, and a few bundles couldn't be accounted for... OPR was investigating. I said the investigation was not known about outside OPR, and our office. I think he believed me."

"Was any part of what you told Stafford true? Was there a loss of a few bundles of coke during a recent dope burn?"

"No, but he doesn't know that."

Nelson was quiet for a moment, thinking. "Okay..., sounds like you did all right. It's a good thing you called me. I'll keep an eye on Stafford. No need to report this incident any higher."

Nelson hung up on Dupree without letting him reply. He immediately dialed another number on his personal cellphone.

"Yes?"

"This is Nelson, HSI Agent in D.C. I need to speak to Bravo Two."

"Stand by." There was a short wait.

"Yes?" A different voice said.

"Is this Bravo Two?"

"Yes. Go ahead with your message."

"Sir, El Paso ICE Agent Dupree just told me about an inquiry from hostile HSI headquarters personnel concerning missing cocaine. Agent Dupree panicked when he was asked a routine question, and may have made himself the target of an investigation." There was silence from the other end of the line, so Nelson continued, uncomfortably.

"I believe I have the situation contained here, but Agent Dupree is in a panic. He gave an explanation that can be easily disproved. I believe he is a threat to our group operation. In my opinion, he must be dealt with, sir."

"I see. Thank you for sharing your concern, Agent Nelson. Continue monitoring the situation at your location, and advise me of any change. We will handle Dupree."

"Yes, sir. I will continue to monitor and advise."

"Well done, Agent Nelson." The connection went dead.

Nelson closed his phone and started back to his desk. He knew that Stafford was the man to watch. Maybe Stafford would have to be dealt with too. Taking care of Stafford, if he got too smart, might earn Nelson some good will from the people at the top, whoever they were. He figured Stafford might be onto something about the reduced cocaine seizures. Nelson knew there was a connection, but didn't know what it was. He smiled as he walked back inside. He thought about what it would feel like to watch the life leaving Stafford's body.

Chapter 10

For Stafford, the rest of the afternoon was thankfully uneventful. Nelson had some good ideas about where the "missing" cocaine was. "You know... seizure figures don't always have to add up... because of the international market influences on cocaine trafficking."

"What market influences?" Stafford said.

"If cocaine has a higher profit margin in England or France compared to the United States, the traffickers simply shift their supply to where it's more profitable. Maybe the price of coke is better in England or France."

"I hadn't thought of that, but I don't believe that's what's happening," Stafford said. He flipped through the report again. He could not have missed anything, he had looked at it a dozen times before. Nelson shrugged and turned to his own reports.

Nelson's explanation makes sense, but the U.S. was still the largest market for cocaine in the world. Why shift away from that?

The amount of cocaine Customs seized was staggering, but it was a small fraction of the total amount shipped. Some said the amount seized was only ten percent, but that was just a guess. No one knew how much dope was coming in undetected, except the dope smugglers. Stafford was thinking out loud. Nelson turned around to listen.

"You know..., it's possible the smugglers have found a totally new way to smuggle the dope in. I think I'll compare the current commercial importations report for the ports along the Mexican border, with the one from last year. The numbers might show an increase in one of the harmonized tariff numbers that has been flat or non-existent before. That might give me a clue."

"Harmonized numbers? What are you talking about?" Nelson said. He had a concerned look.

"We had classes on it in FLETC..., remember, Pete? Everything that is imported into the United States has a classification number, which makes it easier for computers to handle the information. It also makes it less confusing for the importers, and Customs. Was that a pin with an I, or a pen with an E you want to import? See what I mean? The classification number is called harmonized because several dozen countries agreed that the first seven digits of the classification number will be the same in every country for the same item. For example..., if you know the French customs classification number for fingernail files, the U.S. classification number will be the same up to the seventh digit."

"That's very interesting, but how is a harmonized number going to help you find out where the missing coke is..., or even if there *is* missing coke?"

"Because there's a computer record of all commercial importations coming into the U.S. We can do a computer search of the information. If, for example, there were no importations of bagged cement last year, and this year there are 305, then those shipments of cement would be suspect until they were verified. Seek and ye shall find! I think I may be on to something," Stafford said smiling. Nelson wasn't smiling.

"But for now, I've about had it with eyeballing these reports. I think I better give it a rest." Stafford good naturedly threw the printouts against the wall in front of his desk.

"That's a good idea. Put the reports away for a week or two, and then take another look. Maybe you'll see something you didn't see before," Nelson said.

"That is excellent advice. Quitting time people! Don't let the screen door hit you on the fanny on the way out," Stafford said loudly to the entire office.

He grabbed his jacket, and headed for the door. Just as he reached the door, he remembered he was supposed to meet Frank Hernandez in the gym. If it wasn't for the gym in El Paso, and the heat, Stafford might have been overweight. He drank gallons of beer during his bar-hopping, woman-hunting forays.

The women he chased, and sometimes caught, were not the kind you took home to meet your mother. After the initial excitement faded, he found himself depressed and unhappy. He knew the reason why, but he ignored it. He neglected his spiritual side because it would have gotten in the way. He had no use for God.

He left the office and went to the gym. It was crowded, as it always was after five o'clock. In the locker room, Stafford changed into his work-out clothes. The other men in the locker room were in varying conditions of physical fitness. Some of them might have given him a run for his money, if he were to fight them hand to hand. Others looked like today might be their last day on earth.

At least they're trying.

He made his way out of the locker room and over to the free weight area. There were several men and women working out there already. The men were strutting like peacocks, breathing hard like they'd just climbed a mountain. They sneaked glances at the women who were working out. All they needed was a place to serve drinks.

After stretching and warming up, Stafford used two 25 pound dumbbells, and a high number of repetitions over three sets, to build strength and stamina. He did wrist curls, and flys.

"Most police officers are killed with their own guns." Stafford's father had told him that, and he had never forgotten it. Statistically, that was no longer the case, if it ever had been, but weapon retention was always in his mind during his strength training. He had doubts about how an average woman could keep her weapon from being taken away by a large male attacker. Stafford was pretty sure that somebody would have scars for life if they tried to take his weapon away from him.

After he had been working out for about 15 minutes, Stafford saw Frank Hernandez arrive. He and Frank exchanged chin nods, and Frank went to change clothes.

Stafford finished his third set of reps and sat down on a mat to wait for Hernandez. He stretched a little and mentally went through the fighting techniques he wanted to show him. Hernandez came out of the locker room dressed in fluorescent green spandex bike pants. He walked over to where Stafford was sitting, stunned.

"You look really spiffy in those shorts, Frank. How often do you change the batteries?"

"Ah, you just wish you had the nerve to wear these."

"You got that half right..., you gotta have a lot of nerve to wear those."

"Yeah, well, whatever." Frank was getting peeved.

"Okay, Frank..., I have some ideas about what I want to show you. But first, do you have something in particular you want me to help you with? How about edged-weapon defense?"

"Yeah, I have some ideas, but why don't you go ahead and show me knife defense first."

"Okay-fine. Let me explain something about knife defensive tactics." Stafford crossed his arms in front of his chest and went into teaching mode.

"If you get into a knife fight, you are probably going to get cut. Count on it. Unless stealth is a priority, just shoot your attacker if at all possible. Aim high on the torso, and let the bullet impact knock them back away from you. If your attacker is right on top of you, and your weapon is not already out and ready to fire, you aren't going to have time to draw and shoot. That is also true if the attacker is moving quickly toward you. If they run at you from within about 30 feet, they'll reach you before you can recognize the threat, draw your weapon, and fire. There might be exceptions, but if your attacker knows what he's doing, it's too late for you to react. That's not to say you shouldn't put up a fight. He might give you a fatal wound, and you kill him before you go down. If an amateur attacks you, they tend to make mistakes in the first few seconds. For example, they yell to scare you into submission. You have a chance against an amateur."

"You're not exactly building my confidence. Basically, what you're telling me is I'm probably going to get killed if the attacker is an expert?"

"Probably..., and you're *definitely* going to get cut. But remember, odds are the person attacking you is most likely inexperienced."

Hernandez didn't like what he had heard and was unsettled. He pursed his lips, and crossed his arms in front of him. He was standing with his feet spread about shoulder width apart, in a classic defensive posture.

"I can't believe I wouldn't be fast enough to shoot the attacker," Hernandez said.

"Nobody is fast enough to use a pistol to defend against a surprise knife attack from close quarters. If you can push them off and get some distance, then maybe, and that's a big maybe," Stafford countered.

"I think I'm fast enough. I'm *very* fast out of the holster."

"I thought you used to be a police officer. They never told you about this when you were in the police academy?" Stafford said.

"I don't remember them saying anything about not having a chance."

"I know they touched on this subject in FLETC..., you didn't hear it there either?"

"Yeah, well they said a lot of things in the academy to try and scare people into quitting."

"Okay, Frank, I'll prove it to you." Hernandez frowned, as if he knew he was about to be made a fool of. He uncrossed his arms, getting ready.

"Yeah, prove it to me, but take it easy, okay?"

"Okay, I won't hurt you. For demonstration purposes, let's assume I have a knife in my right hand, and you have your weapon holstered on your right side. I'll stand here, about three feet away from you."

"Okay."

"Are you ready?" Stafford said.

"Ready," Hernandez answered as he moved his right foot back a half-step, but it wouldn't be enough.

In a flash, the back of Stafford's left hand tapped Hernandez heavily on the end of his nose. Hernandez jerked his head away from the strike, and involuntarily closed his eyes for a split second. He raised his arms attempting to block whatever was coming next. Realizing his mistake he tried pushing away with his left hand as he brought his right hand down towards his imaginary holstered weapon. He knew it was too late for a good response.

Stafford stepped forward as Hernandez recoiled. He continued around to his left, parried Hernandez' left arm away with his right forearm, and wrapped his left arm counterclockwise around Hernandez' right arm. This trapped Hernandez' forearm in Stafford's left armpit. Stafford made a quick slashing motion with the edge of his right hand across the left side of Hernandez' neck, about three inches under the ear. The entire demonstration had taken less than two seconds.

"You're now dead or dying, partner..., you just don't know it yet. Your gun hand was not a factor," Stafford said quietly. He released his hold on Hernandez, who was starting to struggle to get free.

"I think I've seen enough for today," Hernandez said. He rubbed his nose and neck.

"Hold on. Let me demonstrate a good technique against what I just showed you."

"Oh, so there *is* a defense against it then?" Hernandez said.

"It might work well on an amateur..., like I said."

"Okay..., show me," Hernandez said.

Stafford demonstrated on Hernandez. He showed him how to seize an attacker's weapon arm, and by applying pressure to the back of the shoulder and elbow, move the attacker to the ground to disarm him.

"There are other techniques, but they are more deadly. I can show you if you like," Stafford said.

"No, this was good enough. I think I'll do a little workout and then call it a day. Thanks for showing me."

"You're welcome, Frank. Let me know if there is anything else you'd like me to show you."

"Will do. Later, man," Hernandez said as he walked away, rubbing his arm.

I hope you remember what I told you.

Stafford finished his workout, showered and left the gym for his commute home. He considered himself a student of people. The truth was, he just liked to watch people make fools of themselves. During his rush-hour walk and commute home via the Metro, he entertained himself by watching the ballet of white collar bureaucrats rushing home.

Stafford thought the women walkers were especially interesting. Apparently, there were two forms of female footwear. One was for walking to and from the Metro, and one was for looking good in the office.

Why go halfway? Why not wear your housecoat all the way to the office and change there? In fact... wouldn't it be more efficient to stash your makeup and clothes at work and totally change when you got there? Why wear clothing and shoes that are uncomfortable? Tradition?

If patience was a virtue, there was not much virtue to be found in D.C. People were pushing and shoving at the bus stops, and late arrivals at the Metro came from the back of the crowd and cut in front of others who had been waiting longer. Usually, nobody did more than mumble, or frown at the line cutters.

Stafford noticed a man, walking in his direction, who was walking square-shouldered. He was purposely not turning his shoulder aside to prevent a collision when someone passed by in the opposite direction. Occasionally, someone who wasn't paying attention received quite a jolt. Stafford smiled in amazement.

Funny I never noticed that before. That's one way to get rid of your daily frustrations... like sucker punching somebody. No way am I going to stay long in this town. Look at that... someone's not paying attention again. They're going to meet. This ought to be good.

The two men were on a collision course. At the last second, the man from Stafford's direction side-stepped and avoided a collision.

He missed him... What a chicken!

Stafford adjusted his stride and aimed himself toward the square shouldered walker coming his way. Stafford looked left and right nonchalantly, pretending he wasn't watching where he was walking. Stafford made a slight adjustment to the left, and so did the other man.

He's heading for me... ten feet.

Just before the collision, Stafford lowered his left shoulder and stepped off hard with his right foot.

Stafford's shoulder hit the mark and knocked the air out of the other man. The collision sent him staggering to his right. As he staggered, his arms flew up, he dropped his briefcase, and tripped over it. He tried to catch himself with his right hand, but hit the ground hard. Momentum carried him over from his right side onto his back. His feet flew in the air, and he nearly did a backward somersault. Stafford stepped over to him as he was sitting up.

"Are you okay, pal? You really ought to watch where you're going. Somebody could have gotten hurt. Are you okay?"

The man got to his feet, red-faced with anger and embarrassment. He retrieved his briefcase and rubbed his hand, which was pink and had loose skin dangling from his palm.

"Yeah, I'm okay. Maybe we *both* ought to watch where we're going," he said. He started walking again, brushing off his clothes with the back of his bleeding hand.

"You are so right. Sorry about that. YOU BETTER TAKE CARE OF THAT HAND!" Stafford said to the man's back. He walked away, smiling.

After walking for a couple of minutes, Stafford entered the Metro station and went to the platform to wait for his train.

"Ben, I saw what you did to that man," a woman's voice said. He turned around and saw Beth St. James, frowning.

"I think that was a rotten thing to do. You should be ashamed of yourself. Oh…, and by the way, don't even *think* about calling or coming to see me." She turned on her heel and walked back to the stairs. Stafford was momentarily speechless.

"Beth, wait a minute. What are you talking about?"

"You know very well what I'm talking about. Good-bye," She said over her shoulder.

"BUT IT WAS AN ACCIDENT!" Stafford yelled up the steps at her.

Beth kept walking. She was still pretty, even going away.

His train arrived. He boarded and stood near the door, holding the bar. The car was crowded and smelly. His best chance to end his loneliness was getting farther away by the second.

Chapter 11

Stafford got off the train at his stop, and started walking to his apartment. The neighborhoods he walked through were pretty nice. Some of the houses were well cared for, and a few looked like nobody lived there. Most were built in the 1940's and 50's during the boom. Yuppies owned them now. Their expensive designer dogs were pooping on the lawns and the yuppies were picking it up like lose change. What a way to live. Stafford was no yuppie, and proud of it. He spent most of his money on expensive vacations and cars, instead of in the stock market or real estate. His eyes were not on the future.

The apartment buildings near his were a mixture of 1940's, 50's, and 60's. A few were so new they looked out of place. His apartment building wasn't much to look at. It was one of the many that were built to house the servicemen returning from World War Two. The sun was getting low in the sky, as he walked through the building's main entrance. It had been a beautiful day outside, but he had spent all day in a steel, concrete, and glass box.

The door was propped open to let in some fresh air. He stopped to pick up his mail. The mail box was as old as the building, and had been painted numerous times. Bubbles of rust surrounded his apartment number.

He climbed the steps to his second floor apartment. His liked renting above the first floor because he didn't want to worry about a burglar coming through the windows.

He unlocked the door, walked in and saw the message light blinking on his answering machine. The machine sat on a cardboard box he was using for an end-table. In this case the box wasn't at the end of anything, since he didn't have a couch or arm chair. He tossed his mail down beside the answering machine and pressed the play button.

"Ben, this is your dad. I've got some bad news. Rennie Gordon's daughter Carrie was found dead in her apartment in Dothan today. Rennie was the one who found her. I know you two used to go to school together, so I thought you'd want to know. Your mom and I are fine. Hope you are too. Call me when you can." The machine beeped and played the next message.

"Ben Stafford… this is Bill Williams. We just had a get together today at Rancho Deluxe, and the fellas were all wondering what was happening with you. I told them a little of what I knew, but I said I'd call you and find out how you were doing, and so I have. Give me a call when you can. Bye."

Billy didn't mention Rennie's daughter, so he didn't know about it when he called. He didn't leave his number either. I can get it from dad if I need it.

Stafford called his father. It only rang three times before he answered. Stafford knew he would probably be sitting in his recliner with his hands behind his head, the television remote balanced on one arm of the chair, and the wireless phone on the other. His mother would be in the kitchen cooking supper.

"Uh, Hel-lo?" He sounded sleepy.

"Hey, Dad. Did I wake you up?"

"Nope… no. I was just sitting here watching some TV."

"I figured. I got your message about Carrie Gordon."

"Yeah, it's a shame isn't it?"

"How did she die?"

"They're not sure yet. Drugs, I'm guessing. Rennie is beside himself over it. I knew he was a friend of yours, and thought you'd want to know. Are you planning on coming down for the funeral?"

"I don't think so, I'm pretty busy here."

"Well, if you need some money for a plane ticket, I can loan you some."

"No, it's not the money. Rennie just isn't in my circle of friends any more. It's too bad about his daughter, but it's really not that big of a concern for me."

"I'm sorry to hear you say that, Son. I thought I raised you better than that."

"Ah… come on, Dad."

"Well, you let me know if you change your mind. I hope you do. The funeral will probably be next week sometime. I'll call and let you know."

"Okay. I'll talk to you later."

"Yes, you will. Bye." His father hung up. The disappointment in his father's voice was obvious. Stafford slowly hung up the phone, put his hands on his hips, and looked down at his feet.

When did I become so callous? Is this what war does to you?

He shook his head no, in disapproval of himself, and looked around. The living room was almost bare of furnishings. The television was sitting on the floor. He didn't have much furniture when he lived in El Paso, and hadn't bothered to buy any after he moved to D.C. The lack of furniture was a combination of not having enough money after he first got hired, and the fact he was too lazy to go furniture shopping. He thought about renting a furnished apartment, but the unfurnished ones were cheaper by a couple of hundred dollars, and he didn't have the money right now.

Stafford had brought his two most prized possessions from Texas. One was a large framed print of John Wayne. Stafford hung it on the living room wall. The Duke was dressed as a cowboy, of course. All his weight was on one leg. He held a lever action rifle in one hand, and the other hand was pushing down the butt of his pistol. The expression on his face said "Yeah..., you heard me." The characters John Wayne played in the movies were everything Ben Stafford wanted to be. They were always strong, fair, moral, brave, and expert shots with a rifle or a pistol.

Stafford's other prized possession was a framed watercolor of a rattlesnake, which he hung on his bedroom wall. He liked the symbolism of a snake being in the bedroom, although he wasn't sure exactly what it symbolized. The snake painting would have been over his bed, if he had a real bed. His bed was a foam mat on the bedroom floor.

He turned on the no-name big screen TV he had bought at the local big-box store, took off his suit coat, and hung it from a nail on the wall. There was a picture there once upon a time, most likely of dogs playing poker. Underneath his coat, was an old folding lawn chair he used for watching TV. He got lucky one morning, and found the chair in the trash in front of the building. He also had a table lamp he had acquired the same way. He kicked off his shoes and walked into the kitchen, leaving sweaty footprints on the twenty year old peel-and-stick tile floor.

He reached into the freezer without really looking, grabbed a frozen dinner, and put it in the microwave. He punched in seven and a half minutes, which was a good time for heating almost anything small and frozen, and went back to watch the news. He sat down carefully in the chair, not wanting to rip the webbing further, and listened to the bleach-blond anchorwoman blather about the economy, car crashes, plane crashes, shootings, murders, missing women, and drug deaths.

Do all women dye their hair? Is it some kind of law? Do they think people can't tell? I bet I'd have to go to Sweden to find a real blond.

The newswoman was speaking again.

"Police in the district and surrounding areas have noticed a sharp increase in the number of drug overdoses in recent days. So far this week, 28 people have died from apparent drug overdoses compared with 15 deaths in the previous two months. As yet, police have no explanation for the increase in deaths."

The microwave dinged, and Stafford retrieved his dinner. He sat down in the lawn chair again, and used the remote to turn off the TV. He wanted silence so he could think.

Strange that Carrie Gordon died about the same time there was this upswing in local drug deaths. No connection though... Alabama is a long way from D.C. I wonder if drugs killed her. Maybe the purity was higher than normal, or maybe she just overdosed. I'll check on that when I get back to the office.

After dinner he took a shower, put on his lay-around-the-house clothes, and looked at the junk mail and bills the mail dude had brought him.

He turned the TV on again, and channel surfed continuously. Finally, he got sleepy, shut everything off and lay down on his sleeping mat. As he relaxed, he remembered, as he did every day, the men he served with in Iraq and Afghanistan. He remembered how some good friends had died, and how some had been wounded. He thought about the men he had killed. They were with him always.

He choked back the lump in his throat in time, and wiped the tears from his eyes. He needed to cry for them, and for himself, but he couldn't. He was afraid if he started crying, he wouldn't be able to stop.

He fell asleep, but he dreamed his recurring dream again this night.

"Echo three this is echo five. Say again your position and situation... over."

The radio handset was loud in his ear but he was still having trouble hearing. There was heavy firing going on, and Stafford was trying to direct his squad leaders by hand signals and yelling. Mostly, his men were where he wanted them, but his lead squad was pinned down. Their Humvee had been hit by an RPG. The soldiers from that vehicle had taken cover behind a mud-brick wall to the right rear of the vehicle. Two of them were wounded. The number two Humvee had pulled around in front, and was laying down a steady stream of return fire from the .50 cal in the roof turret. The situation wasn't good, but it wasn't getting any worse either. He answered his radio.

"Echo three... this is echo five... over."

"Echo five... this is three... go ahead."

"This is echo three. Our position ten clicks north our base on Balad road. I have one vehicle disabled by R-P-G. Heavy small arms fire from a hundred-fifty meters our east. Have two W-I-A. Request immediate dust-off. Break." He stopped transmitting to yell at Sergeant Bailey, the third squad leader.

"Watch our left flank!"

Sergeant Bailey nodded and gave an okay sign with his fingers. He began yelling and pointing to reposition his squad to the left. His men immediately moved, rifles up, scanning high and low for targets. Stafford went back to the radio.

"Echo three this is echo five... over."

"Echo five... three... go ahead."

"This is echo five. Do you have any Apache's up?"

"Echo five this is echo three. Your dust-off is in route. E-T-A 30 mikes. Negative Apaches. One Kiowa will arrive with dust-off..."

Stafford saw something streak by from behind and to his right. It struck the .50 gunner and keep going. There was no explosion. The gunner's helmet flew into the air and landed behind the vehicle. What was left of him dropped down inside the vehicle. The .50 was silent. Stafford felt sick. He could hear men in the vehicle yelling. He saw something dark arc in over his head, bounce, roll, and come to a stop near Sgt. Bailey. Bailey saw it too.

"GRENADE!" Bailey and Stafford yelled simultaneously. Bailey dove over a low mud wall.

Stafford hit the ground and rolled over on his back as he brought his rifle up, aiming at the roof of the building nearest him. The grenade went off.

Stafford flinched but kept looking through the dust and smoke at the roof. He saw something move. A man stood up and started firing an AK-47 on full automatic, spraying the area below with bullets. The AK rounds kicked dirt onto Stafford's face as he fired three quick shots, and saw the bullets hit the man's chest and head. He dropped his rifle over the roof's edge, and fell back out of sight.

"MAN DOWN! MAN DOWN! MEDIC!" Someone yelled behind him. Stafford rolled onto his stomach. It was Sgt. Bailey.

Stafford awoke and jerked into a sitting position. He took a deep breath and exhaled slowly. He inhaled deeply once more and rubbed his hands over his face and head, trying to reach inside and pull the memory out for good. He knew he couldn't.

"Thank you, Lord, for keeping me safe. Please protect our soldiers. Please stop the war. You have the power. You can do it with a thought. If I had your power... if I were Emperor of the World... I'd stop it."

He lay back and closed his eyes. He could smell the battle. He tried to empty his mind of negative thoughts so he could sleep. He thought about Beth. She was upset with him, and he hoped she would get over it. He had pleasant thoughts about her anyway. He had hopes. He fell asleep.

Chapter 12

T he morning was cool and clear. It was the beginning of a beautiful day. Stafford could see the sky from his mat on the floor because there were no curtains on the windows. The sun was not up yet, and he could see two or three stars through the glow from the city lights. He liked this time of day. Each morning was somehow connected to every other morning in your life. Mornings as a boy, when you hated going to school. Mornings in the Army, when someone was yelling at you before you could get your eyes open. Mornings in Washington, when you wondered whether any of the other mornings made a bit of difference to anybody, anywhere. He eased himself into a sitting position, wrapped his arms around his knees, and yawned. He began his daily routine. After breakfast and a shower, he was out the door, heading back to the office on the Metro.

Why do people live this way? Why did people stop farming? I'd rather be feeding the chickens.

Before he realized it, he was sitting at his desk again. It was as if he had never left. Today would be a carbon copy of yesterday, with reports, reports, and more reports. Stafford had 50 official emails to read, but had not been able to read them. He could never keep up. His favorite email messages were the open-source compilation of possible terrorism related incidents from around the country. Someone outside the government gleaned it from news stories and sent it to law enforcement agencies. There were county and state departments of homeland security all over the country, working to stop terrorists before they did more damage.

So far, the effort was paying off. There was always the lone person acting out a plot, like the Muslim gunman at the mall in Idaho randomly shooting people, but the attack was not coordinated with other people. To the FBI, an attack by a single person was never a true act of terrorism. It was all in the definition of terrorism. Stafford thought that approach was designed to keep the public feeling safe, when in fact no one really was.

Today's compilation of incidents was interesting. Army Criminal Investigation reported substantial amounts of military weapons, ammunition, explosives, and equipment had been stolen from several military bases near the Mexican border.

"Hey, Pete. Did you see this email about stolen Army equipment? The bases being hit are near the Mexican border. I'll bet drug gangs are involved. I wonder if the stolen Army equipment is connected with my missing coke," Stafford said.

"I doubt it," Nelson said. What could cocaine and Army equipment possibly have in common? It's probably a book-keeping error by some supply clerk."

"No way. It says here that ammunition storage bunkers were broken into. That's no bookkeeping error."

"Stafford, if you can connect those dots, I'd like to see it."

"Yeah, you're probably right... that would be a stretch for the drug guys, and too easy to track if heavy weapons started showing up in Mexico, or on the black market."

The morning passed quickly, and lunch time had arrived. Stafford called Beth to see if she had calmed down since yesterday's confrontation in the Metro, and to ask if she would be his lunch partner again today.

"Customs, St. James," she answered.

"Oooh, you're going to get in trouble," he said, stretching out the words like a teasing adolescent. "You didn't say the official headquarters greeting. I'm gonna tell your daddy!"

"What do you want, Ben? I haven't got time for your foolishness."

"I'm sorry, Beth. Would you please have lunch with me today?"

"Not today... I'm too busy. I brought my lunch and I'm going to eat at my desk. Maybe some other time."

"Listen, Beth, I want to explain about what you saw me do yesterday. It's really not what you think."

"How would you know what I think? I'll let you know when I want to eat lunch with you again. Good-Bye."

I really messed up a good thing. Maybe she just needs more time..., like a couple of years.

Nelson had been sitting quietly behind Stafford, eavesdropping. He wondered what Beth had seen Stafford doing yesterday.

"Hey, Pete..., want to go get something to eat?"

"Sure. Let's go eat," Nelson said.

"Hold all my calls people, I'm going to lunch!" Nelson said loudly.

Everyone in the room turned and looked at Nelson, to see if he had said it instead of Stafford. Even Stafford looked at Nelson strangely.

"What?" Nelson said, holding both arms out from his side, palms up in the universal gesture of innocence. He headed for the door with Stafford a few steps behind him, smiling.

Both men were eating light today. Stafford was pining for Beth, and Nelson was following Stafford's lunch food lead. They found a spot, sat down and nibbled on their salads. As Nelson and Stafford were eating, Anne Dawson and Sam Person walked over, carrying their lunch trays.

"Mind if we sit with you two?" Anne said.

"Not at all. Have a seat," Stafford said.

"Is Beth coming down today?"

"No..., afraid not. She's tied up today. So how are you two?"

"I'm doing well, thank you," Anne said.

"Ahm joost fime," Sam said. His mouth was already loaded with food. He looked like a chipmunk with his cheeks bulging out.

"Ya'll, this is Pete Nelson. He works with me upstairs in Intelligence. Pete, this lovely lady is Anne Dawson, who works with Health and Human Services, and this hungry fellow is Sam Person. He works for the FBI."

"Nice to meet you both," Nelson said, as he gave them a head nod. He hadn't offered to shake hands, and neither had Anne or Sam, who were eating with their hands.

Anne was in a talkative mood. She began telling Stafford and Nelson about her work at HHS. Stafford paid attention, since he didn't have a good idea what the people at HHS did for a living, and he wanted to know. After five minutes of talking about who the laziest employees and managers were, Anne switched the subject to current events. Sam kept eating.

"Did you see the newspaper this morning, Ben?" She was holding her eyebrows higher on her forehead. She relaxed her brow and didn't wait for a reply.

"There's a big rise in reported drug deaths across the entire region. Our CDC Director is very interested in statistical spikes like that. He thinks they may be indicative of some underlying epidemiology." Now Stafford's eyebrows went up. Nobody had used words like that around him since he was in college.

"What's CDC stand for?" Stafford said. He was trying to cover up the dumb expression he was wearing.

"The Centers for Disease Control, silly. You never heard of the Centers for Disease Control before?"

"Oh yeah…, the CDC…, of course. That's very interesting, Anne. What could the other underlying epidemiology possibly be?"

"Well, there might be something poisonous in the drugs, besides their usual ingredients that is. That's what I think."

"You mean like a contaminant?" Stafford asked. Nelson slowed his chewing so he could hear their conversation better.

"Yes. Maybe something went wrong in the processing of the drugs. I understand some of the labs are pretty primitive. It wouldn't be unusual for someone to use the wrong chemical in the processing or diluting," Anne said.

Sam had finished his meal and was speaking normal English again. "Or they could be mixing it with something to increase the high and instead, they got a new low…, so to speak."

"You know, a friend of mine in Alabama had a daughter who just died mysteriously. I imagine it was due to drugs," Stafford said.

"That's awful. Are you going down for the funeral?" Anne's expression showed she was expecting a yes. She helped him decide.

"You know, you're the second person to ask me that. I think I might go down to pay my respects, and see some family and friends. Maybe I'll check into that poison drug angle too. Anyway, we have to get back to work. Nice talking to the two of you." Stafford and Nelson left together and walked to the elevator.

Nelson's mind was working. He knew about the missing cocaine, but he didn't know anything about poison drugs. He wouldn't put it past the people he worked for to want to kill off some dopers. He thought about what he could do to stay ahead of Stafford, and if he couldn't stay ahead of him… how to stop him permanently.

*   *   *   *

On the way back to their office after lunch, Stafford and Nelson were both thinking about what to do next. They got on the elevator together.

"I'll see you back at the office later. I've got some people I need to see upstairs."

"Funny you should say that, Pete. I've got people I need to see upstairs too."

They rode past their usual floor, got off together on the sixth floor, and walked away in opposite directions. Neither had any idea where the other was going, but Nelson was the most curious. He took five or six steps and stopped, turning around to look at Stafford.

"See ya later," Nelson said.

"LATER, PETE," Stafford said loudly, still walking away. Nelson, turned again, and continued on hi way.

"YOU WANNA HOLD IT DOWN OUT THERE?" said a man's voice coming from a nearby office.

Stafford couldn't resist. He headed to the office the voice had come from, and stepped inside. The voice had a face and body, and the face showed he was not happy.

"Sorry, chief, Stafford said. "I didn't mean to wake anybody. Was I talking too loud?"

"Very funny, sport..., and yes you were."

"Sorry about that, chief."

"Don't call me chief. Ah..., you're Stafford, aren't you? I've seen you around here before. What's your business on this floor?"

"I have an appointment to go to, chief."

"Don't call me chief…, sport." Face was frowning.

"Who you calling sport…, chief?" Stafford said. "I'm just trying to find room 7-6-5-3 point 3-4-A. Can you give me some directions?"

"I said… don't call me chief!" Face glared at Stafford.

"Sorry about that..., sir."

"Did you make up that room number? There's no such office number on this floor…, but I can still tell you where to go anyway," Face deadpanned.

"I thought the number I gave you was a good one. I would appreciate any directions you could give me. I'm looking for Supervisor Beth St. James, sir."

Face sighed and opened a small book on his desk. He scanned a page with his eyes following his finger.

"Her office is room 7-34 point 56-A, and it's that way," he said pointing in the direction Stafford had come from.

It was clear that he wasn't simply indicating a direction, but immediacy as well. Stafford couldn't leave without one more provocation.

"Thanks a lot, sport!" Stafford said smiling. "Oh..., could you call her and tell her I'm on my way?"

"You really like to press your luck, don't you, chief? Tell her yourself. Now get out of my office."

Stafford didn't reply. He might have said something more, but was fresh out of smart-alecky remarks. He smiled and nodded his head once, then turned back in the direction Face had pointed.

Nelson was alone on the smoking balcony. He sauntered over to the sunny area, near a large window. There were silver reflective blinds on the window, so he felt the warmth on his face as well as his back. It felt good. He opened his personal cellphone and called his controller. The call was answered on the first ring.

"Hello?" a man's voice said. Nelson was surprised. The voice didn't belong to the assistant who usually answered his calls.

"Who *is* this?" Nelson asked.

"Who's calling?"

"HSI Agent Peter Nelson, at Customs headquarters."

"You have something to report, Nelson?"

"Yes. I need to speak to Bravo Two."

"This is Bravo Two. Go ahead with your report." Nelson took the phone away from his ear and checked the number displayed, then checked it again. It was the correct number. He put the phone back to his ear. Something didn't seem right.

"Nelson? I said go ahead with your report."

"Yes, sir. I have a new concern about Agent Stafford. He may be getting close to... I'm sorry, sir. You sound different today..., and what happened to your assistant?"

"I have some congestion today. It's nothing for you to be concerned about. My assistant is out of the office at the moment. Continue with your report."

"I'm sorry, sir, but I will make contact again via secondary protocols. Goodbye, sir." Nelson closed his phone.

Stafford had been walking past the smoking balcony window, and saw Nelson on the phone through blinds. Stafford heard part of Nelson's conversation and stopped. He definitely had heard Nelson say "Agent Stafford."

Who was bravo two? He said "I need to speak to bravo two?" Why was he using code? Why was my name mentioned? Was he talking to OPR? A couple more letters and they'd be Oprah. They're on this floor... I better go see them, before they come see me.

Nelson finished his call. Stafford continued in the direction of Beth St. James' office, as well as the Office of Professional Responsibility. In police departments, they were called Internal Affairs.

*   *   *   *

In the electronic intercept room at FBI headquarters, Director Brad Clement had been listening in on Nelson's phone call. Clement oversaw the FBI's Domestic Anti-Terrorism Section. Because the Nelson-DHS investigation was one of the most important cases the FBI had going, Clement was personally supervising the daily activities, and reporting any progress to the Secretary of the Justice Department. Clement yanked off his headphones and slammed them on the desk, startling the man who had been playing the part of Number Two.

"Nelson hung up! He knows something isn't right!" Clement said. He leaned forward and put his clenched fists down on the table top.

"Supervisory Agent Sanchez," he said slowly "What is the secondary protocol? Who is Agent Stafford? Which agency does Stafford work for?"

Supervisor Sanchez and the other five agents in the room looked back and forth at each other, and shrugged together in ignorance. Sanchez opened his mouth to speak, but didn't get the chance.

"Well, *somebody* better find out, and I mean NOW!" Clement said angrily. His face turning red.

Three of the agents scurried out of the room, with Sanchez on their heels, barking orders as they went. The young Agent who had been role playing as Number Two sat looking at Clement, his mouth open in surprise.

"Close your mouth, it'll raise your perceived I.Q. by 20 percent," Clement said. The young Agent closed his mouth and swallowed hard.

 "What's your name, Agent?"

"Bonifay Schwartzchild, sir."

Clement rubbed his forehead with his fingers, shut his eyes, and dropped his hands to his hips. Then he stood up straight, opened his eyes, and looked down at the man..

"Bon-ni-fay Schwartz-child? Are you putting me on?" Clement said.

"No, sir. That's my name, sir."

 "Well, Bonnie-Faye... may I call you Bonnie-Faye?"

"Certainly, sir."

"Unless you've got something more to say to me, and your name was plenty... don't you think you had better get your butt in gear?"

"Director, sir, shouldn't we leave a person, like another assistant, here to answer the phone in case it rings again?"

"Good idea," Clement said quickly. "At least somebody around here has an idea about how to do their job. Find somebody else to answer the phone."

Schwartzchild jumped from his seat and ran out of the room, leaving the communication specialist to tend to the intercept equipment. Clement, head down and hands still on his hips, walked slowly into the hallway. Schwartzchild was already out of sight.

"Who's going to answer the phone now?" Clement said to himself. He went back into the intercept room and looked at the communications specialist, who had a deer in the headlights look on his face.

"You guys had better not be the best we've got, or we're in deep trouble."

Chapter 13

S tafford was walking near Beth's office. He heard her voice coming from an open doorway, and her voice was getting louder as he got closer. She was telling someone she would be back in a few minutes. She walked into the hallway and stopped when she saw him. Her look of surprise quickly changed to one of mild irritation. He pre-empted the expected verbal jab.

"Hi, Beth. Sorry, but I can't talk right now. I've got an appointment," he said, as he walked past her. She never took her eyes off of him. He didn't look back.

"Wait just a minute!" she said firmly. Stafford stopped and faced her.

"I need to talk to you," she said in a softer tone. Can you meet me after work today?... on the first floor, near the Wilson Center?" Stafford was pleased. He didn't think she would return to normal so quickly.

"Sure..., say a little after five o'clock then?"

"Yes, that's fine. I'll see you then." She offered Stafford a shallow smile. Stafford smiled weakly back, and continued on his way.

I wonder what she wants to talk about... me I suppose. Women... talk-talk-talk-talk-talk.

Stafford found the OPR office and went inside, shutting the door noisily behind him. A thin young man was seated behind a small desk, looking intently at his computer monitor. Stafford walked over to him and waited to be greeted. The man was obviously the receptionist, but was in no hurry to receive anyone. After 30 seconds, which was long enough to irritate Stafford, he reluctantly stopped what he was doing.

"May I help you?" he said cocking his head to one side without looking up.

"Yes. I'd like to talk to an investigator about some possible misconduct."

"Do you have an appointment?" he said with a nasally drone, finally looking at Stafford.

"No."

"You should really make an appointment. All of our agents are very busy right now," he said with a false smile.

"Would you like me to go out in the hall, call you on my cellphone, and make an appointment for right now?

"There's no reason for you to get snotty."

"*You* would be the reason. But you're right, I shouldn't have been snotty. So why don't you go ask whoever is here if I could talk to them?"

"Don't tell me how to do my job!" he nasaled again.

"What is it with that nasally sound? One sentence you have it, and the next sentence you don't."

The young receptionist smirked as he picked up his phone and pressed four numbers. He put the phone to his ear and looked at Stafford.

"I have a gentleman out here who is trying to give me a hard time. Can you come out please? Thank you." He set the receiver down and placed his hands on the desk in front of him, intertwining his fingers. He tapped his thumbs together and smiled at Stafford.

"Someone will see you in a moment." He didn't nasal this time.

"Oh, I guess I'm in for it now huh?" Stafford said. He shoved his hands in his pants pockets and smiled.

The door in the back of the room opened, and a gray haired man wearing a white shirt, power red tie, and navy blue trousers emerged, and walked over to Stafford.

"I'm OPR Section Chief Turner. What seems to be the problem here?" he said, looking at Stafford and then the receptionist.

"This yo-yo told me if I didn't go out with him, he wasn't going to let me talk to anybody today. What kind of office is this anyway?" Stafford said. Turner looked down at the receptionist, whose mouth was open like someone had just stomped on his toe, and then back at Stafford.

"There's no need for name calling. Well, Andy, is that what you said?" Turner asked smiling, and sensing a jokester. Andy regained his composure quickly, although his face was still flushed.

"It most certainly is *not* what I said! This… this *man* offered me 50 dollars to go with him to the men's restroom, and I refused."

"Okay, okay," Stafford said. "I give up. I just wanted to talk to an IA investigator about some possible misconduct."

"Would the *possible* misconduct be your own?" Turner said, folding his arms over his chest.

"If only it was that simple, sir. No, it's about an agent I know on the Mexican border."

"Okay mister funny man, why don't you come with me while I've got some time," Turner said. He turned and headed back the way he had entered, with Stafford following.

Stafford winked at Andy as he passed, and Andy stuck his tongue out at Stafford in return.

"What's your name, grade, step, and section?" Turner said. It sounded more like a demand than a question.

"Agent Benjamin Stafford, GS-12 step five, HSI intelligence section, sir."

"Intelligence huh? I love oxymorons," Turner said.

"Thank you, sir," Stafford said.

"You're quite the comedian aren't you, Stafford?"

"I try, sir. My father says, "A feeling man cries, and a thinking man laughs.""

"That's a pretty good saying, Stafford. I've got one my father used to tell me. I think it was from the Bible. "Better to keep your mouth shut and be thought a fool, than to open your mouth and remove all doubt.""

"So, which do *you* do, sir?" Stafford said. Turner stopped short, and faced Stafford.

"And here's a saying of my own... don't let your mouth overload your abilities."

"I like your saying better, sir. I'm going to remember it."

"I think you'd better." Turner turned and continued walking.

Turner's office was at the end of the hall. It was a comfortable office, but had only one small window. There was the usual "Me" wall with diplomas and plaques telling the world what a great guy Turner was.

"Nice office," Stafford offered after he walked in.

"Have a sit." Turner said. He went around his desk and sat down heavily in his executive chair.

"So, what's the misconduct you want to report?" Turner asked.

Stafford told Turner about his call to Agent Dupree, Dupree's reaction to the question about missing cocaine, and about his suspicions that an agent in Headquarters was probably already talking to OPR about him.

"How well did you know Dupree?" Turner asked.

"Not very well. I only saw him at the office. We never socialized."

"What headquarters agent do you think reported you to us?"

"Peter Nelson, sir." When Stafford had mentioned Dupree's name, he saw Turners eyebrows rise slightly. When he said Nelson's name, he saw Turner stiffen.

"Agent Stafford, I want you to go back to your office and get back to work. I'll call you later after I've talked to some people upstairs." Turner stood, and Stafford stood too, with a puzzled look on his face.

"Upstairs? *This is* upstairs."

"I'll call you later..., probably tomorrow. Now go back to work, and don't tell anyone you were here."

"Can you tell me why the need for secrecy?"

"It will be common knowledge soon anyway. Agent Dupree was killed this morning."

"Under what circumstances?"

"I can't say. Don't say anything to anyone else about this until it's public knowledge. Go on now, get out of here."

"Yes, sir." Stafford headed to the front office and into the reception area. Andy glared at him his as he walked past to the door. He was shocked by the news of Dupree's death, but still had to have the last say.

"You don't need to leave the light on for me," he said. Something hit the door just as it shut behind him.

Stafford had a lot to think about as he ambled back to his office. Nelson was turning things over in his mind, as well. He needed to make contact with his controller, but he had to go through a different procedure, using another more secure method of communication. He would try later. He looked around to see if anyone was watching him.

If Nelson felt he was being watched, he was right, but it was the FBI that was doing the watching, not other HSI agents. He didn't know it, and neither did the agents watching him, but there were a few traitors at the FBI, as well.

ICE OPR division had not been informed Nelson was under FBI surveillance. The investigation had been classified "TOP SECRET" by FBI Director Clement, and he didn't believe anyone at DHS or HSI needed to know about it, not even the DHS Secretary.

After talking to Stafford, Chief Turner made a quick call on his personal cellphone.

"Hello?"

"This is Chief Turner. I need to speak to Delta Four."

"Wait one." After a minute of silence, another person answered. Turner recognized the voice.

"Delta Four. Go ahead."

"Sir, we have a problem. I believe our Agent Nelson may have been compromised by an HSI Agent named Stafford."

"We are familiar with Agent Stafford, Chief Turner. Take whatever measures you think appropriate to keep Stafford out of our way. The operation has started, and results so far are very good."

"Can you tell me anything more about the operation, sir?"

"Only that the future of this country may depend on you doing your job. Keep following orders, and you'll be well rewarded. Now back to Nelson and Stafford..., if you decide it's necessary, use Nelson to terminate Stafford, and then terminate Nelson as a precaution. Do you understand?" Turner let the other man's words sink in.

"Is that how Nelson is going to be rewarded, sir?"

"Chief Turner, Agent Nelson has been uncontrollable in the past. We do not tolerate insubordination or variance from orders. The only reason he still works for us is because he provides very useful information. Don't forget, we can be your best friend, or your worst enemy."

"I understand, sir."

"Keep me informed of your progress on Stafford. Do you have anything else to report?"

"No, sir..., nothing more to report, but I do have a question. If the need arises, whom should I use to terminate Nelson?"

"You can handle that yourself. He has your trust. It should be a simple matter. The important person is Stafford. We can't have him getting in our way, or asking too many questions about our activities. If you think Nelson can't handle Stafford, then take care of Stafford yourself."

"Understood, sir."

"Good. Delta Four out."

Chapter 14

F ive o'clock arrived faster than usual for Stafford. With all he had on his mind, he was glad the workday was done. Work would be one less thing to worry about. He thought about the meeting he was going to have with Beth St. James. He hoped they could iron out their differences, because he wanted to get to know her, in the Biblical sense, of course.

As Stafford left the office for the day, he noticed that Nelson had not returned from his break. He assumed he was on another personal trip somewhere around the building. Nelson had left the office for a short time after Stafford returned from the OPR. From the ring tone on Nelson's phone, Stafford knew he had received a personal call. Nelson then left for a time, returned, and then left again without saying where he was going.

Stafford rode the elevator with the other workers who were hurrying to get to the Metro, the car park, the grocery store, and all the pleasures of their homes in the suburbs. They stood silently together in the elevator, like wooden sentinels, watching the floor numbers change on the display board over the door. Staring at the changing floor numbers was the accepted method for coping with the uneasiness people felt when forced to stand too close to strangers. Stafford turned around and faced the back of the elevator. He smiled and looked as many people in the eye as he could. It was typical Stafford, taking joy in annoying people. He waited, wanting to exit the elevator last. He was ready for more fun.

"After you," he said to everyone. They all left, except one woman.

"That's okay, you go ahead," the woman answered.

"No..., ladies first," Stafford said. He made a gesture at the open door with one arm, and bowed from the waist.

The doors started to shut, and with a sigh of exasperation, the woman walked out. She moved obliquely for a few steps, trying not to give Stafford a full view of her rear.

Stafford exited the elevator and stood watching her walk away. She turned to see if he was looking, and saw him watching her. He gave her two thumbs up, and a smile.

"Creep," she said. She marched away disgusted, which had been his intention all along.

Beth was waiting in front of the Wilson Center, pacing and thinking about what she wanted to say, and how she wanted to say it. The center was used mostly by upper level administrators when they wanted to talk to the employees, and have a good photo opportunity.

Stafford finally walked away from the elevator, and saw Beth. She thought his smile meant he was glad to see her. That was part of the reason for his smile, the smallest part.

Beth noticed Stafford was smiling, but not as broadly as when they had last met for lunch. After seeing him knock the man down on the street, and confronting him about it in the Metro, she wasn't surprised he looked less than enthused to see her.

"Hi, Beth, I hope you haven't been waiting long."

"No, not long. Let's go inside and sit down, if you have the time."

"Of course..., I've always got time for you."

She smiled at his too sweet compliment, and went with him into the center. They sat in the last row of seats in the back of the auditorium. Beth perched on the edge of the seat, facing him at an angle so she could look more directly at him.

"Maybe this isn't a very comfortable place to sit."

"This is fine, Beth. What's this all about?... the man you saw me bump into on the street?"

"That's part of it. I've been thinking about a lot of things the past couple of days. I'm just going to start talking and hope I cover it all."

"This sounds serious."

"This *is* serious. This has to do with life and death, and life *after* death."

"Uh-oh, are you going to preach to me?"

"Ben, please hear me out."

"Okay, I'm sorry. You talk, and I'll listen." She breathed deeply and looked directly into his eyes while she sent up a quick prayer.

Heavenly Father, please give me the right words to say to him, to open his ears, and to remove the scales from his eyes so he may see The Light. I pray this in Jesus' name. Amen.

"Ten years ago my older sister Beverly died of cancer. She left behind a husband and two children. I thought it wasn't fair. She had everything to live for, and she died..., not suddenly in a car or plane crash, but slowly and painfully, of cancer."

"After she died, I was angry at God for letting her die like that, and I had a lot of questions for Him. Like, why does God allow so much suffering? Why do good people die so young, and bad people die of old age? Does God really hear our prayers? Does He answer our prayers? If He does answer our prayers, what was his answer to the prayers of six million Jews, who died at the hands of the Nazis? His answer was no? The world just didn't make sense to me. Before Beverly died, I thought I had it all figured out, but I discovered I didn't understand anything. Do you know what I mean?"

"Yes, I do. I've asked myself the same kinds of questions many times. I've seen more than my share of suffering and death, and none of it makes sense. If I was emperor of the world, I'd put a stop to the sufferings of the innocent."

"I imagine you *have* seen a lot. It's too bad you *aren't* emperor of the world, with the power to put an end to suffering, but God is the creator of the universe, which trumps being the emperor of the world."

"So why *doesn't* the creator of the universe put a stop to all the pain and suffering? He certainly has the power," Stafford said.

"He could stop it, but He allows us to make our own choices. If we would follow His ways, there wouldn't be so much suffering and pain. But we're human, and this is a broken, sin-filled world, that rebels at following God's ways. So..., we struggle to understand and to cope with trouble." Neither spoke for a short time. Her words were falling like gentle rain on his parched spirit. Stafford shook them off.

"I'm trying to understand... trying to ask the right questions," Stafford said.

"When you questioned God, did He answer you?" Beth asked.

"God never answered me. I found the answers for myself."

"Well, Ben, I hope they were the right answers. God answered some of *my* questions, but others He left unanswered."

"Which questions did He answer for you? How did He answer? Did you hear a voice?" Stafford asked, genuinely interested.

71

"He answered me from His Word, and with the words of His followers. I had never read the Bible before, but Roger, my sister's husband, suggested I read the Bible, and pray for the answers to be made clear to me. Roger often quoted from the book of Luke, Chapter 11. "I say unto you, ask, and it shall be given you; seek, and you shall find; knock, and it shall be opened unto you. For every one that asks, receives; and he that seeks finds; and to him that knocks, the door shall be opened.""

"That sounds wonderful," Stafford said. Beth nodded in agreement.

"Roger certainly had it together. He was just wonderful with Beverly and the children. I don't think I ever met a more loving and generous man. It's easy to see why my sister married him. He handled her death very well."

"Anyway, Roger gave me Bev's Bible to read, and at his suggestion, I started reading the Bible every day. You know, I had a lot of misconceptions about the Bible. I had always said I didn't understand it, but I had never bothered to read it. My sister tried to talk to me about Jesus, but I didn't want to hear it. I was having too much fun living life in the fast lane."

"Really? Somehow, I just can't imagine you in the fast lane, Beth."

"I was shameless…, but never mind about that. After reading Bev's study Bible for about a year, things finally began to make sense. I had been looking at life with the wrong perspective."

"Well, Beth, it sounds like you've got it figured out. Tell me how to make sense of the world, I'm dying to know." Stafford crossed his legs and intertwined his fingers over his knee.

"This life isn't the end, Ben. Our souls will last for eternity. How and where we spend eternity depends on who we place our faith in."

"You mean Jesus, right?"

"Yes, I mean Jesus." Stafford uncrossed his legs, leaned forward, and put his elbows on his knees. He hung his head, looking at the floor.

"I learned that we all are made by God, and everything that happens to us is part of God's plan. Our earthly friends and loved ones may leave us, but God promised us He will never leave us, or forsake us. God loves us more than we can understand," Beth said.

"He has a strange way of showing His love for us sometimes," Stafford said.

"He gave His only Son to die for us."

"I know the story of Jesus and His crucifixion, Beth."

"I don't think people really understand what Jesus did for us on the cross. In ancient times, God's people made animal sacrifices, asking God to forgive their sins. The sacrificial animals had to be as perfect as possible. As perfect as the animals were, they were not absolutely perfect. Because the sacrifice was not perfect, the high priest of the temple had to make the sacrifice every year, asking God to forgive the sins of the people over and over again."

"The truly perfect sacrifice, could never be an animal. It had to be a perfect human sacrifice. The perfect sacrifice was Jesus. He was the only human who never sinned, because He was God in the flesh. He was sent to save all of us from death. Jesus took all the sins of the world on Himself, so that God would forgive our sins for all time. The only thing you have to do to have everlasting life, is to believe that Jesus was God's Son, and He died to save you. That's the good news, Ben... the gospel of Jesus Christ!"

Beth waited for some kind of response. Stafford said nothing. He was still leaning forward with his elbows on his knees, looking down. He leaned back in his seat and looked at her.

"Beth, I want to thank you for telling me all that, but I was raised in the church and I've heard it before. I just don't think God cares about our everyday lives."

"Then you *do* believe Jesus was God's Son, who died on the cross for you don't you? You *are* saved, aren't you?"

"I don't know, Beth. There was a time when I would have said yes immediately. I'm not so sure any more." He stood, and Beth stood up with him. He opened his arms, and she stepped inside and hugged him. He squeezed her close.

"You're one of the sweetest women I know. Thank you for taking the time to talk to me about Jesus... it shows that you care about what happens to me." He relaxed his embrace, but continued to hold her close. She pushed away gently, politely breaking his embrace, and stepped back.

"I *do* care what happens to you. I care very much. I think you're a good man, and you could be even better, if you opened your heart to Jesus again."

"Thanks, Beth. I'll think about what you've said."

They walked slowly to the door, side by side, not speaking. She held onto his arm like a school girl at the prom. He felt her hands on his arm, and liked the feeling. He wanted to get used to feeling her close to him. To do that, he knew he was going to have to make some changes.

*   *   *   *

Nelson was standing near the stairs, waiting and watching for Stafford and St. James to emerge from the center. He held his cellphone to his ear, rolling his eyes as Turner blathered on.

"Stafford must not be allowed to put all the pieces together. He thinks you reported him to OPR, and he suspects Dupree is involved in something illegal. Stafford told me that himself. According to our weekly brief, the big plan, whatever it is, has already begun, and it won't make any difference *what* Stafford finds out after a few more weeks. But if he were to turn over the right rocks now, he might cause a major disruption. That can't be allowed to happen."

"I know that, Turner. Stafford is not stupid, and he's not going to stop until he finds the missing coke, or gets a good explanation about why the numbers don't add up. But, I'm not stupid either. I know enough about the information I've been supplying to know somebody is using it to smuggle huge loads of coke. Today, Stafford told me about a new angle he's going to use to try to figure out how the loads are coming in. If he makes it work, he'll be another step closer."

"As I said, Nelson..., that could have serious ramifications. Have you had a chance to pass your latest conclusions about Stafford to your controller?"

"Not yet. I should use the backup protocols to try and contact Bravo Two. Can you arrange that for me?"

"I'll consider your request. Haven't you been reporting about Stafford all along? Why do you need to use your backup? Has your primary method been compromised? Have you compromised your other contacts?"

"Sir, I think it best that I don't tell you more than you need to know."

"I recruited you, remember? If you've been compromised..."

"Just the same, sir, I want to be able to enjoy my retirement, if you know what I mean."

"You're right, Nelson. Don't tell me more than I need to know."

"Are there any new instructions for handling Stafford?"

"He must be kept from getting too close. You are authorized to eliminate him as soon as possible."

"You could have told me that before," Nelson said.

"I wanted to hear what you had to say about him first," Turner said.

"Aren't you clever? Well..., I think we've talked enough," Nelson said. Turner was irritated, and hung up before Nelson could. Nelson closed his phone with a snap.

"Today, Stafford..., today you are going down for good," Nelson said quietly. He headed for the main exit, unaware of the three men watching every move he made, and three more men outside, waiting to grab him when he left the building.

Chapter 15

As Stafford and Beth were leaving for the day, Stafford's government cellphone vibrated on his belt. He snatched the phone off his belt.

"This had better be important..., it's past my quitting time," he said, looking at Beth with a frown. His walk slowed. He answered the call, but didn't recite the usual speech.

"Customs, Stafford."

"Stafford, this is Boyer, I need you to come to my office right away. There's something very important I need to see you about."

"Sir, can this wait until tomorrow?"

"No argument Stafford. This can't wait. Get back here."

"Roger that, sir, I'm on my way." He snapped the phone shut and made a sour face.

"I've got to go back upstairs and see the boss. I'll see you tomorrow..., all right?"

Beth had a sad look on her face, but Stafford barely noticed. He was already backing away from her, toward the elevators. She had no chance to ask the half dozen questions she wanted to ask.

"Okay, Ben, I'll see you tomorrow," she said after him.

She watched him walk away. She continued to watch for a time. She wondered what God had in store for him, and for her. She realized she was changing her feelings for him. She was caring more, but liking him less. What could explain the way he made her feel? So angry, and so alive at the same time? She wasn't comfortable with the realization, or the feelings.

She left the building and blended in with the people hurrying along. She felt like her life was being squeezed out of her. She wanted to turn around and follow him to his office to talk with him more, but she kept going, farther away from her want.

Stafford was rounding the corner of his office, when Boyer met him at the door, with his cellphone to his ear.

"He just walked in. We'll be there in a couple of minutes." He closed his cellphone and dropped it in his jacket pocket.

"Let's go," Boyer said. He walked past Stafford and into the hallway.

"What's this all about?" Stafford said, as he followed behind.

"The Commissioner wants to see you. That's all I know."

"Commissioner Gomez wants to see *me*? And you don't know what this is all about?"

"The Assistant Commissioner called and told me to get you up to the Commissioner's office right away. Have you done something I need to know about?"

"Probably, but I wouldn't know where to start. Whatever I've done, I'm sorry."

Boyer looked sideways at Stafford, pursed his lips and shook his head. They walked onto the elevator, rode to the executive floor, got off, showed their credentials to a guard, and got onto another elevator.

Stafford saw that Boyer was trembling slightly. Boyer stared at the buttons on the control panel, and didn't speak. Stafford was getting butterflies in his stomach. He felt like he was about to make his first parachute jump. Stafford watched the control panel buttons with Boyer. When the elevator stopped, they stepped out into a marble-floored, wood paneled, reception area.

"Right this way, gentlemen. You're expected," a young woman said. She gestured for them to follow her.

They walked across the reception area and down a hallway to a security door. She touched a pass card to a metal sensing plate on the wall, and pressed a code into a keypad. The door clicked open, revealing a small room with walls covered with small compartments. Some of the compartments contained cellphones, or other electronic devices.

"Please place your hand held electronic devices in a cubby. No electronic communication or recording devices of any kind are allowed in the conference room." They both did as they were told.

"That's a good idea," Stafford said. "I understand some investigations have been compromised by tech-savvy criminals who knew how to turn a cellphone into an eavesdropping device."

"You are quite correct, sir, which is why we ensconce all the aforementioned devices in this room before anyone enters the conference area," their escort replied. "You may reclaim your items on your way out. Please remember your cubby number."

Ensconce? Aforementioned? Cubby? Why can't women speak plain English?

"Are you kidding?" Boyer said. "They can turn cellphones into listening devices?"

"Yes, it's true, sir. I believe there is a Customs Directive advising all CBP investigative personnel, with government issued cellphones, on how to mitigate that risk."

Mitigate? There she goes again, and Boyer is shot down in flames.

After shutting the door, she led them through a well-furnished office, and into a large conference room. Ten men were sitting around an oval conference table. At the head of the table sat Customs and Border Protection Commissioner, Eduardo Gomez. He looked sharp in a dark suit, green tie, and white dress shirt.

"Welcome, Agent Stafford. Please take a seat. Thank you, Supervisor Boyer. Would you close the door on your way out?"

"Of course, sir. Should I wait for Agent Stafford?"

"Yes, if you'd like. You can wait by the elevators. Someone will brief you later." Boyer left, accidentally shutting the door with a slam. Stafford sat down in the only chair that was unoccupied.

"One of the reasons the Commissioner asked you here today is because you know how to get the job done and keep your mouth shut," said Charles Peterson. Stafford looked at the folded name card in front of him. It said he was the Assistant Commissioner of Intelligence and Operations Coordination.

A name probably created to make the acronym IOC... International Olympic Committee. That's easier to remember than the Division of People Who Keep Other People From Messing Up Somebody's Intelligence Operation.

Stafford glanced at the name cards in front of the other men at the table. Some didn't have cards, but for those that did, he saw Drug Enforcement Administration, Federal Bureau of Investigation, U. S. Army Intelligence and Security Command, and Alcohol Tobacco and Firearms.

"Chuck, let's not get ahead of ourselves, or Agent Stafford," Gomez said.

"I'm sorry, sir, but we don't have a lot of time for niceties."

"No, we don't, but I want you all to start at the beginning, and tell Agent Stafford what he needs to know. Colonel Allred, why don't you begin?"

The man behind the Army name card looked at Stafford, and then at the papers in the folder in front of him. He shut the folder and placed his forearms on the glass tabletop, scrunching his shoulders, and making his neck disappear.

"Agent Stafford, I'm Colonel Allred. I work for Army Intelligence and Security. As you can see, there are several other agencies represented here that normally do not work together. Indeed, before the terrorist attacks of September 11, we were forbidden by law to cooperate with each other, but the rules have changed."

"Three months ago, a DEA informant, in the employ of a Mexican narcotics trafficker named Claudio Roja, overheard Roja address a visiting American by the title *General*. Later, the informant heard Roja calling the American visitor Andrew. The man named Andrew has visited the Roja estate several times, and according to the informant, was present during the murder of a man Roja suspected of disloyalty."

"DEA headquarters thought this information was important enough to try to identify the General. With the help of the Department of Defense, all living active duty or retired United States military personnel with the rank of General, and with a given name of Andrew, were identified. There were only six people who met those two criteria. From photographs, the DEA informant identified Major General Andrew Jackson Miner, U.S. Army, retired, as the man he had seen with Roja."

"Under the provisions of the Patriot Act, DEA headquarters notified the FBI. The FBI investigated and found indications that active duty military personnel were involved with General Miner in smuggling war material out of the United States to Mexico, and it is assumed, to Roja. As our colleague from ATF has already informed us, many of the weapons Mexican authorities have confiscated from narcotics gangs have been identified as stolen from United States military bases near the Mexican border."

"The FBI notified the Department of Defense Criminal Investigation Division, who in turn notified my unit. Together, we and CID began an investigation of the active duty military officers suspected of working with General Miner."

"As our investigation of the active duty officers progressed, we found evidence General Miner may also be involved in smuggling drugs into the United States. Eight general grade officers, active and retired, were identified by our investigation as being in frequent contact with known drug smugglers, as well as General Miner."

"Due to the threat to national security posed by the possible involvement of high ranking members of the military, the FBI and U.S. Army Intelligence were authorized by the Foreign Intelligence Surveillance Court, to intercept any communications to or from General Miner."

"From our intercepts of some of his communications, which were unencrypted, we identified a nationwide network of several dozen active and retired military officers and enlisted men, federal agents, and civilians, who are actively involved in a conspiracy to murder hundreds, if not thousands, of United States citizens."

"We know the killings have started, because we've intercepted communications between the members discussing the number of deaths. There are no reported incidents of mass murder anywhere in the United States or Canada. We are not sure how these killings are being carried out. Nor are we sure what the group's ultimate goal is, or even if there is a goal." The Colonel sat back in his chair, looking tired. It didn't happen very often, but Ben Stafford was speechless.

"Thank you, Colonel Allred. Deputy Director Morgan, would you please make your presentation?" Gomez said.

Stafford looked around the table but didn't see a name card with Morgan on it. Someone sitting on Stafford's left cleared their throat, and Stafford leaned forward to see who it was. Seeing Stafford searching for the next speaker, the two men sitting between Stafford and Morgan leaned back in their chairs. Stafford moved his chair so he wouldn't have to crane his neck to see.

"Agent Stafford, I am DEA Deputy Director Patrick Morgan. The DEA became aware of the previously mentioned smuggling conspiracy, and began investigating..., trying to identify Roja's drug shipments, and their destinations. We hoped to be able to confirm the involvement of those persons already identified, as well as identify others that had escaped detection. We were somewhat successful in determining the destination of some of the drug shipments, but have not been able to determine the method of importation."

"The Commissioner has informed us that you are aware of a large decline in the amount of cocaine being seized on the southern border. There has been an increase in the amount of cocaine seized within the U.S., and the street price of cocaine has declined significantly. This indicates that there is an increase in the amount of drugs available on the street. We know it's coming in, we just don't know where, or how."

Stafford wondered how Gomez knew he was asking questions about the decline in coke seizures.

"Thank you, Deputy Director Morgan," Gomez said. The FBI representative didn't wait for Commissioner Gomez to prompt him.

"Agent Stafford, I am FBI Senior Special Agent Elwin Myers. In my opinion, you shouldn't be attending this conference, or listening to highly classified reports of investigations."

Gomez leaned forward in his chair. "Agent Myers, would you like me to get the FBI Director on the phone so you can confirm your instructions with him personally?"

"My title is *Senior Special* Agent, sir. And no sir, that won't be necessary. I just want it understood that I think this briefing is not intended for lower ranking government employees. It was only to be given to senior officials from the various...."

"I don't care what your opinion of this briefing is, or who you think should, or shouldn't hear it. Just do as you've been instructed, *Agent* Myers," Gomez said.

"As you say, sir." Myers cleared his throat.

"Agent Stafford, the FBI has quickly and..."

"That's *Special* Agent Stafford," Stafford interrupted.

"Excuse me?" Myers said, looking at Stafford. He had no trouble seeing him. He was sitting directly across the table from Stafford.

"I'm *Special* Agent Stafford..., *Senior* Special Agent Myers."

"Noted," Myers said, trying not to show his irritation. The Commissioner smiled.

"As I was saying, the FBI has quickly and quietly identified and arrested several conspirators. Based on information obtained by ATF agents during interrogations of suspected Mexican arms merchants, several co-conspirators, as well as a former U.S. military officer code named Bravo Two, were identified."

"As authorized by the Patriot Act, arrest warrants were issued after secret indictments. The FBI has held the suspects incommunicado since their arrests. During questioning, one of the suspects told us about a conspiracy to use poisoned drugs to kill large numbers of Americans. The FBI has been unable to verify that statement."

"We have recently learned that Bravo Two was a subordinate of General Miner when the General was the base Commander at Fort Hood, Texas. Unfortunately, one of our agents fatally shot Bravo Two when he attempted to escape from custody shortly after his arrest."

Stafford had to ask about an obvious possibility. "Are you certain the suspect who was killed wasn't assassinated by the Agent who shot him?"

Myers couldn't believe his ears. "Of course not!" he answered quickly.

"Agent Stafford, you have a knack for hitting the nail on the head, which is one of the reasons I asked you here," Gomez said.

"May I ask another question, sir?" Stafford said.

"Go ahead," Gomez said.

"Agent Myers..., if you've been intercepting General Miner's communications, you must have identified most of his regular contacts. Why didn't the FBI identify which ones were co-conspirators, get warrants, and arrest *all* the top people in this murder conspiracy? And..., what was the name of the man who was shot by your Agent? Why do you only refer to him as Bravo Two?"

Myers hesitated, and then said, "I'm not at liberty to answer those questions, Agent Stafford."

"I bet I can guess the answers to those questions," Stafford said. "The FBI didn't arrest the leaders of the conspiracy because they don't know who they are. They don't know who they are because the FBI only has the capability to wiretap land-lines, cellphones, and microwave transmissions, to and from low level players. The *main* players are communicating over video chat networks, and the FBI can't wiretap the internet... they'd need help from the NSA to do that. If the FBI asked NSA for help, they'd have to share operational intelligence and, more importantly for the FBI, any future publicity. Reluctance to share intelligence is also the reason why you won't tell us who Bravo Two is. So, have I guessed about right, Agent Myers? And by the way, does the FBI academy still give classes on how to dress for press conferences?" Myers glared at Stafford.

"Go ahead Myers, answer him," Gomez said. He clasped his hands over his stomach and leaned his chair back on two legs.

"Just a minute, sir." Myers said, holding up his hand. "I resent the implications Agent Stafford made. The FBI Agent Stafford referred to as a possible assassin, shot the escaping suspect only as a last resort, and in defense of his own life. As far as asking another Federal agency for help installing a wiretap..., the FBI would do whatever was lawful and necessary to keep the American public safe, regardless of which agency gets credit afterward!" Someone snickered. Myers heard it, but ignored it.

"Before Bravo Two was killed, he gave us valuable information that allowed us to take over his contacts. From those contacts we learned that Agent Stafford is considered a threat by one of the Gadsden Council's members. We believe Agent Stafford's life may be in danger."

"Stafford's life has been in danger for almost all of the past 15 years," Gomez said. "The Deputy Secretary of ICE was notified only moments ago about Stafford being considered a threat by the Gadsden Council. Evidently, Stafford's activities in the intelligence section might uncover something the Gadsden Council wants to keep secret. Amazingly, the Deputy Secretary's notification by the FBI was the first time *anyone* in his office heard that HSI agents were part of an investigation by the FBI."

"I'm sorry, sir, but I have no control over things like that," Myers said.

"I don't doubt that for a second," Gomez said.

The door opened, and Gomez' receptionist entered. All eyes followed her. She walked directly to Gomez and handed him a slip of paper.

"I'm sorry to intrude, sir, but I have an important message for you." Everyone watched her leave. Gomez read the note silently, pocketed it, and set upon Myers again.

"Let's get back to the shooting of Bravo Two, Agent Myers. The escape attempt and shooting occurred when your Agent was alone with the suspect *after* the interview room security cameras had been turned off. Isn't that correct?"

"Sir, what Agent Stafford and you are suggesting is ridiculous."

"Ridiculous? What is Bravo Two's name? Are the main conspirators using internet video networks to communicate, or not?" Gomez asked. Myers adjusted his sitting position in his chair.

"I can't say, sir. I am not here to answer your questions. I am here to give a briefing to the Task Force and provide the information I think...."

"The information *you* think? Not here to answer my questions? I'll tell you what Myers..., I've had enough of your tap dancing and insolence. Gather your things, and get out of my sight. I don't want to hear another word out of you."

"I'm sorry, Commissioner. The Director of the FBI ordered me here to...,"

"Are you deaf, Myers? I said not another word."

Myers collected his paperwork, stood up, pushed his chair back, and walked to the door, which was the first sign of having good sense he had shown. As he opened the door to leave, he turned to face the men at the conference table.

"This investigation is the most important, and best run, anti-terror investigation the FBI has ever undertaken."

"That's not saying much," Stafford muttered.

"MYERS! I CAN STILL HEAR AND SEE YOU!" Gomez shouted, but wasn't angry.

Myers backed through the doorway and shut the door quietly behind him. No one spoke. The DEA man cleared his throat. Each man at the table was either looking at Gomez, or at the paperwork in front of them. Stafford had more to say.

"Sir, I think what needs to be done is obvious. We get NSA to do a video chat wiretap…, identify the names and locations of these perps for us, and then hit *all* of the traitors simultaneously, *and* with overwhelming force. If they resist us, we vaporize them. If they surrender peacefully, and cooperate fully, they get a life sentence instead of an execution. Simple as that, sir." Gomez smiled at Stafford.

"And that, Agent Stafford, is the other reason you're here."

Chapter 16

The room was quiet. Commissioner Gomez was savoring the feeling of sending an FBI Agent to bed without his supper.

"Sir, this may sound like a silly question, but just what *am* I doing here?" Stafford said.

"Gentlemen, will you excuse us for a moment?" Gomez said. He stood and walked to the door. "Agent Stafford and I will be back in about ten minutes. While we're gone, why don't you all discuss what you believe our course of action should be from this point on." Stafford followed his boss out of the conference room and around the corner into the Commissioner's office. Gomez shut the door.

"I want to show you something," Gomez said. He opened the bottom drawer of his desk and pulled out a photo album. The album looked as if it had been around for some time. It was the inexpensive kind that used very sticky paper to hold the pictures in place, never to be removed again without peeling the paper off the back of the photo. Gomez opened the album and flipped a couple of pages, then turned it around and held it open for Stafford to see.

"Do you recognize any of the men in this picture?" he said as he wiggled his thumb over one of the pages.

All the men in the picture were young, and dressed in faded green military fatigues. They were carrying an assortment of weapons, including a belt-fed machine-gun, M-16's, a scoped rifle, and an old style grenade launcher. Stafford immediately recognized one of the men in the picture as his stepfather. It was a photo taken at a base camp. He could see the perimeter concertina wire in the background. Stafford didn't recognize any of the other men in the picture.

"That's my dad there," Stafford said, as he pointed to his father in the picture. Where did you get this picture, sir?"

"The man with the M-60 is me," Gomez said smiling. Stafford did a double take at the picture, and Gomez. Seeing Stafford's reaction, Gomez chuckled and said, "that picture was taken a *long* time ago. I can still feel the weight of that M-60. I hated lugging it around."

"My dad never said anything to me about serving in Vietnam with the Commissioner of Customs. You'd think he would have mentioned it."

"I don't believe he knew about me being in CBP until just a few years ago. He must have seen my name and picture in a Customs newsletter when I was a Port Director out west. He called me once and let me know he was working for Customs, too. Some coincidence, huh?"

"No kidding, sir. It must have been a strange feeling for my dad, finding out one of his Army buddies outranked him in civilian life."

"Well, I didn't outrank him in Nam. We were both Spec-4's assigned to the same unit. We were not the best of friends, but I definitely remember your father as being one of the finest soldiers I ever knew."

"You saved each other's lives and all that?"

"No…, nothing that dramatic. But I saw your dad do incredibly brave things over there. I know he saved *other* people's lives." Stafford felt his chest puff out with pride.

"But let's not get too serious, there were some funny times too. Ask your dad to tell you about the time he burned down our only outhouse."

"I'll do that, sir." Stafford smiled at the picture he had in his mind.

"Being Dan Stafford's son was enough for me to put you in that conference room. I knew if you were his son, you would be the kind of man I could count on. But that's not the only reason I chose you to sit in today. I've heard some things about you since you got here, and some were not so complimentary. In fact, there are a more than a few people who would like to see you disciplined, or even fired. Normally that kind of thing is handled on a lower level than my office. So…, I did some checking on you. I looked at your military record, and the reports of investigations you worked on the southern border. I was impressed by both." Gomez stopped talking long enough to move in front of his desk and sit down. He motioned for Stafford to take a seat next to him, which he did.

"You're intelligent, and a thorough investigator. I think your intelligence is one of the reasons you get yourself reported so often. People like you think they're smarter than everyone else. You may well be, but believing you are smarter than everyone else can make you overconfident. I happen to think extra confidence is going to be required to get this job done."

"You've led men, seen combat, and are an expert shot with a pistol or a rifle. I'd wager you're better than average in hand to hand as well. Those are abilities you may need to call on before this is over. So, you're perfect for this assignment. Now…, there are a few other things going on that you don't know about yet."

"After what I've already heard, I'm afraid to ask what they are, sir."

"No need to ask, I'm going to tell you." He reached into his desk and pulled out a piece of paper. He handed it to Stafford.

"Read it. It's not very long." The paper was from the Secretary of Homeland Security, addressed to Gomez, and was marked 'SECRET' at the top. Stafford read.

As per our telephone conversation this date.

Under the direction of The President of the United States, I am hereby informing you that Immigration and Customs Enforcement will be the lead agency in the investigation of the Gadsden Council, and their alleged involvement in the conspiracy to smuggle drugs and war material. Any collateral investigations resulting from this initial investigation are to be coordinated through Headquarters ICE/HSI.

Due to the broader responsibilities of Customs and Border Protection, your office, and the Director of ICE, will share operational responsibility.

The President has directed me to inform you that this investigation is of the highest priority and you, or the Director of ICE may request the assistance of any other agency of the Federal government, including the armed forces, in your enforcement efforts.

Signed, etc., etc.

"Sir, I don't believe The Secretary of DHS can authorize you to use the military to go after these people. The posse comitatus act prohibits the use of military personnel in civilian law enforcement roles."

"This Gadsden Council has officially been designated a terrorist organization," Gomez said. "Terrorism is a recognized threat to our national security, and the military can be used against threats to national security. That sounds pretty simple, but if need be we'll let the lawyer's figure this out *after* it's all over. I wanted to let you know that I'm not crazy, and that I *do* have the authority to do what I'm doing."

"The FBI doesn't like CBP in this role because *they* are supposed to be the lead agency in any terrorism investigation, but this had *nexus to the border* written all over it. Nexus to the border means it's our baby. I sold the nexus thing to the Secretary of DHS, and he sold it to the President. As I expected, the FBI now drags their feet big time when we ask them for anything more than a paper clip..., but let's get back on subject," Gomez said.

"The day after you called Agent Dupree, he was shot and killed in a grocery store parking lot during a *supposed* robbery. A surveillance camera across the street caught the shooting on video. Dupree didn't have a chance. He was shot in the head at close range. The shooter grabbed Dupree's wallet from his pants after he hit the ground. I think Dupree was killed for another reason..., probably to shut him up about the missing cocaine you asked him about."

"How did you know about that, sir?" Stafford said.

"I've got a hot line on my desk. Every time you open your mouth too wide..., somebody calls me."

"I'm sorry, sir. I had no idea." Stafford felt terrible. He wondered how much Gomez knew about him. He thought he better tell him everything.

"As you are probably aware, sir, I spoke to OPR Chief Turner today, about my call to Dupree. Turner told me about Dupree's death, and said not to tell anyone about it until after it was public knowledge."

"That doesn't change a thing. Turner is involved with your buddy, Peter Nelson. Nelson was arrested by the FBI outside the building just before you came up. We're still looking for Turner." Stafford was dumbfounded.

"Sir, I told Turner everything I knew, and Nelson sat at the desk right behind mine."

"Well, that can't be helped. There are HSI and FBI agents at Turner's home right now. If he shows, they'll get him. In the meantime, you better watch your back. Turner and Nelson were heard discussing your murder." Gomez saw the look on Stafford's face and tried to calm his mind.

"Agent Stafford, I know this is a lot to digest all at once, and you aren't sure who you can trust..., but you *can* trust *me*. We have lots of ground to make up, and we don't know how much time we have. This group has very long arms and they aren't afraid of reaching out and killing lots of people. They've got to be stopped. The drug shipments are involved somehow..., maybe to finance what's going on. We really don't know."

"Sir, what if the drugs are bankrolling this, as well as being the means for killing thousands of people?"

"Myers mentioned that, and it's an interesting idea, but how can they kill large numbers of people with drugs, unless they give poisoned drugs to a large number of people at the same time," Gomez said.

"What if the poison drugs and deaths are spread nationwide and not in a single place?" Stafford said.

"What would be the point of doing that? Is it just to kill people? What could their motive be, besides mass murder? This thing has way too many people involved for it just to be about murder. Do any of your reports support your nationwide killing hypothesis?" Gomez asked.

"No, sir, my reports only show a downward trend in drug seizures..., there was nothing about any increase in deaths. I heard on the news last night that there was a big increase in drug deaths in D.C. that couldn't be easily explained. I had lunch today with a woman who works at Health and Human Services. She told me there was an increase in the number of drug deaths all over this region, and the Director of the Centers for Disease Control was very interested in statistical spikes like that. If the increase in drug deaths is nationwide, then thousands of people may have already been killed," Stafford said. Gomez cursed.

"What was the woman's name you had lunch with?"

"Anne Dawson, sir." Gomez wrote her name down on a pad on his desk.

"I'm going to call the CDC Director, and see what info he's got on these drug deaths. I want verification that mass murder by drugs is actually happening. If it is, the CDC needs to make an announcement to warn the public."

Gomez tapped his pen on his desk, then dropped the pen on top of the pad of paper, and sighed. They were both quiet for a minute; thinking.

"Stafford, the key to this whole thing has *got* to be the drugs. We need to know how and where the drugs are coming into the U.S., and stop them. When you find out how and where, you'll have a good idea about who was behind the killing of Dupree. That's going to be your job. I'll clear it with your Director. I want you to be ready to leave for El Paso tomorrow morning. You'll be investigating the drug shipments and Dupree's murder. You'll need some help. Think about who you want to go with you to assist."

"Yes, sir. I know just the man for the job. I'll let him know to pack his bags."

Chapter 17

Gomez talked to Stafford for another ten minutes about the various methods of drug smuggling. Stafford had heard about most of them, but some were new and very ingenious. Unlike most Customs commissioners, who were political appointees, Gomez had worked his way up from Customs Inspector, and was aware of smuggling methods and ways of altering drugs to make them harder to detect.

"I think you have all the information we have on the Gadsden Council," Gomez said. "The FBI is probably holding out on us, but I think we can work around them. I'll be calling the Deputy Secretary of ICE, and asking him to name you the acting Assistant Special Agent In Charge of the Dupree murder investigation. Go home and get some rest. You'll need to be on your best game in El Paso."

"Thank you, sir. I appreciate your confidence in me," Stafford said softly. He watched Gomez re-enter the conference room, then left the Commissioner's office and headed back to his own. When he got there, there was a light on in Boyer's office. He peeked inside. Boyer was sitting at his desk, working at his computer. Stafford walked in and stood near the door.

"Mr. Boyer, were you informed about the reason I was asked to the Commissioner's briefing?"

"In general terms, but I was told not to ask for more information, so I'm officially not asking. Right now, I'm just glad I still have a job."

"Sorry you got blind-sided like that, boss. Just so you know, I may be leaving for temporary duty, starting tomorrow. I better get home and get some sleep."

"Break a leg, Stafford." Boyer gave him a smile and a sloppy salute. "Go ahead and get out of here."

"Thanks, boss. See you tomorrow."

Stafford left the building and entered the dwindling, but steady, stream of people heading home. Since he had been in D.C., he had never left work this late. The sun was very low in the sky, and there was a chill in the air. If he was lucky, and there were no delays, he would be home in an hour. Stafford called Hernandez' government cellphone as he walked to the Metro.

"ICE..., Agent Hernandez."

"Frank, this is Ben. I know this is short notice, but the Customs Commissioner has given me a very important assignment."

"Oh yeah? Are you going away?" Hernandez said.

"Yep..., back to El Paso awhile. He told me I could have the assistance of anyone I wanted to get the job done, and I want you."

"Whoa..., slow down a minute. Me? Gomez isn't your boss..., and what kind of assignment did he give you?"

"That's all I can say for now, but you should pack a bag and be ready to go on official travel for let's say... two weeks... starting tomorrow. Tell your boss to check with the Commissioner's office, and mention my name."

"What if I don't want to go?"

"Trust me on this, Frank, you can name your next assignment if all goes well."

"And if it doesn't go well?"

"Gotta go now, buddy. You're starting to break up. I'll tell you all about it tomorrow."

"That's great. With friends like you, I don't need enemies, huh?"

"You're still breaking up. You'll be thanking me later, dude. Bye." Stafford shut his phone.

The trip home was uneventful, and except for a few very attractive women, was boring. That was good, because he had had enough intrigue for one day.

He arrived at his apartment in good time. There was still enough of the day left for a quick meal and some relaxing before bedtime. He checked the mail as he always did, but hadn't gotten even junk mail. He stepped deliberately up the stairs to his door. He had his key ready to unlock the door, when he saw the door was open a crack. He thought back, thinking maybe he had forgotten to shut and lock the door when he left for work that morning. He dismissed the idea. He remembered locking the door when he left.

He drew his SIG Sauer pistol from its holster, and slowly pushed on the door. It swung quietly open. Looking around the door frame to the left and right, he saw no one in the living room, or dining room. He paused and listened, but didn't hear anything. He stepped softly inside and looked left and right again. He still didn't see or hear anything. There was a light on in the kitchen. He didn't remember leaving the light on. He thought whoever had broken in had left it on.

The TV is still here. How can I tell if anybody has stolen anything if there isn't anything to steal? I'll just have to hope they kick in the door every time.

He decided to make sure there was no one in the apartment. He knocked five times on the door with his free hand.

"HELL-LO… U-P-S DELIVERY" he said loudly in a high voice. "IS ANYBODY HOME?"

"JUST LEAVE IT BY THE DOOR THANKS, I'LL GET IT LATER," said a voice coming from the kitchen.

Stafford pointed his pistol toward the kitchen door. He lined the weapon up without using the sights, by simply looking down the top of the slide. His trigger finger was resting lightly above the trigger guard, ready to move to the trigger in a split second.

He kept most of his attention focused on the kitchen, but did a visual check behind him to make sure there wasn't another person in the room. He noticed the message light was blinking on his answering machine.

"YOU HAVE TO SIGN FOR THE PACKAGE, SIR," he said in his high voice again from the open door.

After saying 'SIR' he carefully took several steps to his left, away from the door, and closer to the kitchen door. He was in what would have been the dining room of the apartment, if he had a dining table.

The ambient light coming in from the windows and door provided some light. It wasn't difficult to see. Stafford heard footsteps in the kitchen. Someone was coming out. He was still pointing his SIG at the doorway. His point of aim was chest high and a little to the right. He already had a lead on whoever was going to walk through the door.

A man stepped from the kitchen into the dining room. Stafford took a mental snapshot; dark suit coat, dark pants, short gray hair, fair complexion, average height and weight. It was Turner.

Turner took another step into the room. Stafford could see he was holding a pistol behind his back. Turner saw the door standing open and stopped abruptly. Out of the corner of his eye he caught sight of Stafford.

His head snapped to the right as he brought his arm out from behind his back.

"FREEZE! DROP THE GUN!" Stafford yelled.

Turner didn't stop moving. His arm was coming up fast in Stafford's direction. He was looking directly at Stafford. His expression made it clear that he had been taken off guard.

Stafford knew they were both going to shoot.

Stafford's reaction was automatic. He had been mentally preparing himself for different shooting scenarios for most of his adult life. He mentally practiced when to shoot, when and where to take cover, and when to retreat.

He had seen Turner's gun in his right hand, and knew when a right-handed shooter rushed a shot, he tended to jerk the trigger, and therefore the entire gun, to the right, spoiling the shot. Stafford stepped to his right as he and Turner fired.

There were three explosions in such quick succession that the first two shots sounded like one. A microsecond later Stafford fired another shot. Turner's snap shot missed by inches. The bullet punched a hole in the wall to the right of where Stafford was standing. Both of Stafford's shots hit Turner. As the bullets hit him, he rose on his toes before bending over and falling face first onto the floor. Stafford kept his pistol pointed at him. His finger was on the trigger as he edged closer to where Turner was lying on the floor. Turner moaned.

Keeping his pistol aimed at Turner, Stafford used his left hand to pick up Turner's semi-automatic and slip it into his own rear pants pocket. Next, he stepped backwards to the open apartment door, glancing back and forth between Turner and where he was heading. He held his weapon at the low ready position, using both hands. He found the wall switch, and turned on the overhead light. From his framed picture on the wall, John Wayne had seen everything. The Duke would have been proud.

He cautiously approached Turner again. He could see blood coming from the wounds. One wound was in the shoulder area, and another at the waist. Turner rolled over on his side, and tried to draw his knees up. Stafford holstered his weapon, took out his handcuffs, and secured Turner's hands behind his back. He bent forward so his face was directly in front of Turner's. Turner moaned and opened his eyes, but they weren't focusing on anything.

"Hey, Chief..., I bet that hurts. Consider yourself Mirandized," Stafford said, and stood up. Turner moaned again.

Stafford drew his SIG again, and searched the rest of his apartment, but found no one else. Nothing seemed out of place, other than Turner bleeding on the dining room carpet. He re-holstered his weapon and tried to collect his thoughts. His ears were ringing. He heard well enough to hear someone shouting from the bottom of the stairs.

"HEY…, WAS THAT A GUNSHOT I HEARD?"

"YES! CALL 9-1-1 AND TELL THEM A FEDERAL OFFICER WAS INVOLVED IN A SHOOTING. THE SUSPECT NEEDS AN AMBULANCE," Stafford yelled back. He heard a door slam, and then police sirens. Someone had already called 911.

As the sirens got closer, he took his credentials and badge out of his pocket and draped the badge on his jacket pocket, so the police could see it clearly. Next, he went into the kitchen and grabbed the hand towel that always hung on the oven door. He tore it in half and brought it back to where Turner was lying. He pressed half the towel against the stomach wound and the other half onto the shoulder wound, which wasn't bleeding too badly. Stafford walked slowly out of the apartment, and onto the landing at the top of the stairs.

No sense getting shot by a nervous cop…. I know someone is going to be pointing a gun my way.

He pulled Turner's pistol out of his back pocket and laid it on the floor inside the apartment door where he could see it. He took a deep breath and exhaled loudly as he sat down on the top stair-step.

He held his trembling hands out in front of him and rubbed them together, spreading the blood around and drying it. It felt sticky. He was glad it wasn't his own blood. Stafford had a familiar feeling. He realized there were still people around that wanted him dead.

This is like old times…, I've got somebody's blood on my hands again.

Chapter 18

As Stafford expected, he had more than one gun pointed at him before the police verified his identity. After a quick questioning by the arriving uniformed officers, a fire engine and an ambulance arrived. The apartment was filled with policemen, firemen, and EMT's. The firemen helped the EMT's put Turner on a stretcher and carry him down the stairs to the ambulance.

The police detectives arrived about twenty minutes later. They questioned Stafford briefly about what had happened, and searched the apartment. They found nothing out of the ordinary, except for the fact Stafford slept on a mat on the bedroom floor.

The detectives were particularly interested when Stafford told them the man he shot was a supervisor in the DHS equivalent of Internal Affairs. They both had that *oohhh* look of understanding. Of course they didn't understand at all, but thought they had found the motive for the shooting, until they discovered the outstanding Federal arrest warrant for Turner.

The detectives put him in the back of an unmarked police car for the ride to the police station. They wanted to question him in more detail, and get his written statement. Stafford expected the investigation to take the rest of the night.

After they got to the police station, Stafford was allowed to call the DHS communications center. He reported he had been involved in a shooting, and asked the communications officer to have Boyer call him immediately.

Boyer called within minutes, and Stafford told the whole story again. As policy required, Boyer called the ICE Situation Room to make an official report. All shootings involving HSI personnel had to be reported to the Situation Room, and from there, to the Deputy Secretary of ICE.

The HSI shooting investigation team arrived at the police station about an hour and a half later. The two HSI men were negatives of each other. One was a tall, thin, black man and the other was a short, pudgy, Caucasian. Stafford nicknamed them Flip and Flap. The police detectives were satisfied with Stafford's explanation of self-defense, but listened in as the HSI agents questioned Stafford. The HSI men had some questions for the detectives, as well.

The detectives didn't appreciate being questioned, but gave the agents the information they needed to make their shooting report. It wasn't every day that someone shot an IA Agent and got to go home afterward, but that was what was going to happen this time.

The HSI agents called the hospital to see how Turner was doing. They were told Turner was out of emergency surgery, and was in intensive care in critical condition.

The police released Stafford in time for breakfast. He wasn't hungry, but thought he had better eat anyway. He asked Flip and Flap to go through the drive-thru at a fast food place near his apartment. He wolfed down two sausage biscuits and a cup of coffee.

The two agents wanted to see the scene of the shooting. Stafford was tired, and felt like he needed to throw up, but pushed on.

The apartment was a mess. At one point, there were a dozen men in the apartment. There were dirty footprints, pieces of tape, paper wrappers from bandages, and intravenous tubing on the floor. The door frame was broken, and the carpet in the dining room had a large blood stain in front of the kitchen door. Stafford did a replay of the shooting. He looked them both in the eyes as he ran through it for them, and then told it one more time. He told the agents everything, and acted out the moves he made as he talked.

He knew he had done everything correctly. The agents said they thought so too, seeing as how there was an arrest warrant out for Turner. Flip and Flap were satisfied, and left an hour after they arrived. Stafford shut the door and sighed in relief, and fatigue. His cellphone vibrated on his belt, and he answered without thinking.

"Yeah, hello."

"Is this Stafford?"

"Hello? Can you speak louder, please?"

"I said..., is this Agent Stafford?" the voice said a little louder.

"Yes..., who's this?"

"This is Commissioner Gomez. Are you all right? I heard you shot Turner."

"I'm sorry, sir. Yes, sir, I'm fine. I guess I'm a little tired, and my ears are ringing."

"That's okay. I wanted you to know that Nelson isn't talking. He clammed up, and wants an attorney. Nelson must have told Turner about your interest in the missing drugs. I think Nelson was supposed to keep you out of the way, or kill you, and when he was arrested, Turner went after you instead. It wasn't very smart of him to break into your apartment."

"It might have worked, if he hadn't been dumb enough to answer my knock on the door. It would've looked like I surprised a burglar."

"You knocked on your own door?"

"I saw the door was open, and I knew I had left it shut and locked. I really thought someone had broken in and left, but I played it safe, and surprised Turner."

"Well, I guess he *was* surprised. Lucky for you."

"Yes, sir, lucky me."

"I can predict with certainty, you will be back on duty as soon as the ICE Deputy takes a look at the shooting report. Keep your bag packed and report to your supervisor regularly. We don't want to have to go looking for you. If you need to request anything big, like artillery support, call me directly. Save my direct number, is it showing on your phone?"

"Yes, sir, I see your number. I hope you were kidding about artillery support though."

"Yes, I was kidding, but not much. Whatever it is, if you've absolutely got to have it and can't get it, let me know right away."

"Roger that, sir."

"You take care, Stafford."

"Thank you for calling, sir."

Artillery support... God, I hope I'm not going to need THAT.

Chapter 19

It was early morning, but Stafford called his landlord anyway. He wanted to tell him about the shooting, the broken apartment door, and the blood stained carpet. He expected to get an answering machine, and was surprised when his landlord answered the phone.

Stafford played down the seriousness of what had happened. He simply said he had surprised an armed burglar, and he was forced to shoot the burglar in self-defense.

"I'm sorry to hear that your apartment was burgled and someone tried to kill you, Mr. Stafford, but the door repairs and carpet cleaning will be coming out of your security deposit. I'll have a repairman there to fix your door this morning."

"I can live with that. If you'll send me a bill, I'll voucher the repair costs back to the government since the shooting was in the line of duty," Stafford said.

"I'll send you the bill, of course. Unfortunately, I can't tolerate a shooting in my building, Mr. Stafford. You will be receiving official notice that I will not be renewing your lease."

"Well now, that *is* a shame, because the rats and I were just getting to be on a first name basis."

"Good bye, Mr. Stafford. I hope the remainder of the day goes better for you."

"Better than not being shot but getting evicted? What could be better than that?" The landlord hung up.

"How do you like that? I'm being kicked out. Who am I talking to?"

Stafford slammed his phone shut and threw it at his TV-watching lawn chair. The phone bounced off the webbing, flew back and hit him on his foot before bouncing like a ball across the floor. It came to rest near the blood stain on the carpet.

"Was that my phone, or the government phone? Oh... the government phone... drat."

Stafford high stepped to the phone and picked it up. He opened it and checked to make sure it still worked. It was still working, and Stafford made another call.

"DHS, HSI, Boyer, how can I help you?"

"Morning, Boss. This is Stafford."

"Stafford, are you all right?"

"Yes, sir, I'm good..., just a little tired. How about I get some sleep and come in after lunch?"

"Sounds okay to me. The Customs Commissioner and the ICE Director are aware of the shooting. I can give you two days of administrative leave, effective immediately. Get some rest. By the way, Commissioner Gomez said to tell you well done."

"I *feel* well done. I'll still be in after lunch. I've got to do some data queries on imports from Mexico."

"Suit yourself. We'll see you then."

"Thank you, sir."

Stafford wanted to sleep, but his door was broken. He wanted some kind of warning in case there were more uninvited guests. He went into the kitchen and got two drinking glasses and some silverware, and brought them to the broken door. The entry area had wood flooring for about ten square feet around the door. The rest of the living room and dining room was covered in worn, but fairly clean, wall-to-wall carpet.

He pushed the door shut as tight as it would go, and placed one glass top down on the floor next to the door. He placed the second glass bottom to bottom on the first glass, and placed the silverware inside the top glass. It was a home-made burglar alarm. If anyone pushed the door open it would knock the glasses over and make plenty of noise. Satisfied, he went to his bedroom and lay down on his sleeping mat fully clothed, including his gun.

He was quickly asleep. He dreamed his recurring dream of helplessness. In his dream, it was mid-day and he was standing in the middle of an airfield. He could see bullets hitting the concrete all around him. The bullets kicked up dust and sparks. There was no cover in any direction as far as he could see, just concrete. The ricocheting bullets whizzed by him from every direction, making a terrible sound as they went by. He ran, but the bullets kept coming at him. He lay down on the concrete, but that was worse because the bullets stayed near the ground after they hit. It was only a matter of time before he would be wounded or killed. He awoke in a cold sweat, surprised he had slept at all. He got up and went into the bathroom, splashed water on his face, and dried with a hand towel. From the smell of the towel, he knew it was time to do laundry, another day.

He checked the time, and saw he had slept for about two hours. He heard knocking on the door and then the sound of glasses and silverware crashing to the floor.

"EXCUSE ME. BUILDING MAINTENANCE. I HOPE DIDN'T BREAK ANYTHING," a man's voice said.

"COME ON IN," Stafford called out as he walked out of the bedroom. He placed his hand on the grip of his pistol, just in case he was being fooled the way he had fooled Turner. He turned part way to his right, which concealed his weapon and put him in a ready position for whoever was at the door.

The door was pushed open by a gray-haired black man, carrying a large tool kit. Hearing the glasses rolling around on the floor, he looked behind the door and saw the glasses and silverware, and then looked up at Stafford.

"Good morning, sir. That there's pretty smart. Made yourself a little alarm, eh? I'll have to remember that one for myself. I'm Henry Johnson. The landlord called and told me you got a door that needs fixing? I guess it'd be this door here. Somebody broke in, huh?"

"That's right," Stafford said. He relaxed his stance and took his hand off his weapon.

"My name's Ben Stafford."

"And I hear you also got some carpet that needs... good Lord... what happened there?" He was looking at the large blood stain on the carpet in the dining room. He walked over to get a better look.

"I cut myself shaving. I'm quite a bleeder," Stafford said. Henry frowned.

"From the blood on the wall there, I'd say somebody got popped good. Do the cops know about it?"

"Oh, you bet. I just got back from the police station. I was there all night. A burglar pulled a gun on me and I had to shoot him."

"He dead?"

"Not yet."

"Got what he deserved, looks like to me. Darned kids. I'll get to work on that door, and I'll bring a carpet shampooer tomorrow maybe... okay?"

"Sounds good. I'm gonna make some coffee while you work... maybe watch some TV. You want some coffee?"

"Wouldn't bother me none. Cream and sugar for me, please."

Stafford made their coffees, came back out of the kitchen, and handed Johnson his coffee. He turned his lawn chair around and sat so he could watch Johnson work on the door. He didn't turn on the television. Johnson sipped his coffee.

"Thank you. That's good coffee," Johnson said.

"It's instant. Instant coffee is hard to mess up," Stafford said. Johnson placed the cup carefully on the floor outside the door.

"I see you wear a gun. I guess you're the police, or a G-man or something, huh?"

"Federal Officer." Stafford took his badge and credentials out and showed them to Johnson.

"So I guess it was a pretty long night for you," Johnson said. He started prying off the door frame.

"Yep..., pretty exciting too. That burglar scared a few years off of me." Henry stopped what he was doing, and looked at Stafford with one eye squinted, sizing him up.

"I think I read people pretty good. You don't look like a man that scares too easily. You were in the service I bet."

"Yeah."

"Marines?"

"U.S. Army Rangers."

"You fight in Iraq and Afghanistan?"

"Both."

"Too bad the burglar didn't know that." Stafford thought for a moment.

"I think he knew," Stafford said.

"Well, then he was some kind a fool." Johnson pulled a tape measure from his tool kit, and measured the height of the open doorway. He let the tape zip back into its case with a loud snap.

"You know, that reminds me of a story my daddy used to tell me. Can I tell it to you?"

"Sure, I love a good story. How much longer will you be with the door? I'll be leaving in an hour or so," Stafford said.

"Oh, I'll be done by then, sir. This kind of thing happens more often than I like, and I'm good at fixing stuff. I may be slow, but I do a good job."

"I can see that. Please don't call me sir. My name's Ben."

"Okay, Ben. Like the Benjamin from the Bible?"

"That's the one."

"Your momma's name wouldn't be Rachel, would it?"

"No. My momma's name is Marie."

"That's a good one, too."

"Well anyway see, my daddy had this old cat that used to hang around the back of the house. Seems that something happened to the cat when it was a kitten, and it just didn't have all its senses about it... got brain damaged I guess."

"So one day my daddy was sitting on the back porch, watching this cat sitting in the backyard. This old cat saw another cat walking through the yard and he went over to see what the other cat was up to. The other cat sees the dummy cat coming at him and gets all bowed up, making itself big like they do. He was hissing and spitting and making all his fur stand up like they do, you know. He was giving this stupid cat *all* the signs that said watch out and stay away, or else you going to get hurt, you know?"

"Yeah, I've seen cats do that. So what happened?"

"Well, Mr. Ben, this old cat walked right up to the other cat... never slowed down a bit... just came straight at him, meowing like everything was cool. This old goofy cat didn't know any better. When they were about a foot apart, the other cat just turned around and ran straight up the side of the house and jumped down on the other side of the yard, getting away from that crazy cat. Daddy said he'd never seen anything like it in his whole life. He never forgot it."

"That's a pretty good story. What'd you say your name was again?"

"My name's Henry Johnson, sir..., I mean Ben. You can call me Henry though..., everybody does."

"The point I was trying to make Ben, was that to this crazy cat, the other cat wasn't dangerous at all. Young people and fools, they think like that too. Now the normal cat, well he saw things a different way. He was giving all the right warning signs you know... hissing and spitting, and this other cat just keeps coming. I imagine this normal cat had never seen anything like that before. He wasn't sure he could win a fight with a cat that wasn't afraid. See what I mean?"

"I think so, Henry."

"I'll say it plain in case you don't get it. You won that fight there because you weren't afraid, and you weren't no fool either. Sometimes fear is a good thing, because it makes you cautious, and sometimes it just gets in the way and slows you down. And being a fool, well that never helps at all, but sometimes it doesn't hurt. See what I mean now?"

"I certainly do Henry. You… are a very wise man."

It also helps if you're not afraid to die.

Chapter 20

S tafford arrived at work just after lunch. When he walked in the door of his office, the other agents crowded around him. They had heard about the shooting, and wanted to hear about it firsthand. Boyer heard the commotion and came out of his office to see what was going on.

"Agent Stafford, come into my office for a moment please. The rest of you can get back to work."

"Good morning, sir." Stafford was smiling sheepishly from all the attention he had gotten.

"Good afternoon, Stafford. Come in please," Boyer said. They went into Boyer's office and Stafford shut the door. Neither of them sat down.

"I'll get right to the point, Stafford. I was authorized to give you some time off. My supervisor reminded me today that it is mandatory that you be placed on administrative leave until the report of the shooting has been reviewed and approved by the Deputy Secretary. So…. get those data queries you wanted done A-S-A-P, and then go home until we tell you to come back."

"Sir, I was supposed to be going on temporary duty to El Paso today."

"I was told that's officially on hold. Agent Hernandez was here earlier asking for you. I assume he was going with you to El Paso?"

"Yes, sir. In fact, Hernandez can still go, and I can catch up to him in a day or two."

"That might be a good idea," Boyer said.

"Am I forbidden from doing any official duties while I'm on administrative leave?"

"That's correct, so get as much done as you can in the next couple of hours, and then go home. Take a short vacation or do whatever you want.

We just need you to call in once a day, especially if you leave town. Understood?"

"I hear you, sir." Stafford left Boyer's office. As he approached his desk, he saw Hernandez come in.

"I'm glad to see you're okay. I'm sorry to hear about you having to shoot that guy last night. Did you get any sleep?" Stafford shook Hernandez' outstretched hand.

"Thanks, Frank. Yeah, I got a little sleep this morning after the investigation was done. I'm only in for a couple of hours. They're putting me on admin leave until the shooting report is approved."

"I heard they arrested an Agent named Nelson yesterday. What was that about?" Hernandez asked.

"Nelson sat right there," Stafford said, pointing to the desk behind his.

"Nelson's arrest, and Turner trying to kill me are connected," Stafford said. Hernandez' eyebrows went up.

"Really?"

"Really," Stafford said. He looked around the office. Half a dozen agents were looking at him and listening to his conversation.

"Let's find someplace else to talk. There's no sense telling the whole office everything I know," Stafford said. He and Hernandez stepped into the hallway outside his office. Stafford stopped to get his bearings, and rubbed his chin.

"There's an executive conference room down this way, let's see if it's empty," Stafford said. Hernandez followed Stafford to an open door. They walked into a darkened room.

"This is the place." Stafford found the light switches and turned them both on. The room was brighter than necessary, so he flipped one off.

"That's better. Now listen up."

Stafford talked for fifteen minutes. He told Hernandez everything he knew about the missing coke, Dupree's murder, the poisoned drugs, the meeting with the Commissioner, and his shooting of Turner. Hernandez asked a couple of pertinent questions, but mainly listened. The longer he listened the more he frowned. Stafford finished talking.

"I think I need to sit down," Hernandez said.

"You *are* sitting down, Frank."

"Oh..., yeah."

"What's the matter, Frank? You look a little peaked."

"Man, don't you think we're just a little bit out of our depth here? Why not let the FBI handle this?"

"Because there's too much at stake, Frank. There's something very big going on behind the missing coke and the drug deaths. The FBI can't get the job done quickly, but working from another direction, we can. Saving time means saving lives, and God knows what else."

"Can I say no?"

"Sure, you can say no," Stafford said, as he tried to drill a hole in Hernandez' head with his eyes. Hernandez stared straight ahead. His right leg bounced up and down nervously.

"This goes against my better judgment, but I'll do it. But, I think I'm going to be sorry I ever got involved in this." He stopped frowning, and smirked. His leg was still bouncing.

"Just don't make me sorry too. Okay, Frank?"

"I'll try not to. So what's the plan?"

"I'm going to do some data queries and see if anything unusual pops out. You're going to El Paso to help with the investigation of Dupree's murder, and follow any leads that develop. If anything looks good from the queries I do, I'll call and tell you about it. I'm going to take my required admin leave, and in three or four days I'll catch up with you in El Paso."

"I'm glad I already packed a bag," Hernandez said. "I'll put my travel authorization in the computer as soon as I tell my supervisor. He's not too happy about finding out you were my supervisor too. Oh…, and my wife sends her regards." Hernandez laughed as he got to his feet.

"I'll bet she did. Sorry on both counts, Frank. It couldn't be helped."

"I know," Hernandez said seriously, still smiling from his laugh. He and Stafford shook hands like old friends who might not see each other again. The possibility was not lost on either of them.

"I'll see you in El Paso. Don't leave me hanging," Hernandez said. His smile was gone.

"It'll never happen Frank, not as long as I've got breath. I'll see you in El Paso. Get going as soon as you can."

"Okay, boss." They walked back to Stafford's office together. Hernandez kept walking as Stafford stopped at his office door. He looked at Hernandez as he walked by.

"Stay safe, Frank." Frank answered with a low wave.

Stafford set to work on his data queries. The computer seemed especially slow. He needed to run two queries. One for the period before the decline in seizures, and another for the period afterward. The query filters would limit the results to show frequent and infrequent importations by known and unknown importers. Any examination results would be listed, as well.

The computer finally accepted his data requests, after making him start over twice. He arranged it in a format he could understand and read easily. Now all he had to do was wait for the computer to process his job request. There were a dozen requests ahead of his in the system. Stafford had hoped he would get the results back before he had to leave.

While he waited, he checked his voice messages. One message was from Beth St. James. The time stamp in the message indicated she had called before lunchtime today. She asked him to call when he got in. He called her immediately, anxious to hear her voice again.

"Good afternoon, United States Customs and Border Protection, Supervisory Officer St. James, how may I help you?"

"Hi, Beth."

"Ben…, why did you let me go through my entire speech? Why didn't you say something?"

"I like hearing your voice, and I wanted to hear you ask how you could help me. Can you help me?"

"Very funny."

"I was thinking about how you've already helped me. Tell the truth now Beth, you were praying for me yesterday, weren't you?"

"Are you making fun of me?"

"No, I'm not making fun of you… well… you were praying for me, weren't you?"

She didn't want to tell him the truth. She *had* been praying for him, but she decided there was a good reason he was asking, he probably needed to know someone truly cared about him.

"Yes…, I prayed for you in the center before we talked, and I prayed for you after you went back upstairs."

"I don't know what you prayed about Beth, but I'm glad you did."

"I heard about the arrest of one of the agents in your office, as well as about you being involved in a shooting yesterday."

"News gets around this place pretty fast."

"I knew you were okay. I just wanted to talk to you and see if there was anything I could do. I know it must have been tough on you…, having to shoot that man."

While he was listening to her talk, he saw he had an answer from his data query. He routed the finished job to a printer in his office.

"No, I'm okay with it. I'm sorry, Beth. You could probably hear me typing. I'm officially on admin leave in an hour, and I have some things I have to nail down before I go. I have to hang up now."

"That's okay. Call me before you leave, okay?"

"Will do. Bye now."

Stafford retrieved the printout, but it was too much information to wade through in an hour. He needed to refine the results of his query. He saved the data to another format, and opened a software application package that CBP paid some vendor too much money for.

After having to open and read the software help feature a half-dozen times, he figured out how to get the data arranged the way he wanted it.

He saved the file, and emailed it to Hernandez. He sent the file to his own email address, as well. By sending the message to himself, he could access it even if he wasn't on the headquarters LAN. He called Hernandez to let him know the data was waiting for him.

Hernandez answered. "United States…"

"Frank…, this is Stafford, I got some info for you."

"Uh…okay, what've you got?" Stafford heard traffic noise in the background of Hernandez' end of the line.

"Where are you, Frank?"

"I'm on the way to the airport. Where did you think I was?"

"Oh yeah, sorry. I just emailed you some names and addresses of companies that need looking into when you get to El Paso. It's all in the email. Have a good flight."

"Thanks, boss… See ya there."

Stafford went to Boyer's office. Boyer was leaning over his desk, holding his forehead in his hand, looking intently at a duty schedule for the office's agents.

"Excuse me, sir. I've sent Hernandez an email with the data I found, and I am officially going home now. Hope I haven't messed up your duty schedule."

"No, no, it's all right. Enjoy the time off if you can, but remember to watch your back."

"Oh, you bet I will."

"Hey, Stafford, didn't you ask about time off to attend a funeral? This might be a good time to get out of town, if you know what I mean."

Stafford crossed one arm over his chest and used it to support his other arm as he rubbed his chin. If he had been sitting down, he might have looked like a copy of *The Thinker*, by Rodin.

"That a good idea, boss. I'm definitely going to check into that. I'm gone as soon as I make one more phone call." Stafford went to his desk and called Beth. The call went to her voice-mail, so he left a message saying he was sorry he missed her, and left his home phone number. He remembered Beth saying she knew it must have been tough having to shoot Turner. He thought about the first man he ever shot.

No need to dredge that up now. I'm off for a few days... with how many people looking to put a bullet in me?

As soon as I get home I'm calling dad, and then the airlines. I can taste Mom's cooking already.

Chapter 21

The Metro was blissfully un-crowded. Stafford was tired. He was tired from not getting enough sleep, and tired from too much thinking. He didn't want to do any more thinking until tomorrow. He shut his eyes for a moment.

He couldn't help it. His mind started working on what he had heard from the men in the Commissioner's intelligence briefing. Then picture of Turner bleeding on his carpet came into his head. His ears were still ringing.

"Hey, mister… do you mind if I… sit here?" a woman said breathlessly.

He was about to be annoyed, since he knew there were plenty of empty seats throughout the car. He opened his eyes and looked up.

"Beth! What are you doing here?"

"I took the rest of the day off. I thought I would treat you… to a home cooked meal at your place. You look exhausted, and hungry."

"And you look out of breath. What are you doing on my train? This isn't your way home, is it?"

"No. I was hoping to catch up to you… before you got to the Metro, but I saw you were… way ahead of me. I caught up with you just as the train pulled in. I almost missed it," Beth said as her breathing began to slow.

"I'm glad you caught me, but a meal at my place wouldn't be a good idea. I haven't cleaned up from the shooting, and besides that…, my refrigerator's empty." He stood up so he wouldn't have to look up at her. "It's a very nice offer, but I'll have to say some other time."

"Well then, since your place is a mess, why don't you come with me to my place and I'll make you a meal there?" His eyes opened wide.

"I don't know what to say," he said.

"Say yes..., and say yes right now..., because my stop is next." She smiled at him, and his reluctance melted.

"Okay, yes. Thank you very much. I'd be happy to accept your invitation."

They got off at the next stop and made their way to the surface. Beth talked about the news of the shooting, and how her day had gone. He was not paying as much attention to her as he usually did. People still wanted to kill him.

He looked around at the people walking behind him. They didn't seem to be paying attention to him, and he saw nothing that remotely looked threatening. Just the same, he tried to raise his awareness level a few notches.

Beth continued talking. "...plus I really did want to cook you a nice dinner. I didn't think about there being a mess at your apartment."

"My apartment was a mess *before* the shooting. I don't entertain guests very often, well not at all really, so I never saw the need to buy things like furniture, tables, or chairs."

"So where do you sleep, on the floor in a sleeping bag?" She laughed at her joke, until she saw he was frowning.

"Lady, you've really got my number," he said looking at his feet.

"Oh, Ben, I'm sorry. I didn't mean to insult you."

"No, it's okay, and it *is* funny. It happens to be the truth. I sleep on a mat on my bedroom floor, and if it's cold I use a sleeping bag." She stopped walking. He walked a step farther, but turned around to look at her.

"Ben, I am so sorry. I would never intentionally say anything hurtful to you like that. I would never make fun of you."

He saw the concern in her eyes. She thought she had said something to hurt him. He liked the feeling of knowing she cared whether she hurt him or not, and he wanted to feel more.

"I know you wouldn't. Don't fret yourself over it, okay?"

"Okay." They started walking again.

"Don't *fret* myself over it? What exactly does don't fret yourself mean anyway?" He looked at her and saw a gleam in her eye.

"It means don't fret yourself none. I'll do all the fretting for both of us..., okay?" He reached over and pulled her to his side as they walked. She responded by putting her arm around his waist and pulling him closer, as well. After a few steps, they both released the hold they had on each other, and then looked left and right into each others eager faces.

"Just a couple more blocks, hungry man," she said with a smile that showed most of her teeth.

"No problem, lady." He smiled back.

The air was cooler today than yesterday. The sky was bluer today than yesterday, and the emptiness they both felt in their hearts was less now than yesterday, or any other day they could remember. They reached her building and went inside.

"Let's take the stairs. We don't get enough exercise riding elevators and escalators at work," Beth said. She led the way up the stairs, and Stafford followed, having fun looking at her shapely legs as she climbed the steps ahead of him.

"Did you say something?" Beth asked as she stopped on a landing to face him.

"No. I was talking to myself I guess. Could you hear me?"

"I heard you mumbling. What did you say?"

"I said you're very beautiful."

"Thank you. I would appreciate your compliment more, if you had been looking into my eyes when you said that."

"I'm sorry, Beth. I guess you can't teach an old dog new tricks. Maybe inviting me here was a mistake."

"Ben…, this may be difficult for you to hear, but I'm going to tell you what I think. You have lived by Army rules, ICE rules, and your own rules, for much too long. You would do well to live by God's rules. Following His rules helps you deal with the complexities of living in a broken world. Now, you are not a dog. You can behave long enough to have dinner with me, can't you?

"I guess so."

"I guess so. You sound like a little boy. Now why don't you go ahead of me? Go to the next floor, and exit to the right."

"Okay." He stepped past her and started up the stairs. He reached the next landing and began to climb the next set of steps.

"Stop staring at my butt."

"Ben, I was not staring at your butt."

"Yes, you were."

"I was not."

"Well, what *were* you looking at then?"

"I was looking at your big feet. What are they, size 15?"

"They're the same size as my big mouth, it makes it easier that way."

Chapter 22

Beth's meal was delicious. He told her so. She had already told him she would clean up, although he had offered his help. He got up and walked around her apartment while she cleared the dishes from the table.

He went to her balcony and looked out, but there wasn't much of a view. He watched the cars going by on the street below. A faint odor of exhaust drifted in through the open sliding glass door.

"This is a pretty nice apartment. You're pretty nice, too. I'm definitely going to see if there are any vacancies here," he said, as he walked back to the kitchen.

"I already checked. There aren't any vacancies, but they expect some in a few months. There is a pretty good turn-over of people here," she said, as she rinsed her hands under the faucet. "Besides, I wouldn't want you moving here on my account. We haven't even been out on a date yet. We got sidetracked from our bike ride, remember?"

"Well, I wasn't the one who sidetracked us. If you remember, you told me not to bother calling you."

"So I did. But that had a lot to do with you. Maybe you can explain why you knocked that man down on the way to the Metro."

"Do you really want to get into this? You made a wonderful meal, and I'm feeling pretty positive right now. Why ruin it?"

She was standing with her rear against the front of the closed silverware drawer, her hands resting comfortably on either side of her on the counter top. She thought about what he said. She didn't want to ruin his positive mood, but pressed on.

"Maybe this *is* a bad time to talk about it. You've had a bad couple of days. One day soon though, we need to talk about it."

"And we will, Beth."

"I better be getting back to my place. I want to call my dad and see if I can fly home on short notice, and possibly go to a funeral," he said. He took a couple of slow steps to the door.

"I'm sorry, Ben, but I've changed my mind. I can't let you go yet."

"I can't go? Why can't I go?"

"I don't want you to leave until you and I have a completely honest conversation; just one honest conversation."

"What would you call the other conversations we've had? I was being honest with you. Weren't you being honest with me?" Stafford said.

"Yes, I was honest. I meant you can't leave before I have *another* honest conversation with you."

Oh brother, here we go again... the beginning of the end.

He didn't have them very often, but honest conversations always made Stafford sorry. Usually, it meant that a woman was about to tell him she didn't want to see him any more. Not only was he not used to being completely honest about himself, he knew the observational profile training from the academy, and started trying to hide the physical signs of his dishonesty.

"Okay, Beth. Completely honest again it is. Why don't you start?" He folded his arms over his chest, remembered that meant someone was being defensive, and uncrossed them.

"All right, but first let's get comfortable. Why don't you come and sit down on the couch?" she said.

Stafford had an *aw shucks* look about him. It was the same look he used to get when he knew his mother was about to give him a talking to. He walked slowly to the couch and plopped himself down. Beth sat near him in a side chair. She patted him on the knee and then rested her hands in her lap.

"I have mixed feelings about you, Ben. I like you, and enjoy being around you, but you frequently leave me with a bad feeling..., like there's a part of you that you're hiding, and I wouldn't like if I knew about it. The incident with that man you knocked down is a perfect example. I want to get to know you, but right now I'm not sure that would be what God wants for me. Can you tell me why you knocked him down? You obviously did it on purpose."

He wanted to go on the defensive, but he could see that she was being honest about the way she felt about him, and so he tried to explain.

"You didn't see all of what happened. The man I ran into was running into other people on purpose. I just gave him a taste of what he had been dishing out. He got what he deserved."

"You gave him what he deserved?"

"That's right," Stafford said, as he leaned back and put his hands on his thighs.

"And what do *you* deserve?"

"What do *I* deserve? What do you mean? I guess I deserve whatever I get, too." She thought about that for a few seconds, and then repeated his words back to him.

"I guess I deserve whatever I get." Beth continued.

"Deserving what you get may be true. If you've heard the gospel, and knowing who Jesus is, you refuse the gift of salvation through Christ's sacrifice on the cross..., then you *will* get what you deserve. If you are in Christ, having accepted Him as your savior, then in a way of speaking you get what you *don't* deserve..., which is God's mercy and grace. Do you see what I mean?"

"I told you I know the story of Jesus, Beth..., and I thank you for telling me about it again that day at work."

"But do you believe it, Ben? From what I've seen, and from what you told me, I'm not sure you ever really accepted Christ as your savior."

"I was baptized when I was ten years old. I got dunked in front of the whole congregation."

"Did you understand the significance of being baptized? Did you understand what you were doing? This is an honest conversation remember?"

He thought about the feeling he had on the street when he had been honest with her. Being honest might make him feel embarrassed at first, but he felt good after telling her the truth. He wanted to feel good again.

"No..., I didn't know what baptism was all about."

"But you know now, don't you?"

He sat forward and put his elbows on his knees and hung his head, placing his face in his hands. Tears came to his eyes. Beth leaned forward and put her hand on his back. Stafford sniffed, trying to keep the tears from flowing.

"Why don't you open your heart to Jesus, Ben? He loves you and wants you to allow Him in."

"I don't know how."

"Would you like me to help you?"

"Yes, please... tell me what to do."

Every day of Ben's life had been part of God's plan. He was alive and in this city, in Beth's apartment, listening to Beth witness to him, because this was exactly where he was supposed to be. His life experiences, and his brokenness, were the fertile ground upon which Beth's words were now falling.

He sniffed again and raised his head to look at her. His eyes were red and damp with tears. She took his hand and squeezed it gently. He gripped her hand tightly, and then loosened his hold.

"The scriptures say if you confess with your mouth that Jesus is Lord, and believe in your heart that God raised Him from the dead, you will be saved. These aren't just words. Saying it and believing it mean you are giving yourself completely to God, and you are going to try to live by his will. Do you understand?"

"Yes," he said softly as he nodded his head.

"I suggest you pray, and ask God for forgiveness for all the sins you have committed. Thank Him for the wonderful gift of salvation He has given us through the sacrifice of His Son. You can pray silently. Why don't you do that now, and tell me when you've finished."

But you don't know the things I've done.

Stafford closed his eyes and bowed his head. He let go of Beth's hand and slid himself forward off the couch and onto his knees, clasping his hands together in front of his chest. He was silent for a time, and then he raised his head, opened his eyes and said, "I've finished praying."

"Now say this after me... Jesus is Lord."

"Jesus is Lord," he repeated.

"He died for my sins, and God raised Him from the dead."

"He died for my sins, and God raised Him from the dead," Stafford said.

"You're saved, Ben. Praise God.... You're saved!" She stood up and put both hands straight up in the air. Her smile was the prettiest he had ever seen. She danced around the room laughing and clapping her hands together. She had never been happier.

Stafford got up and started clapping and dancing around the room, too. His eyes were still full of tears, and he was sniffling, but he was a new man; a new creation. He felt wonderful. He ran to the balcony's sliding glass doors and slid the screen open. He stepped out onto the balcony, turned his face to the sky and said loudly, "Thank you, Jesus! Thank you, Jesus!"

Stafford walked back in from the balcony and shut the screen door. Beth was watching him, her hands held together down low.

"Oh, Ben, I'm so happy for you. I feel like my feet are about a foot off the floor. I'm on cloud nine!"

"I don't know how I can ever thank you, Beth. This is the greatest thing that has ever happened to me."

"That will go down as the biggest understatement of your life. But don't thank me. It's not about me, or you... it's about Jesus," she said, while pointing at the ceiling with her finger.

Stafford nodded his head in agreement. He clapped his hands again. He couldn't stop smiling.

This time, I'm really saved. But you don't know the things I've done.

After things calmed down, Stafford knew it was time to head for home. He had a completely different feeling about everything now, and his mind was going a mile a minute.

"Before you go, I'd like to give you something." She went to the end table and picked up a Bible.

"I'd like you to have this. It was one of the first study bibles I bought. It's very easy to read, and there are notes and ways for you to apply the lessons of the Bible to your life."

"I can't take your Bible, Beth. I'll get another one at the book store."

"Well, until you do, you can use this one. I have another Bible. I'd like to go with you to the book store when you decide to get one. I can help you pick a good one."

"In that case, thank you very much."

He took the Bible from her, and walked to the door. He stopped with his hand on the door handle. Beth reached for the door and her hand rested on top of his. He read something into the moment that wasn't there yet, and leaned forward to kiss her. She put her other hand up, covering the lower part of his face and mouth.

"Not so fast, hungry man. One thing at a time. You've got to crawl before you can walk," she said. She pushed down with her other hand, opening the door behind him. She dropped her hand from his face.

"I guess this changes everything doesn't it?" he said. He still wanted to kiss her, but didn't try.

"It's supposed to..., but we still have a date to go on, remember?"

He remembered imagining what she would look like sitting on her bike. He felt embarrassed as the image he had created of her came to his mind again.

"Yeah, I remember…, but I have a feeling this is going to be a whole new ball game for me. When I get back from my T-D-Y in El Paso, I'd like to take you to dinner, to a place that has cloth napkins and tablecloths."

"That sounds very nice, Mr. Stafford, I'll be looking forward to it. You know, I hate to bring this up now, but seeing as how Agent Nelson has an arrest warrant out for him…"

"Yes?" Stafford said, sounding interested.

"He and I had a couple of dates. It was really nothing. He made some unwanted advances, and I didn't go out with him again. I think he had a crush on me for a time after that."

"No wonder he always sounded like he wanted to punch me in the face…, he was jealous. Thanks for telling me."

"You're welcome. Of course I'm not going to see him again, and I'm glad."

"Me too. If you did see him again, you'd have to arrest him."

Beth slapped her forehead, and laughed. "Oh yeah…, forgot."

"Well, good night, Beth. Thank you for everything."

"You're welcome, Ben. Good night, and God bless you."

As Stafford walked out of the building onto the sidewalk, he started whistling a hymn. The hymn had a new meaning for him this time. *What a friend we have in Jesus!*

The Bible felt strange in his hand. He looked at it closely. The outside cover was made of cloth, which Beth had placed there to protect the book from dirt and dust. 'Holy Bible' it said in gold lettering. When he was a boy, he used to call it the Holly Bibble. He chuckled at the memory.

Stafford brought the book to his face and pressed it against his forehead for a couple of seconds and lowered it back to his side as he walked. The Bible smelled like Beth. He brought it to his nose, breathed in her scent again, and then dropped the book to his side. He prayed again, thanking God for saving him, and for bringing Beth into his life.

Although he felt mentally better than he had in a long time, he was physically tired, and had to slow his pace as he walked to the Metro. He used his commuter pass, and found his way to the proper platform. His feet hurt, so he sat on a bench. Pedestrian traffic was low, but there were plenty of people waiting for the train. He looked left and right, trying to pay attention to the people standing around him. He imagined all of them hoped to be first on the train when the doors opened.

"Hey preacher, when's the next service?" someone laughed.

Stafford looked to his left and saw a young man standing with his hands in his jean pockets. He was looking at Stafford's Bible, grinning.

"Are you talking to me?" Stafford said in an even tone.

"Yeah, I'm talking to you preacher-man. When's the next service?" He laughed again.

Stafford got up and took a couple of steps toward the laughing man. He was about a foot away from the man when he stopped and said quietly, "There'll be a funeral service right here tonight. Would you care to attend?"

"Hey man, it was like a joke, ya know? Don't go getting yourself all amped up over it."

"Yeah..., like why don't you go for a walk, junior?"

"Absolutely, man. No problem." Laughing man's smile was gone as he turned and walked to the other end of the platform. Stafford walked back to his seat and sat down again.

Everybody's a comedian. I'm supposed to be the comedian.

My light's not shining so bright now, is it? Go and apologize to the man you scared away.

Stafford felt strange. He could hear the voice, but wasn't sure if it was his imagination, or something else.

I'll be speaking to you in different ways. Sometimes you will hear me, and sometimes you will simply know what to do.

Stafford walked to where the young man was standing. He glanced at Stafford as he approached, and looked concerned when Stafford stopped in front of him once again.

"Listen, I'm sorry I sounded off that way to you. I know you were just having fun with me," Stafford said.

"No problem, man. I don't know when to keep my mouth shut sometimes. Sorry if I offended you." He offered his hand, and they shook. They smiled and Stafford walked away as the train pushed the air out of the station, and stopped.

Stafford watched the people surging at the opening doors, not leaving enough room for the people getting off to get through. Some people swam upstream, fighting their way on board even as the crowd tried to get off. Somehow, everyone who wanted to get off, got off, and everyone who wanted to get on, got on. Stafford waited until the pushing and shoving had stopped and then calmly entered and held the hand-bar.

People.

And I love every one of them, Son.

Then I do too.

And I do know the things you've done.

He made it home and was glad to see his apartment door had not been kicked in again while he was out. As he opened the door, he smelled soap. The rug had been shampooed, and the stain was gone. He could see the rug was still wet. He glanced at the wall with the bullet hole in it.

Nya nya ya missed me.

"Thanks, Henry, you did a good job, but I'm not going to miss this place," he said to himself.

Stafford walked into the kitchen and tore off a small piece of paper towel and wet it under the faucet. He squeezed the water out and walked back to the dining room wall with the bullet hole. He rolled the paper into a ball between his palms, and stuffed it into the bullet hole, pressing the paper in level with the surface of the wall. He stood back and admired his ingenuity.

He saw the answering machine light blinking, and remembered it had been blinking yesterday. He walked over to punch the button when he remembered he had forgotten to check the mail. He stopped in his tracks and thought for a moment. He had been through worse days than this, and was puzzled that he was a little confused. He still had the Bible in his hand. He put the Bible down and walked downstairs to check the mail. He found he hadn't received any.

He re-climbed the stairs and shut the apartment door, checking the fit of the door and whether the lock worked. He realized Henry obviously had a key, or the rug couldn't have been shampooed while he was out. He decided not to worry about it for now. Finally making it to the answering machine, he punched the message button. The machine said there were two messages. The first one from yesterday was a hang-up.

I'll bet that was Turner checking to see if I was home.

The next message was from this morning.

"Ben, this is your dad. The funeral for Rennie's daughter is in the morning. Rennie moved the funeral so some of his family wouldn't miss too much work. I know it's too late to do anything about it now, so you won't be able to come. Talk to you later. Sorry, Son. Bye." He picked up the phone and called his father, who answered on the fourth ring.

"Jerry's pool hall..., Jerry speaking."

"When did you change your name to Jerry, Dad?"

"Hey, Son. I don't know what gets into me. I get a lot of telephone solicitors calling, and sometimes I mess with them a bit before I hang up. I guess now you know where you got your weirdness."

"I've always known that. Mom's too normal."

"I suppose you're not coming to the funeral..., it being tomorrow and all."

"I'll be coming if I can get a flight, but I doubt I'll be in time for the funeral. Do you mind if I stay with ya'll a couple of days?"

"Of course not, but why the rush to get here if you can't make the funeral?"

"I want to see you and Mom, that's all."

"Who you trying to fool, Son? What's going on?"

"I'm tired, Dad, and I don't want to talk about it right now, if that's all right with you. I'll tell you when I get there. Everything's okay though."

"You sure?"

"I'm sure. I'll call you from the airport before I leave. Don't worry about me okay?"

"I'm your father. It's my job to worry about you. I'll be seeing you sometime tomorrow then."

"Bye, Dad, I love you. Tell Mom I love her too."

"I will. Bye, Son." Dan Stafford hung up the phone and looked at his wife with concern on his face.

"What's wrong, honey?" Marie Stafford said from the kitchen table.

"Ben just told me he loved me, and said to tell you he loved you too."

"What's wrong with that?" Marie said. She stopped snapping pole beans and walked over to her husband.

Dan hugged her, and wrapped his arms completely around her shoulders. He kissed the side of her head through her thinning gray hair, and then loosened his hold enough for her to look into his face.

"The last time he said he loved us, he was on his way to Afghanistan. Something is happening. I don't know what it is, but he said he'd tell us when he gets here tomorrow."

Chapter 23

Bangladesh was where Stafford guessed the airline representative was talking from. He spoke English well, but Stafford hoped that the man's mastery of the English language extended to a mastery of the airline reservation system, or else he might be ticketed to Denver, Colorado instead of Dothan, Alabama.

He departed from Reagan National, and after landing in Atlanta for his connection to Dothan, called his dad and told him what time to expect him. The connecting flight was a half-mile away, and so he walked until he was tired, and then caught the train. He got off and found his way to the concourse. He recognized a couple of people as being on his flight from D.C. to Atlanta.

I bet I know them.

He chuckled as he remembered how many times he had heard his mother say that about strangers going in the same direction they were going, even on the interstate. They had Alabama tags on their car, and that was enough.

It was a hassle flying armed, but he felt it was necessary under the circumstances. TSA had to be dealt with, and the pilot had to approve, but afterward he got to sit in first class if a seat was available. Once or twice he sat near the Federal Air Marshals.

When he did sit near them, he discreetly identified himself to them as a courtesy. They already knew who he was because the airline alerted them to the presence of other armed agents or police on the plane. The FAM's usually informed him that unless they asked for his help, or were losing a fight, to stay out of the way. That arrangement was fine with him. He had seen one of their training sessions in FLETC. They drew their weapons and fired faster and more accurately then anyone he had ever seen. There weren't any Air Marshals on the flight today that he could see, but that didn't necessarily mean anything.

Maybe they've changed their appearance from the military haircut and business suit uniform I've seen them wear.

First class was full, so he sat in coach. Stafford tried again to ignore the pre-flight announcement, but it was so loud it was impossible.

As annoyed as he was of the required safety briefing, he was careful enough to glance at the emergency card, and locate the nearest exit in front and to the rear of his seat. After that, he tuned out the flight attendant as well as he could.

Whenever he flew, he always remembered flying in a Chinook helicopter over some God-forsaken part of Afghanistan. Chinooks were incredibly noisy, and a huge target. He could still smell the turbine exhaust and hot transmission fluid that sometimes leaked into the interior of the helicopter.

As he used to do while he was riding the Chinooks, he imagined what it would be like to be in an aircraft full of people who knew they were about to crash and die. He looked around at the other passengers sitting near him.

Screaming... praying... crying... cursing... shouting... staring straight ahead.

Not a bad way to go really. You'd have just enough time to tell Jesus how sorry you were... just before He agreed with you about how sorry you were... and hopefully not how sorry He was.

It was going to be one more uneventful flight. A crash was not likely. He had speed read the inflight magazine in a matter of minutes on the first leg of his trip. He picked the magazine out of the seat back pocket and flipped through it again, lingering over the full figured woman's brassiere ad.

What was it about a semi-naked woman that attracted a man? Is that a stupid question?

He saw an interesting looking food story he had missed.

Cooking Grits the Bama Way! Does anyone really care how they cook grits in Mobile? Momma made the best grits... lots of butter. He decided to pass on the story again.

Someone had already done the magazine's crossword puzzle in ink. Next he flipped through the in-flight shopping catalog again. He wondered if anybody ever bought any of those bathroom slippers with LED lights attached to them for $49.95, or spent $895 for Swahili lessons on six CD's.

For $895 they better send somebody to my apartment to cook my supper in Swahili.

It wasn't long before the plane was landing. He knew the drill. Stafford also knew statistically that take-offs and landings were when planes crashed, and people died. He always said a small prayer, just to hedge his bet that they weren't going to die.

Please LORD... put your angels around all of us, and keep us safe from evil and harm.

They landed without crashing, in answer to his prayer, but Stafford didn't acknowledge it.

Stafford only had one carry-on bag, and retrieved it from the overhead compartment. He did the marriage march down the aisle, holding his bag in front of him. He followed the crowd and soon saw the main airport entrance, where his father was waiting for him.

Stafford's step-dad was hard to miss. Dan Stafford was six feet two inches tall, and weighed 220 pounds. He had the build of a wrestler. The thing that always annoyed Ben Stafford when he saw him, was that his step-dad never had to work out to stay fit. The Staffords had been farmers for several generations. All the hard work and hard times had squeezed the weak genes out of the Stafford men a long time ago.

"Hey, Son, it's good to see you again," his father said, and gave him a bear hug. Ben grunted as he squeezed him. Stafford let go of his bag, laughed, and returned the hug. He squeezed until his dad grunted in return.

"That's a big hug, Boy... trying to squeeze the stuffin' outa' me?"

"Yep. It's good to see you too, Dad. Where's Mom?" he said looking around for her.

"She's home whipping up one of your favorite meals."

"Pancakes with maple syrup and sausage patties?"

"You guessed it."

"Let's get a move on then... I'm hungry."

Stafford and his dad walked to the parking lot, found the family car, and got in. It was an older car, mechanically sound but aesthetically a disaster. In a dozen places, rust was popping through what was left of the faded blue paint job. The windshield had scratches where the wiper blades had rubbed grit against the glass for over 20 years. Duct tape covered the many holes in the upholstery.

Dan Stafford would not part with a car until replacement parts were impossible to find. He had done the same thing to other cars his entire adult life. Some of Dan's friends said he squeezed a penny until Lincoln screamed.

"Dad, when are you going to break down and buy a new car? I know you can afford it."

"Affording it is not the point. I'll buy another used one when this one breaks down and I can't fix it." Dan laughed. Ben appreciated hearing his father laugh.

"It's really good to see you again, Dad. I need to get down here more often."

"I've been telling you that for years, Son. You know us crusty old guys don't need to see their sons very often, but your mom misses you something terrible." Dan Stafford looked over at his step-son. He had always felt that Ben was his flesh and blood, even though he wasn't. He had raised him as if he was. That was the best he could do.

Dan snapped out of the heavy thoughts, and back-handed his son good naturedly on the chest. Ben grabbed his chest and looked at his step-dad, a man he considered to be more of a father than his biological father, in surprise. The elder Stafford laughed as the younger Stafford rubbed his chest, tingling from the slap.

"What was that for?"

"Just breaking up some of that old crust, Son."

"Take it easy will ya? I bruise easily."

"Wimp," Dan said. They both laughed at the notion.

"It's good to see you, Son." They drove in silence for a couple of minutes, savoring the old feelings; a father for his son, and a son for all that had once been so familiar to him.

Ben Stafford looked, and smelled, and breathed in the air of his childhood and teenage years. He remembered the times he had driven down this road with friends on the way to school, and home from dates with moonbeams in his eyes for whatever girl had let him kiss her on the first date. He was home again.

He purposely didn't let himself remember the darkness that had come over him like a blanket when he was ten years old. The memory of it would come again, but for now he kept it locked away.

"Ben, I wanted to mention that even though the funeral for Carrie Gordon is already over, there'll be a gathering at Rennie's house later today. You might want to go over and pay your respects."

Ben turned back from his memories, and thought about Rennie and how much it must have hurt to find his daughter like that.

"After I eat and say hello to Mom, not necessarily in that order, I'll go over and see Rennie. I haven't seen him in a long time." Dan Stafford nodded his head.

"Here we are!"

"Looks like it always did," Ben said.

The neighborhood, if you could call it a neighborhood, hadn't changed much since he was home last, that had been four Christmas's ago. He noticed there were a few trees missing from the tornado that blew through last year. His father had told him about it. Nobody lost their home, but shingles had been blown off roofs, and a couple of metal storage sheds had gotten blown so far away, nobody saw them again.

Houses began appearing on this street about 50 years ago, when a farmer paved a road on part of his land, and sold lots. This was not a deed restricted community to be sure. Some houses were wood framed and constantly in need of paint, and some had a brick facade, at least in the front. About half the homes had paved driveways, and the other driveways were loose gravel. The gravel drives made it easy to pull pick-up trucks to the front door, which some people did. Others used old car tires turned inside out as planters near the road.

The Stafford homestead was the nicest in the neighborhood. Dan had a good pension, didn't work, and so had the time and money needed to tend to the yard and house properly. The driveway was paved, so there was no driving to the front door for the Staffords.

As they pulled into the driveway, Ben saw his mom standing at the living room window, smiling. She was holding her hands together in front of her waist. She never seemed to change. Her graying brown hair touched the top of her shoulders. Time had taken its toll on her figure, and she had put on a few pounds. She waved at them as they came up the walkway, and moved to the front door, where she was waiting when Ben and his father came in.

"Oh, Son, I'm so glad you're here," she said.

As he bent to put his bag down, his mother took the opportunity to clasp his face in her hands and kiss him lightly on the lips. He stayed bent over to give his mother a gentle hug, since she was all of five feet four inches tall, and weighed 115 pounds.

"I'm glad I'm here too, Mom. Is that pancakes and sausage I smell?"

"You sure do!" Marie smiled and then shot a look at Dan.

"Did you tell him I was making pancakes and sausage?"

"I didn't think it was a secret, Hon. Besides…, you can smell them from the road."

Marie gave Dan her 'you're in trouble' look, and headed for the kitchen with Ben following behind her as he had for so many years.

"I hope you brought your appetite!"

"I sure did. All I had today was a sip of water at the airport, and a cookie on the plane."

"Sit down. I'm keeping the pancakes warm for you in the oven. I knew you'd be hungry." She switched the oven off and retrieved the dinner plate from the oven's top shelf, letting the oven door stay open. The kitchen quickly filled with the smell of sausage and pancakes.

Father and son sat down at opposite ends of the kitchen table. Ben's place had already been set with silverware, and a bottle of real imitation maple syrup. The kitchen table was where all the meals in the house were eaten, unless there was more company than the kitchen table could hold. In that case, they would move to the bigger dining room table.

"Well, I don't know why *you'd* be sitting down too... you've already eaten," Marie said looking at her husband of 30 years. She slid a dinner plate stacked high with pancakes and sausage patties in front of Ben, and wiped her hands on her apron. She put her hands on her hips, and looked at Dan again.

"I'm not eating hon… I'm just sitting here. Why don't you get off your feet?"

Ben poured syrup over the pancakes until it pooled around the side of the plate, threatening to spill onto the table.

"I believe I will," Marie said. She pulled a chair from the table and sat down heavily. By the time she sat down, Ben had already taken a bite of sausage, and stuffed a forkful of pancakes soaked with syrup, into his mouth.

"So, how's everything at work?" Dan said.

"For heaven's sake, Dan. Let the boy eat his food."

"Mom, can I have a glass of milk?" Ben managed to say through his mouthful of food.

"You know better than that. Don't talk with your mouth full," his mother said. She placed her hands on the table and started to push herself up. Dan stopped her with a wave of his hand as he stood up himself.

"I'll get it, Honey." Marie sat back.

"Listen, Ben, you aren't company, and you know full well where the refrigerator is. This ain't a restaurant, and she's not your waitress." Marie sighed and looked down at the table. She felt Dan had spoken harshly, but sometimes that was his way.

Ben slowed his chewing and considered his step-father's words for several seconds. He knew his step-dad loved his mother and was protective of her. His obvious love for his mother was one of the reasons Ben respected him so much. There was a time when a verbal cuff from his step-dad would have brought an argument, but he couldn't argue with what his dad said, only the way he said it. He measured his response.

"You're right." He looked at his mother. "Sorry, Mom. I wasn't thinking." He put down his fork and put his hand on top of his mother's hand. He squeezed gently. She smiled her acceptance of his apology. He got up and got a glass of milk, and settled back down into his seat for another large bite.

Ben finished his pancakes in no time. He picked up his plate and glass, put them in the sink and ran some water on them, as his mother had taught him to do.

"I have something to tell you," he said seriously.

"Come sit and tell us, Son," his mother said. Dan sat down expectantly. Ben sat and looked at both of them.

"I accepted Christ as my savior last night."

His mother and father looked at each other. His father held his eyebrows up and grunted. His mother had a puzzled expression on her face.

"Son, I remember when you were baptized. You accepted Christ when you were ten," she said.

"Well, I guess it didn't take…, so I had to do it again," Ben said. He thought his mother would have been delighted at his announcement.

"Well, I never!" she said. She got up and marched into the den.

"Mom, wait a minute!" Dan held up his hand.

"Just leave her alone awhile, Son. I know what you mean, but she doesn't. Let her calm down some…, and then I'll talk to her."

"And just how is it that *you* know what I mean and she doesn't? *I* don't even know what I mean sometimes!"

"I wasn't born 60 years old with a mustache." Ben sat back in his chair and looked at his dad.

"I sure wish I knew you better. Speaking of that…, you never told me that you and the Commissioner of Customs were old Army buddies. I was talking to Commissioner Gomez the other day. He took me to his office and showed me a photo album with pictures of the two of you in Vietnam, mugging for the camera. He said he knew I was your son."

"Really? Well, that's right, we served together. I never told you because I didn't think it was important. Besides, Gomez hasn't been Commissioner for that long... he's only the *Acting* Commissioner. When the President finally makes up his mind about which campaign contributor to reward with a political appointment, he'll name a new commissioner, and Gomez will be bumped back to his old chair."

"Well, Gomez spoke very highly of you. He said you were one of the best soldiers he ever knew."

"Yeah..., well, he'd have to say that."

"What do you mean by that? You don't like Gomez?"

Dan looked at his son. He had secrets his son would never know... that no one would ever know. Every man had secrets like that.

"What's the rest of the story? You were with Gomez in his office? Is something big happening at work?"

"No..., wait a minute. Why would Gomez *have* to say you were one of the best soldiers he ever knew?"

"Because he was one of the *worst* soldiers *I* ever knew. He never followed an order without arguing about it first. When we were outside the wire, he was the last man out from cover, and the first man to call for help when the shooting started. He's lucky he's still alive..., and that's all I'm going to say about it. So tell me why you were in Gomez' office. Were you called on the carpet for something?" Ben was disappointed he wasn't going to get more of an answer, but decided to let it drop.

"I sure thought so at first, and so did my supervisor. We were both relieved when it turned out it was an intelligence briefing."

"About what?"

"Oh come on..., you know I can't tell you."

"What *can* you tell me?"

"There's some major drug dealing going on from Mexico. That's no secret. There are some very big players involved. No secret there either." Ben paused. His father was expecting more. He chose the moment to say what he dreaded to say.

"I'm sorry I didn't tell you this sooner..., but somebody tried to kill me a couple of days ago. Obviously he missed me, and I put two slugs into him. He was in intensive care when I left D.C."

"He tried to kill you? Why was he trying to kill you? Where did it happen?"

Ben told the whole story, as Dan sat back in his chair, trying to take it all in.

"He should be in the morgue," Dan said after Ben had finished talking. "I wish you had told me sooner, I could have gotten some worrying done *before* you got here."

"Please don't tell Mom about it."

"I don't think she would appreciate me knowing about it and not telling her, and she's bound to find out anyway. I'll tell her after you leave. That's the best I can do if you don't want to tell her."

"No, that's okay. You're right. I'll try to tell her before I go."

"Where are you going from here, back to D.C.?"

"No…, back to El Paso awhile. I thought I was out of there for good," he said with a hint of irritation.

"Ben, I don't have to tell you to be careful. When in doubt, shoot it out, is what we used to say."

"I'll be careful, Dad." Dan cleared his throat.

"You better get going if you want to see Rennie today," Dan said. He took the car keys out of his pocket and slid them across the table. "Take her easy. The car pulls to the right a little when you brake."

Ben got up from the table and went to the front door. His father followed him into the front of the house.

"Thanks for the warning about the brakes. I'll call ya'll if it looks like I'm going to stay past suppertime."

Chapter 24

Ben found Rennie's house without any problem. It was across the street from the house where Rennie had grown up. In some places, grown children wanted to move as far away from their parents as possible, but not here. It was a custom often carried over from an earlier time, when farmers used to divide their acreage between their sons as they married and started their own families. Back then, everyone relied on everyone else, and families were held especially close by necessity.

Stafford didn't recognize any of the cars in the street in front of Rennie's house. He parked on the shoulder of the road and walked back to the house. He could hear people talking loudly, and laughing every so often. From the sound of it, and the number of cars along the road, he figured there would be a crowd of people inside.

He knocked on the screen door and heard someone say, "Come on in..., the doors unlatched!" He opened the screen door and went in, letting the door slam behind him.

"HEY!... BEN STAFFORD'S HERE!" Bill Williams yelled. He made his way over and shook Stafford's hand.

"Ben, we were looking for you at the funeral. What happened? Did your flight get delayed?"

"That's a long story. Sorry I didn't make it here in time."

"Well, you're here now, and that's what counts," Williams said.

Other people, some whom Stafford had known all of his life, came from the kitchen carrying grocery sacks filled with empty food containers. They nodded at Stafford. Some said a few words to him about how long it had been since they had seen him. They stood awkwardly, and made polite talk about what had been going on in their lives since they had last seen each other. Then they excused themselves, and gathered their coats and purses. There had been a celebration of Carrie's life, and her friends, as well as Rennie's, were preparing to go.

Rennie Gordon came from the kitchen behind another group of older women that Stafford didn't recognize. Stafford made his way closer to Rennie as the next group of women stopped at the couch to pick up their purses and jackets. There was hugging and kissing of cheeks, and handshakes and one or two hugs between the men.

When he got the chance, Stafford made his way to Rennie and hugged him too. He let his hand stay on Rennie's shoulder.

"I'm sorry about Carrie, and I'm sorry I missed the funeral." It wasn't very comforting to Rennie, but it was all Stafford could think of to say at the moment.

"Thank you, Ben. Let me show my guests out, and I'll be right back." Rennie walked the women, and a few men, to their cars.

"Come on in the kitchen, Ben. It's where everything's happening," Bill Williams said.

"Coming, Billy." Stafford followed him into the kitchen. He was one of the few people Bill Williams let call him Billy.

"Look who's here!" Williams announced as they came through the kitchen door. Sitting at the kitchen table was the weekend gang from the Rancho Deluxe.

"Well, I'll be a monkey's uncle. We were just sitting here talking about you, Ben," Solomon Mooney said. He stood up and shook Stafford's hand, as did Lewis Poindexter.

"It's good to see you all again. It's been a few years. Too bad old friends seem to meet mostly at funerals," Stafford said.

"Yeah…, well…, that's life isn't it?" Lewis said. "Most of the visitors are leaving now. They've been here for a couple of hours. It was too much for Rennie's wife. She went across the street to Rennie's parent's house to lay down awhile. It's really been tough on her."

"I imagine so," Stafford said.

"Rennie's holding up well. He wants to get his hands on whoever gave his daughter those drugs," Lewis said.

"So it was drugs that killed her?" Stafford asked. Sol and Bill nodded their heads yes.

"That was the initial finding. I think the medical examiner was having a hard time figuring it out. The police told Rennie they sent some of Carrie's blood to another lab to do more testing," Lewis said.

"I think I'd like to talk to the police about that," Stafford said.

"Can you do anything about it, Ben? You can't really get involved in a local case like this, can you?" Billy asked.

"Not officially, but I think I'll give it an un-official try anyway." Rennie came into the kitchen and heard the last of Stafford's comment.

"Give what a try?" Rennie asked.

"Sorry, Rennie. Maybe we shouldn't be discussing this now," Stafford said.

"Ben, if there's something you can do to help the police find out what killed Carrie, I want you to do it... unofficially or not." Rennie didn't look sad or grieving to Stafford, he looked determined. Stafford stood and put a hand on Rennie's arm.

"Rennie, officially I can't get into a local police matter, but I can make some suggestions that might help them look in the right direction."

"Thanks, Ben. I've got a business card from the detective who's handling the case. I'll go get it." Rennie left the room and the group sat down at the table, except Williams, who stood near the sink.

"Today has been pretty hectic for all of us. Why don't we relax tomorrow, and meet for breakfast at the Rancho at nine," Sol said. Rennie came back into the kitchen and sat down at the breakfast table with the others.

"I'd like to get my hands on whoever gave those drugs to her. The police better find them first." He handed the detective's card to Stafford, who glanced at it and put it in his shirt pocket.

"I'll do what I can, Rennie," Stafford said.

"Did I hear you all say you were going to the Rancho for breakfast?" Rennie asked.

"We thought it would be nice to have breakfast with Ben while he was here," Sol offered.

"The Lord giveth, and the Lord taketh away," Rennie said. "And the Lord has given us Ben today, and maybe tomorrow too. I'd like to eat breakfast with you all tomorrow, if that's okay."

"That sounds like a good idea. Will you be there, Ben?" We could all probably skip the breakfast bar, but you look like you might have missed a few meals," Lewis said.

"I *have* missed a few meals, Lewis. The Rancho Deluxe it is. I'll be there at 9 AM, with bells on. I hate to leave so soon after I got here, but I better be getting back, boys. I haven't seen my parents much since I've been here, and I'm only going to be here a day or two. I'll see ya'll tomorrow morning." Stafford shook their hands one more time, and hugged Rennie so hard he heard his back pop. Stafford spoke quietly in Rennie's ear as he hugged him.

"I know how hard this is on you and your wife, Rennie. I'm sorry this happened. Please give your wife my regards."

"Thank you. You're a good friend, Ben. I'm glad you're here."

Chapter 25

S tafford drove back to his parent's house, turned the car off, and sat in the driveway. He was thinking about Rennie telling him he was a good friend. He remembered the words he had used when he told his father that he was no friend of Rennie's. He felt ashamed of himself. He knew he wouldn't have been there if he hadn't shot Turner. Ben's father came out of the house and walked to the car. Ben rolled down the window, and rested his arm on top of the door.

"Everything okay out here, Son? Is something wrong with the car?"

"Everything's okay, Dad. I'm just doing some thinking. I'm going to make some calls while I'm sitting here. I have to check in every so often anyway. I'll be in, in a little while."

"All right, Son. Your momma's got some supper ready for you when you do."

His dad went back in the house. Both of Ben's parents had some hearing loss, and so they talked louder than most people. Stafford rolled up the window, but could still clearly hear both of them talking about him. Stafford speed dialed Boyer's cell and reported in.

"I have some good news for you, Stafford. The ICE Cube signed off on your shooting investigation. He wasn't happy about the shooting being in the newspapers, and he was *really* peeved by the fact that Turner was an OPR supervisor, but you've officially been cleared of any wrongdoing. The shooting has been ruled justifiable."

"That's real big of him, seeing as how Turner was trying to kill me. When did you start calling the Deputy Secretary... ICE Cube?"

"I don't remember calling him that."

"It's okay. It'll be our little secret."

"Anyway, it's official. You will be back on the clock at 8 AM on your next work day, which will be... tomorrow," Boyer said.

"I've already got a plane ticket to El Paso leaving Monday afternoon. Naturally, I have to connect in Atlanta. I'll check in with you again when I get to El Paso. Any news from Hernandez?"

"He's checking on the companies you told him about. He said for you to call him when you can."

"Will do. Anything else?"

"Nope, that's it. Talk to you later." Stafford closed his phone and reopened it. He speed dialed Hernandez' number.

"ICE, Hernandez."

"Frank, this is Ben. Anything interesting happening out there?"

"Hey, Ben. Yeah there is. I checked out those companies you emailed me about, and they are all in the same business... importing bulk shipments of anti-freeze. It's always the same broker too... somebody named Sheila Rodriguez."

"Bulk anti-freeze?"

"Yep. Propylene glycol to be specific, and some other chemicals too."

"How is it coming in... by truck?"

"No, by train... railroad tank cars. There was a cargo exam done last week. The examining Customs officer took a sample and sent it to the Customs lab for analysis. The lab reported that chemically it was anti-freeze, but there were some other organic compounds not usually found in anti-freeze. They didn't identify or classify those."

"What *do* they know about the other compounds, Frank."

"They all had big, long, chemical sounding names with every letter of the alphabet in them. I can't even begin to pronounce them all."

"If the lab couldn't classify them, how did they know enough about them to give them names?"

"The lab referred the matter to an import specialist who sent out a CBP Form 28, asking for more information from the importer. Apparently, they think it might be toxic contaminants."

"So the importer was the one providing the basic information to Customs, and not the lab?"

"That's the way a form 28 request works, Ben. They ask the importer."

"Well, this sounds like what we might be looking for, Frank. Can you contact the lab and see if they still have the sample?"

"Sure."

"If they have it, tell them to check for cocaine, or the chemicals that make up cocaine. Tell them to think outside the box, okay?"

"Okay. You really think the cocaine is in the anti-freeze?"

"I remember when smugglers were turning cocaine into plastic pipe, and then chemically changing it back to cocaine after it went through customs exam. Anyway..., it's all we have to go on for now. See if you can find out who owns the companies that are importing the anti-freeze."

"Okay. In the meantime, I asked for any bulk shipments of anti-freeze to be held and sampled," Hernandez said.

"Good idea," Stafford said. "If the lab guys find coke, there will be some major drug seizures happening there pretty quick. What did you learn about Dupree's story about cocaine getting lost at the incinerator during a dope burn?"

"Nobody knows anything about it. I guess he was lying."

"Like I figured. Anyway..., I should be flying in there tomorrow. Where are you staying at?"

"Staying *at*? You know you shouldn't end a sentence with a preposition," Hernandez said.

"Oh, sorry... so where are you staying at... fat boy?"

"The Edison," Hernandez said after he had stopped laughing.

"I'll see you there Monday afternoon. What are your plans for the weekend?"

"I don't have any. I'll probably lie around watching the cable sports channel in my room. How about you? Are you enjoying yourself at home?" Hernandez said.

"Oh yeah. If I stay too long, I'll get fat with all the home cooking. Well, I'll let you go. Watch yourself out there, Frank. Stay safe."

"Okay, boss."

"What's with calling me boss?"

"You're the A-I-C, man... the Agent in Charge. That makes you the boss."

"There's only two of us, Frank. You be Stan, and I'll be Ollie."

Hernandez laughed again. "*You* be Stan, and *I'll* be Ollie."

"This is another fine mess I've gotten you into, eh?"

"Amen to that brother... I'll talk to you later." Hernandez was still grinning when he hung up.

As soon as he ended the call, Hernandez called the Customs lab and asked them to check for cocaine in the anti-freeze. He had just finished the call to the lab when someone knocked on his door. Hernandez looked through the door's peep-hole. He saw a man in a business suit. His hands were folded together in front of him, looking directly at the peep hole.

"Yes?" Hernandez said through the door.

"Mr. Hernandez? I'm Pedro Castile, the hotel manager. We have a problem with your government credit card. I'd like to speak to you about it."

Hernandez was still looking through the peep-hole. He wasn't afraid, he was being cautious.

"Just a minute," Hernandez said. He went to the dresser and picked up his holstered pistol, and slipped the holster clip over his trouser belt. Feeling more secure, he opened the door.

"Come in, Mr. Castile."

"Thank you," Castile said, as he stepped into the room. As soon as the door shut behind him, Castile reached into his jacket pocket, pulled out a photograph, and handed it to Hernandez. The picture was of Hernandez' wife and daughter, getting out of their van in front of Hernandez' house. Hernandez froze.

"Where did you get this?" Hernandez said carefully, barely able to control himself.

"It was taken a few hours ago. If you want to see them alive again, you'll do exactly as I say."

Chapter 26

Hernandez gasped for air. The cloth hood was thick and heavy, and he was barely getting enough air. His hands were cuffed behind him with his own handcuffs. He was momentarily sorry he had high quality cuffs, but knew with sufficient time he could get them off if he wanted to. He dismissed the idea. He had his family's safety to consider.

For a moment, after the man at the hotel had showed him the picture of his wife and daughter, he had thought about killing the man where he stood. The animal part of him had almost taken over, but the intelligent part of him had won out, and so here he was.

He didn't know the who, or why, of his kidnapping, but he did know something about the what and where. He was in a green Ford van. He had seen the van in the parking lot of the hotel before he was hooded. They were heading south. He knew it was south because he could feel the heat from the sun shining on the right side of the van he was leaning against, and it was afternoon. He tried to remember the small things he thought might be important later, if there was a later.

"Hey... can you loosen... the hood... from around my neck?... I'm having trouble... breathing," Hernandez said through the hood, gasping.

"Shut up," a man said firmly. Hernandez felt a hard kick to his leg. He gritted his teeth but didn't make a sound. He didn't want to give the person who kicked him any satisfaction.

"I'm telling you... I need air. I'm having trouble... breathing. I'm gonna... pass out."

"So shut up and pass out."

Hernandez decided passing out was a good idea. He let his chin sag slowly to his chest and then leaned over to his left until he fell over on the floor of the van. He was glad he fell over. The hood came up an inch off his chest, and he began to breathe better. A man laughed.

"Good. Maybe he's suffocating." The driver turned around and looked quickly back and forth at the road and Hernandez lying on the floor of the van.

"The boss ain't gonna like it if he dies, Marty… he's got plans for him."

"He ain't gonna die. I can see him breathing. Just drive the van."

"We're getting close to the border. Put the tarp over him and sit in front." Hernandez could hear the man closest to him moving around, and then the man's voice was close to his head.

"You can hear me Mr. ICE man? If you think yelling for help when we go through Mexican Customs won't get you or your family killed… go ahead and yell." The man laughed again.

Hernandez felt something go over him. It was hot. The laughing man took his place in the van's passenger seat. Hernandez heard a seat belt click. The van slowed and then stopped.

"Welcome to Mexico, gentlemen," another man's voice said in Spanish. Show me your passports or identification cards."

Both men had their United States Resident Alien cards in hand, and although the cards and photographs were genuine, the names and dates of birth were false. The genuine, but fake, resident's cards were provided by the United States Department of Homeland Security. The cards had been difficult to get, but money always makes things less difficult.

The Mexican Customs officer was one they had used before. All he was interested in was money. The van driver placed a folded hundred dollar bill between the cards and handed them to the officer. For all practical purposes, this made the officer blind, unless he knew he was being watched.

"What is the purpose of your visit to Mexico?" he said perfunctorily, as he expertly palmed the money into his hand and then into his shirt pocket. He glanced at the names on the cards.

"We're visiting my Uncle Claudio. He said to tell you hello."

"I understand. What do you have to declare?" the officer said as he leaned forward and looked through the driver's window at the man sized lump under the tarp on the floor of the van.

"I declare it's a nice day to mind your own business," the driver said without smiling.

The officer wasn't smiling either, as he handed the resident cards back to the driver.

"You can pass," he said. With a wave, he dismissed them and watched the van drive away. He patted his shirt pocket with the money in it. He didn't know what the two were up to, but he had heard of Claudio Rojas, and knew not to interfere with anyone associated with him.

"I love this job," he said to himself as he waved the next car forward.

Chapter 27

Stafford decided to call the Dothan police and talk to the detective investigating Carrie's death. He found the card Rennie had given him, and punched in the phone number.

"Dothan Police… Sergeant Mason speaking."

"Sergeant Mason, I'm Agent Ben Stafford, Department of Homeland Security, Immigration and Customs Enforcement. How are you, sir?"

"I'm fine thanks. What can I do for you?"

"I think I may be able to help you on a case you're investigating."

"Oh? What case is that?"

"I'm a personal friend of Rennie Gordon. His daughter Carrie died recently. I understand the medical examiner is having difficulty determining the cause of death."

"I'm not at liberty to discuss the details of the case with you, Agent Stafford. I've told Mr. Gordon all I can."

"I appreciate your position, Sergeant Mason. I shouldn't be talking to you about her case either. I'm sticking my neck out, but I want to help. I can tell you where to look for a cause of death."

"I'm listening."

"Tell your lab boys to look for any chemicals associated with anti-freeze."

"Anti-freeze? You think she was drinking anti-freeze?"

"Not drinking it. I think it was in cocaine she might have been taking," Stafford said.

"Oh, really? And what makes you think that?" Mason said.

"I've already told you too much. I can't say any more," Stafford said.

"Okay, well thanks for the tip. I'll look into it."

"Believe me, you'll be doing yourself a favor," Stafford said.

"Nice chatting with you, Agent Stafford." Mason hung up. For now, Stafford had done as much as he could, and *more* than he should have.

Mason wrote down the information Stafford gave him, but he was not thrilled to be getting pointers from a Federal Agent, especially one that had no authority to investigate Mason's case.

Stafford got out of the car, locked it, and went inside the house. He found his parents sitting in their usual spots in the den, watching television. When his mother saw him, she rose from the sofa and hugged him tightly.

"What's this for, Mom?"

"I'm sorry I got so upset before. Your dad explained things to me. I'm proud of you son. I'm glad that Jesus is back in your life again." She took his face in her hands, just as she had done when he first arrived, and as she had done almost every day when he was growing up. He liked the memories it brought back. She let go, and walked to the kitchen.

"I'll get your supper for you," she said from the kitchen. Go watch some TV until I call you."

Stafford sat where he mother had been. Her spot was still warm. His father was fully reclined in his easy chair, with his hands behind his head, half watching TV. The national cable news was on.

News Anchor: "First off tonight, we have a story from Washington D.C., where the Centers for Disease Control today issued an unusual public health warning. Reporting from Washington is our chief governmental affairs correspondent, Lillian Muldoon. Lillian what brought about this new announcement?"

Reporter: "Today's announcement was a departure for the CDC, from the usual warnings about flu or other diseases Americans might be exposed to. This time the CDC's announcement was aimed at the millions of users of illegal drugs, particularly cocaine. Here's what the CDC Director had to say at his press conference today."

CDC Director: "The latest numbers from our monthly Mortality and Morbidity report show a marked peak in the area of cocaine related deaths. The figures, provided by state and local government coroners and medical examiners, indicate that while deaths from cocaine overexposure are down 38% nationwide, deaths from unknown causes related to cocaine use have increased more than 2,000%. An increase of this magnitude is evidence that something entirely new has entered the equation. From what I have personally heard from medical examiners, exposure to even small amounts of cocaine has led to sudden death."

"If you are a user of cocaine, I urge you to stop. If you cannot stop, I urge you to seek help immediately. Your life may depend on it. The CDC will be verifying future statistics as they are reported, and we will report any new or pertinent information directly to the Secretary of Health and Human Services. Thank You."

Reporter at conference: "What is the total number of people who have died as the result of unknown causes related to cocaine use in the past month?"

CDC Director: "The figure we have for last month is 17,161. The figure for the previous month was approximately 850. If that figure was to continue, the annual death toll would be somewhere around 206,000."

Reporter: "Back to you Bill."

Dan Stafford read the expression on Ben's face. Ben was shocked by the news report. Dan muted the television.

"Ben, do you know anything about what the CDC Director was talking about?"

Ben thought about his reply. What his father was asking was confidential government information, but his father was a retired Customs employee.

"Confidentially…, that's why I'm going to El Paso, to try and get to the bottom of it. We weren't sure it was connected to another issue, but it probably is. Please don't ask me more about it."

"Supper's ready, Son. Come and get it or I'll throw it to the hogs," Marie said loudly from the kitchen.

"We don't have any hogs, Mom," Ben said. He got up and walked to the kitchen.

"Then I'll throw it to the dogs."

"We don't have any dogs either, Mom."

"Quit ruining my fun. Sit down and eat. You're too thin."

"Okay, momma."

"That's a good boy." She mussed up what little there was of his hair.

He straightened his hair, and smiled. His mother sat at the other end of the table and watched him eat. She liked knowing what she did for her family was appreciated, even when they didn't say thank you.

Ben finished his dinner, cleaned up after himself, and went into his bedroom to get his toothbrush. He opened his carry-on bag, found his toothbrush, and his Bible. He placed the Bible on the bed and went to brush his teeth.

When he came back, his father was sitting on his bed thumbing through the Bible. Ben wished he hadn't left the Bible out where it could be seen. Then he kicked himself for the thought. He had nothing to be ashamed of, but it felt funny. The old Ben Stafford would have been mortified for someone to find a Bible in his possession.

"Ben, I got a feeling there's more to this trip to El Paso than you know… trouble I mean." Dan closed the Bible, but kept it in his hands.

"You may be right, Pop. I don't know what I'm going to find, but I may make some big waves for somebody."

"I'm glad to know that Jesus is in your life again. No matter *what* happens, I know we're going to see you again, in this life or the next."

"I don't think you need to worry about me. I can take care of myself."

"I know you can, but worrying is what parents do. Some people say that worrying is a form of atheism. That may be so. In my heart I know we're all in God's hands, but I still can't stop myself from wanting to keep you safe. I suppose that can be defined as worrying. The spirit is willing, but the flesh is weak." He smiled and looked down at the rag rug his feet were on.

"I never told you much about my time in Vietnam. There were things I did that I will *never* talk to you about, but there are a few thoughts I want to pass on to you, without being too specific. Is that okay?"

"Dad, you don't need to tell me anything if it's too hard for you."

"No…, I want to tell you some of what I learned while I was there."

"Okay. Please do."

"Ben, there will be times when you will have *absolutely no control* over what happens next. It happened to me many times. You think you have a situation completely under control, and then it all falls to pieces and comes crashing down on you, and everyone else. People you care about get hurt…, or killed. I was young, brave, and foolish, and so I bulled my way through it most of the time. If I'd been older, I would have been too scared to do the things I did. I didn't know God then either. I shudder to think where my soul would have gone if I had been killed. But I'm wiser now, and after what you've been through already, you should be too."

"I *am* wiser, Dad…, because I'm older and more experienced. I can't tell you everything that I did either. Maybe someday you'll hear about it, but for now I'll carry it by myself. I always try to lessen the risks that I know about, but in the end it all comes down to being smart, hitting hard, and getting the job done." From the expression on his father's face, Ben could see he didn't agree with all that he said.

"Listen, Son, if I learned anything, it's that you can't do it alone. You think you can when you're young…, but that's just stubbornness and arrogance that make you think like that. You can't deal with guilt alone either. You have to forgive the men who hurt you…, and ask God for forgiveness as well. The Bible talks about that…, if you can't forgive, you will not be forgiven."

"A friend told me that the other day," Ben said.

"Well, it's true…, and forgiveness includes forgiving yourself. I'm sure you've asked yourself…, as I've asked myself… why me? Why am I still alive, and other men… better men… are dead?" Ben nodded. He had asked himself those very questions dozens of times.

"Unfortunately, Son, you and I are never going to have a satisfactory answer to that question while we're alive. We have to be content in knowing that we are all in God's hands. Everything that happens to us is from God. He causes it to happen, or He allows it to happen for His own purposes as part of His plan for us. I've found comfort in believing that. It's hard to accept sometimes, but I know it's true." Dan paused.

"You said that it all came down to being smart and hitting hard… getting the job done." His father paused again, weighing his words.

"Ben…, this may sound harsh, or judgmental, or… oh, I don't know. I want you to know how much I love you, and pray for you. I don't want you to learn the hard way like I did…, from mistakes. Now you listen up. Being smart will get you a diploma, a good job, and maybe a nice retirement. But, fear of the Lord will humble you and build your character. Failure and trouble are where wisdom comes from, and the Bible says wisdom is more valuable than gold."

Ben felt tears starting to come to his eyes. His father had never talked to him about their relationship, or told him he loved him and prayed for him. Ben didn't like the feeling of not being in control, and so he tried to talk, to deflect the feelings that were all around him. He took a deep breath, and cleared his throat.

"Dad, I don't understand what you mean by fearing the Lord…, and how does being a failure produce wisdom?"

"I think you might already know the answer to those questions. Wisdom and character seldom come from happiness and success. They come from dealing with problems. You'll understand it better after you start reading the Bible, and praying. Ask God to make the meaning of His word clear to you."

"Seek and ye shall find?" Ben said, cocking his head to one side.

"That's exactly right." Dan stood up and handed Ben the Bible.

"A friend told me that too, the other day," Ben said.

"Sounds like a pretty good friend. As my mother used to say..., the Bible is life's instruction manual. When all else fails, read the instructions." Dan patted Ben on the shoulder and then left his hand there. Ben felt the warmth of his father's hand through his shirt.

"When do you leave, Son?"

"Monday morning. I plan on having breakfast with the old gang Saturday morning at Rancho Deluxe. Want to come?"

"No thanks. Heart attack on a plate," Dan chuckled. He headed for the door.

"Why don't you come out and sit in the den with us? Your mom and I haven't seen much of you since you've been here."

"I know... I'm sorry. I'll be out soon. Thanks for talking to me about this." He held up the Bible and shook it.

"You're welcome. Next time you can do all the talking."

"Okay. There are a few things I should tell you that have been gnawing at me for years. I don't know why I mention it, since I really don't want to talk about it now. I guess I just wanted to give you a heads up about it."

Dan patted Ben on the shoulder and said, "I'm here for you anytime you want to talk. Take your time." His dad stood looking at Ben for a few more seconds, wondering what memories were on his son's mind, and then walked out to take his place beside Marie on the couch.

Ben thought about what his father told him. His father always gave good advice, and he was sure this was more of the same. He was also sure that reading the Bible wouldn't do any harm either. He opened the Bible carefully, and flipped through the pages. He stopped at the book of Isaiah, and picked a verse at random.

Isaiah 39:16. Behold, I have graven thee upon the palms of my hands

He looked at the palm of his hand. He imagined the hand of God, with Benjamin Stafford written on it. He was humbled at the thought.

God knows me, and cares about me.

And I know all that you've done.

Chapter 28

The time had come sooner than Miner liked, but he would still be able to make good use of his assets. He called a meeting of the Gadsden Council on short notice, and therefore not all of Miner's controllers were present for the digital conference call.

"The announcement by the CDC has pushed our timetable forward faster than I like, but there are enough nationwide fatalities to start the document and email insertions immediately," Miner said.

Computer hacking was what Miner was referring to when he spoke of insertions. He disliked the word hacking. Hacking seemed to refer to someone taking an ax to something, or maybe coughing something up. He was not chopping, or coughing something up, he was making something new.

"Take the appropriate precautions when you contact government LAN system administrators. We know the FBI and Customs are actively seeking the identity of our D.C. agents. So far, one agent has been picked up by the FBI near the Reagan building, and one was shot by an ICE Agent named Stafford. It was a mistake to try to kill Stafford. He should have been allowed to waste his time looking for missing cocaine, but no matter that now."

"Sir…, Number Four here. I'd like to explain why I felt it was necessary to eliminate Stafford."

"I said…, no matter that now. We don't have time to nit-pick our mistakes. To continue, one of your colleagues, Number Two, was compromised and had to be eliminated by one of our associates in the FBI. He was able to give information to the FBI before he could be stopped, so speed is essential for carrying out of our plans from here on."

"To be clear, the next action will be the insertion of the emails and other electronic documents into the mainframes of the CDC, FBI, and Customs, as well as the main computer for the White House. The House and Senate computers have already been penetrated. Good job, Number Six."

"Thank you, sir."

"Our assets in the Pentagon will be responsible for sending the martial law and use of force proclamations when we are sure that the President, Vice President, all the cabinet heads, and the Speaker of the House have been located and secured by our units."

"Sir, Number Five here. When will the death toll be sufficient to begin the final segment of Operation Plow?"

"I don't believe it would be too optimistic to say the numbers should be high enough in two days. If any of you have any difficulties, especially with anything that might affect the timing of the disinformation campaign, contact me immediately." There was an affirmative response from every member of the Council.

"I believe that concludes our business for today. From now on feel free to contact me individually and directly."

"Sir, Number Three here. I think I can speak for the other council members when I say it is an honor to follow you in this crusade to take America back from the socialists and Marxists who have weakened us for too long. Thank you, sir, for the opportunity you are giving us."

There was applause from all the members of the Council. General Miner was moved almost to tears.

"Gentlemen, it has been *my* honor to lead you. We only have a little farther to go. Keep up your good work!"

"Yes, sir…, we will, sir," Number Three said.

"Signing off now," Miner said. He had a lump in his throat.

"Good men. So many good men. Thank God for them," Miner said aloud.

Chapter 29

The bed felt strange, but good. Except for some temporary stays at hotels during training assignments, Stafford hadn't slept on a real bed since he moved to Washington, and now he could not fall asleep. He started to throw the bed covers on the floor and sleep there, but decided his mother wouldn't appreciate it. He shut his eyes and prayed for sleep without nightmares.

As he was falling asleep in his old bed, he reminisced about his youth, and the days of fun, and school, and... hunting. He put his arms over his head and rubbed his scalp. It felt comforting. He wanted to forget the last time he went hunting with his father; his dead father. He had almost forgotten about it.

It was so long ago, and he was about ten when it happened. The memories of a ten year old were unreliable and couldn't be trusted. It was the logic of knowing that, that helped him cope. His father had died on that last hunting trip. 'Just one of those things,' everyone said. He and his dad were hunting alone. The safety on his dad's gun was engaged, he was sure of it. His dad was always very careful. The rifle had been leaning against the wire fence, and his dad had reached for the rifle just as it fell over. As it fell, Ben grabbed for it too. The gun went off by itself.

He tried harder to put it out of his mind. He finally fell asleep, but slept fitfully for the rest of the night.

When he awoke, it was early morning. It seemed no time had passed at all. He was awake, looking at the ceiling, wiping the sleep from his eyes. He stretched. Every day felt like Saturday when he was at home, but today really was Saturday.

I used to believe in the sandman, and didn't know God... and now... What time is it?

He turned his head to one side. The clock radio said 7:45, in large red numbers. Over the years he found he didn't need an alarm to get up on time. All he needed was to know what time it was when he went to bed, and then make a mental note to get up after a certain number of hours.

He prepped himself for his long day, by showering, shaving, and dressing in business casual style. He didn't get to dress that way at the office, but he liked flying that way. He checked himself out in the mirror.

I look like a yuppie. Do women like the yuppie look..., or the rugged outdoors-man look? I forgot..., it's the look of a full wallet that attracts the most women. Are there any rich men with unattractive wives? There might be a few.

He laughed at himself, tucked his shirttail in better, and went out to see if his parents were awake. They had been up for hours, and were sitting at the kitchen table drinking coffee.

"Morning, Ben," his father said flatly.

"Morning, sunshine!" his mother sang. "Did you sleep well?"

"Good morning all... yes, I did, thanks." He yawned and stretched, trying to put off what he had to say. "I hate to say hi and bye..., but I'm meeting the old gang for breakfast at the Rancho Deluxe this morning. I don't suppose ya'll would want to come along."

"You supposed right. We ate breakfast hours ago, so go have breakfast with your friends, and we'll be here when you get back. When are you leaving?" his mother asked. She had just said more than Ben had heard her say in a long time.

"I'm leaving for the restaurant right now. We'll have time to talk after I get back."

"Keys are on the rack by the refrigerator," Dan said. "Remember, be careful with the brakes."

"Gotcha. See ya'll later." He found the car keys and said good bye again, as he walked out the front door to the car.

He drove straight to the restaurant without getting lost. He almost missed one turn. There wasn't a strip mall on the corner the last time he was here, and he hadn't recognized the road to turn on until the last second. He pulled into the parking lot and saw Lewis, Rennie, Bill, and Sol, standing outside talking. He parked, got out of the car, and approached the lukewarm group of men.

"Good morning, boys. Have ya'll been waiting long?" Stafford said.

"Naw, we're used to waiting on Bill-Bill. He's usually the last to show up. He would have been last this morning too, if you hadn't been eating with us," Sol grinned. The comment drew a couple of chuckles from the others, except from Bill Williams, who exploded. He spoke quietly but with much emotion.

"Sol..., Lewis..., Rennie..., this is the last time I'm going to tell you all this. I... do not like being called Bill-Bill, or Double Bill, or any... other... cutesy name you all dream up. My name is Bill, or William. If I owe you money, you can call me Billy. If you owe *me* money..., you can call me sir. If you can't remember that, leave me out of your conversation."

"Well okay then," Sol said. "I think we would all do well to remember that. The next time we talk about Mr. Williams, we better be careful what we say."

Williams was still angry. The veins in his neck were standing out. "Sol, so help me..., I will kick your..."

Stafford broke in. "Come on now boys, cut it out. Everybody's on edge, and short of sleep. Let's try to get along long enough to eat some breakfast and talk about old times. Come on... come on now... let's go inside and find us a table."

Bill still looked like he wanted to loosen some of Sol's teeth, so Stafford got between the two of them and ushered everyone into the restaurant. Ben told the hostess they needed a table for five. She had the busboy move tables together to make one big enough for all of them to sit together. The waitress brought their water and coffee.

"The buffet breakfast for ya'll again this morning fellas?" she said.

"That's right, darling," said Lewis, rubbing his hands together.

"Not for me this time, Sarah. I'll just be having coffee. I had plenty to eat at home, but you boys go right ahead," Rennie said.

As usual, they all returned to the table with their plates overflowing with food. Stafford managed to snag a couple of sunny-side-up eggs to go on top of his pile of pancakes and bacon.

"So..., anything exciting going on with you in Washington, Ben?" Rennie said, leaning on the table with his forearms. Stafford held up a finger, gesturing to give him a minute. He cleared his mouth of food, took a drink of water and thought while he swallowed.

Do I really want to tell these guys about the shooting? Why not. It'll give 'm a thrill.

"You could say that. Somebody tried to kill me in my apartment a couple of days ago. I had to shoot him." Everyone stopped eating, and then tried to talk at the same time.

"What?"

"What'd you say?"

"Somebody tried to kill you?"

"You shot somebody?"

"Take it easy fellas. "Take it easy," Stafford said, as he held up both hands. It's okay now. I'm in one piece, and the bad guy's in the hospital."

"Tell us about it, Ben!" Bill said, wide eyed.

Stafford told them the entire story, leaving out the fact that he knew the man he had shot, and why he was trying to kill him. When he finished answering the questions they threw at him, they calmed down enough to go back to the breakfast bar a second time. They all returned with plates nearly as full as the first time.

"Ben, I want to thank you for calling Sergeant Mason for me. He called just before I left the house this morning, and told me you had talked to him."

"You're welcome, Rennie. I wish I could do more."

"There *is* something more you can do for me... for us." Stafford stopped eating. The others put their utensils down and looked at Stafford.

"Name it, Rennie. If it isn't illegal or immoral, I'll do it." Stafford laughed. No one else was laughing.

"Say... what's this all about Rennie? What do ya'll want me to do?" Stafford said.

"I put two and two together this morning after talking to Sergeant Mason. He said you told him what to look for as a cause of death. He couldn't tell me everything, but he did tell me she was poisoned by something in the drugs she took... something that wasn't supposed to be there. After reading the newspaper this morning about the CDC announcement... well, you don't have to be a genius to figure out you know plenty about what's going on."

"Rennie, I can't talk about it." Stafford pursed his lips. He was unhappy that Sgt. Mason had told Rennie what he told him in confidence.

"You don't have to talk about it, Ben. I'll do the talking."

Stafford and Rennie were sitting directly across from each other. Rennie hadn't taken his eyes off of Stafford since he began speaking. The others were looking at Stafford too. He was beginning to feel uncomfortable.

"We know that you're the one who may be putting handcuffs on the people who killed my daughter..., and a lot of other people. We want you to know that if there is *anything* we can do to help you..., all you have to do is ask. You won't have to ask twice, Ben... no matter what you ask for. If you need it and we can get it..., you'll have it."

"That's right," Bill said. "You may laugh at the idea, but I know how to fly…, and Lewis there knows how to fix electronic stuff…, and Sol is an expert shot with a rifle."

"And I've got some money put away from my grandfather's estate," Rennie said …, "so if we don't have what you need…, I can probably buy it."

"Fellas…, I'm really touched by the offer." Stafford thought for a moment, searching for the right words.

"If I'm ever in a jam I don't think I can get out of…, I'll pray, and if I don't get an answer…, I'll call you."

"Can't ask for more than that," Rennie said. "I'm feeling some better now. I think I'll eat."

Chapter 30

Surprisingly, Stafford didn't overeat at the Rancho Deluxe buffet. He loved country cooking, with all the fat, salt, and bread. Fatty food would probably kill him one day, but not any time soon.

He drove home slowly, looking the neighborhood over one more time. After he parked and went in the house, he was surprised to find his parents in the same position he had left them in.

"Hey, Mom. Hey, Dad. Am I ever full."

"It's a good thing you ate big. We already had an early lunch," Dan said.

"So what are ya'll doing still sitting here watching TV?"

"If you haven't noticed…, we're retired. We can do whatever we want, and for as long as we want to," Marie said. It just so happens we want to watch TV."

"How about some fishing tomorrow morning, Dad?"

"Sounds fine, but I don't think much is going to be biting. We've had a lot of rain around here lately," Dan said.

The rest of the day was spent watching sports, and re-runs of 1960's television shows. The Staffords ate snacks, took naps on the couch, and wandered around looking for something to get into. Marie Stafford opened the storage compartment on the china cabinet, and pulled out an old, tattered, Monopoly game box. Ben Stafford saw her from the den where he was watching yet another cop show re-run.

"Oh, Mom, not the Monopoly game…, please."

"I like playing Monopoly," she said. And so the Staffords played until it was time for bed.

When they awoke on Sunday morning, it was off to church with Marie Stafford between her two favorite men.

"The Bible says that pride goes before the fall. If that's so, I'm about to fall down." Marie laughed hard at her joke. Ben and Dan chuckled politely.

Dan Stafford was a fixture at church, but Ben felt out of place. He saw people who used to pinch his cheeks when he was a little boy, when his last name was still Taylor. A couple of older women came back and pinched his cheeks again for fun.

Marie introduced Ben to everyone within reach, and he bore it well. He was a new creation in Christ, but he felt funny being in his old church. He wanted a new start, in a different church. He was sure his mother had told her friends he had accepted Christ again, but nobody mentioned it.

After the sermon, the congregation sang *Just As I Am* four times in a row, and then the service was over.

"You know, Mom, I think the preacher was making the altar call extra long just for me," Ben said.

"That could be, Son. He was looking at you a lot." Marie squeezed Ben's arm tightly.

"Well, frankly, I'm glad church is over. What's for lunch?" Ben said.

"Fried chicken with red-eye gravy over white rice, with green beans and iced tea."

"I love it when you talk that way, momma."

"I like it when you talk that way too, honey," Dan said.

"And after lunch I want to play some more Monopoly with ya'll," Marie said.

"You mean Monotony, don't you, Mom?"

"On second thought, maybe lunch'll be corn soup, oatmeal, and cactus juice."

"Okay, Mom, we'll play Monopoly," Ben said, and rolled his eyes at his dad. Dan kept his mouth shut.

Marie made a delicious lunch, which local folks call supper. They ate too much, and then ate some more. When they couldn't eat another bite, they cleaned up the kitchen and sat down again to talk and laugh until dinner, which is what the same local folks call the evening meal. The words were really interchangeable, so there was always a little confusion around what was going to be eaten when.

They had fun, but they knew the fun would soon come to an end. They got tired of sitting, and moved to another table and the waiting Monopoly game. They played, ate dinner, and played again until it was bed time. Dan was the winner, and Marie didn't like it.

"You always win, you old coot," she said.

"Old coot? Who you calling an old coot?" Ben said.

"Well, I think that shoe fits doesn't it?" Marie said. They all burst out laughing, and got up from the table.

"I'm going to bed. I'll be leaving in the morning you know," Ben said.

"Don't remind us. We'll see you in the morning, Son. Sleep tight," Dan said.

Ben slept better than he had in months. He had a full stomach, a happy spirit, and a mind that was empty of the worries he usually had at work. When he woke up Monday morning, he had the feeling he had slept without moving an inch. He stretched, got up and splashed water on his face, and dressed. He met his parents at their usual places at the breakfast table.

"Morning, Mom. Morning, Dad."

"Morning, Son," his parents chorused.

"What would you like for breakfast?" Marie asked.

Stafford's government cellphone started vibrating on his belt.

"Just a minute..., duty calls," Stafford said. He pulled the phone off his belt and flipped it open. "Stafford," he said informally.

"Stafford, this is Boyer. Have you talked to Hernandez recently?"

"I talked to him Friday. Why? What's up?"

"He was supposed to check in with the ICE office in El Paso this morning, and didn't. He didn't call the communication center either, and he doesn't answer his cellphone, his room phone, or his car radio."

"That doesn't sound good. Who's looking for him?"

"The communications center notified the SAC, and he sent two agents to Hernandez' hotel, but they couldn't find him. The SAC doesn't want to make a big deal out of it yet, but in about 30 minutes he's going to notify the local police. Maybe he met some good looking blonde in the hotel bar, and lost track of time. I hope it's something simple like that."

"That's not likely, sir."

"I know it, he's got a wonderful family at home," Boyer said.

"I'll be flying out there today in any case. Will you call me if he calls in?"

"Sure. If I hear anything, I'll let you know."

"Is someone going to notify his wife?" Stafford asked.

"I don't want to be the one to do it," Boyer said.

"Somebody has to."

"I know…, but I don't want it to be me. Hernandez' supervisor can call and tell her. I'll notify him, and suggest he hold off until the agents have checked the hotel security tapes."

"That sounds wise. Anything else, sir?"

"No…, that's enough."

"All right, I hope you'll be calling me later, sir. Good bye." Stafford closed his phone and looked at his parents, who had been listening to his conversation.

"Who's missing?" Dan said.

"An agent I was going to meet in El Paso. I work with him in D.C. He went to El Paso ahead of me, and now he's missing." Ben put his phone in his pocket and placed his hands on his hips.

"No need to say anything, Son," his mother said. "He's your friend, and you have a job to do. I'll make a sandwich to take on the plane with you." She started to open the refrigerator.

"Just a minute, Mom," Ben said. She stopped and turned to face him. Ben stood still. He was thinking about what he had told his friends at breakfast.

"What is it?" His mother stood holding her hands together in front of her, waiting.

Why couldn't I keep my big mouth shut? Trying to be a big man with the guys? I've got to tell her… if I don't and she hears it second hand before dad tells her...

"Mom, you're not going to like hearing this. I should have told you sooner, but I didn't want to worry you about it." Ben took a deep breath and let a little out.

"Two days ago I had a shoot-out with a man in my apartment. He wanted to keep me from investigating a crime. I shot him. He's alive, but he's in the hospital."

His mother gasped and put her hand over her mouth. Stafford could see her eyes filling with tears. Dan put his arm around her shoulders.

"Momma…, I'm sorry."

"Are the missing agent and the man you shot, connected?" Dan asked.

"I think so. I've got to go see if I can help find him."

"I know. I'll drive you to the airport," Dan said. Marie's tears were rolling down her cheeks, but she wasn't making a sound. Ben saw the tears, and it hurt him to know he had upset her so.

"Momma, I'm so sorry. I don't want you to worry about me."

"I thought I was done worrying about you when you got out of the Army. I guess my worrying days will never be over."

Ben wrapped his arms around her and held her tight. He rested his cheek lightly on top of her head. He could smell her shampoo.

"Let me go. I'm okay," she said, as she pushed him away and wiped the tears from her cheeks with her palms. "I'll go fix you some lunch to take. You go pack." She opened the refrigerator, and Dan helped her take out the sandwich makings, and put them on the counter. He stopped what he was doing when he saw Ben watching them.

"Go on boy... go pack. She'll be okay."

Ben nodded, and went to his bedroom to gather his things. It didn't take him long, since he had barely unpacked. He zipped his carry-on bag closed, carried it to the front door, and set it down.

He called the airline and moved his flight to one that was leaving in about an hour. He needed to hurry. His father came out of the kitchen carrying a paper sack containing the sandwich, and handed it to him. His mother walked slowly behind his father, her eyes red from crying.

"Go ahead and drive yourself to the airport," his father said.

"What about the car? How will you get it back?"

"Leave it in the short term parking lot and put the car keys under the floor mat in the back. I'll have someone give me a ride later to pick it up." Dan offered Ben his hand, but Ben hugged his father instead.

"I'll be all right, Dad. Don't worry about me."

"Of course we're going to worry about you, but we know God's hand is on you. Nothing will happen that God doesn't want to happen." Marie gave Ben a hug and kissed him on the cheek.

"Come back soon, please," she said.

"I will, momma." Ben grabbed his carry-on bag and opened the front door.

"We love you. We'll be praying for you..., but you be careful anyway," Dan said.

"I'm always careful, Dad."

Dan smiled, and patted his son on the shoulder. Ben smiled back, and then walked down the sidewalk to the car. Dan closed the front door, and he and Marie went to the living room window to watch. Ben put his bag in the trunk, got in, and drove away. Ben and Dan began to pray.

Chapter 31

The flight to El Paso, with an obligatory stop in Atlanta, arrived only five minutes late. As soon as Stafford was off the plane, he was on the phone to Boyer. He walked as he talked.

"Mr. Boyer, this is Ben Stafford, any news on Hernandez?"

"I've been trying to reach you. No good news. The two agents the El Paso SAC sent to Hernandez' hotel didn't find anything unusual in his room. The security tapes are being reviewed. Hernandez' car is still missing too."

"The local Police have been notified about his disappearance?"

"Oh yeah... and the FBI, from what I understand."

"Anybody know where he was last seen? Was it in the hotel?"

"I'm not sure. You might ask the SAC in El Paso, his name's Perez."

"I know him, sir. I used to work for him. I'm at the rental car counter now. I'll call him as soon as I get on the road."

"Nobody from ICE met you at the airport?"

"I didn't tell anyone I was coming."

"You won't be reimbursed for the rental if the ICE office has a government car available, so don't put the rental car on your government credit card."

Spoken like a true bureaucrat.

"I'm not going to worry about that now, sir. I'll check in with you again when I have something new to report."

"Please do. If I can help in any way, let me know."

"Roger that, sir. Gotta go now."

Stafford closed the phone and tried to hand the rental agent his government credit card. The agent was typing with both hands, and talking on the phone at the same time. His head was bent sideways almost to his shoulder, as he squeezed the handset against his ear. He looked at Stafford, his head still twisted to his shoulder, and mouthed the words 'just one minute' as he held up a finger.

Stafford tried talking to him anyway. "Official government business... full size car... weekly rental, and make it quick, please."

The agent placed his hand over the phone's mouthpiece and said, "I'll be with you in a moment, sir," and went back to his typing and talking.

Stafford could feel the blood rising into his face. He looked around for other rental car counters. There were three others, but all three were busy with customers.

Stafford decided he shouldn't pull the agent out of his shoes and over the counter. He grabbed his bag and walked out of the building to the curb. He used his cellphone to call the El Paso ICE office. The receptionist answered, and he identified himself and asked her to inform supervisor Perez that he would be arriving at the ICE office in 45 minutes. He didn't want to talk to Perez on the phone out in the open, or anywhere else.

He climbed in the first cab in line, and told the driver the address of the ICE office. After receiving a dirty look from the driver, Stafford rode in silence.

Stafford's mind had been working on the problem of Hernandez' disappearance since he got on the plane in Dothan. Even though he didn't have enough information, he tried to problem solve anyway.

While he thought, he looked out the cab windows at the countryside. The dirt was the color of flesh. The air was dusty, and the sun shone brightly. Soon they were driving toward the North Franklin Mountains, and then alongside the western edge of the mountains. The interstate paralleled the range for some distance. The mountains looked out of place. Millions of years of erosion had shaped them, and made them appear as islands in a sea of sand and rock, beautiful in its own way.

Stafford's problem solving had brought him to the most likely possibility. The disappearance of Hernandez was related to the investigation he was doing.

Since Hernandez said nobody knew anything about the missing coke at the incinerator, Dupree had been lying. His murder, Hernandez' disappearance, and the anti-freeze shipments were probably connected. If Hernandez had been killed as a warning, his body would have been left for someone to find. His body hadn't been found, so Hernandez was probably still alive.

Stafford arrived at the ICE office, paid the cab driver, and walked in the main entrance. His ride had taken a half hour, but he had gone back in time a couple of years. It didn't feel good to be back in the city the locals nicknamed *El Chuco; the Disgusting One*.

Chapter 32

Miner sent his aide away and told him not to return until he called him, and then he made the phone call himself. He didn't want to reveal more of the operations members than he needed to. He realized it was only a matter of time before the FBI, or some other agency, would be coming after him. They were probably working on identifying him right now. He would have to work fast, and make no mistakes. He called Senator Bacster's private number.

"Hello?"

"George... Andrew Miner here. Can you talk?"

"Yes, of course... what can I do for you, Andy?"

"The time has come, George."

"I thought as much. I've been watching the news, and I saw the announcement from the CDC. That was your doing I suppose?"

"Yes. That went very well. There will be some very big numbers to report soon."

"How many do you project?"

"Over 200,000."

"Good-God! You never said anything to me about killing 200,000 people!"

"Don't act so shocked, George. You didn't blink an eye when I said 20,000. Two hundred thousand is only another zero."

"Only another zero? Are you insane?"

"No, I'm far from insane. In fact I may be one of the sanest men you'll ever meet. Besides, do you remember what Stalin supposedly said?... 'one death is a tragedy, a million deaths is a statistic'."

"But two hundred thousand, Andy?... Two hundred thousand?"

"Don't go stupid on me, George. These deaths are going to provide the shock value the nation needs. The people are going to want blood when they find out there is a government conspiracy to kill thousands of lower class Americans, and we're going to give them blood. And don't forget, George…, you're up to your eyeballs in this. If the rest of the operation doesn't go exactly as planned, we'll all hang. So, tomorrow, you had better be convincing during your emergency press conference."

Senator Bacster was silent. This was more than he had bargained for. He might lose his life or his freedom before this was over.

"The emails and documents are all in place?" Bacster asked with heaviness in his voice.

"All the emails and documents are where we said they'd be. Make your formal document requests to the various department heads tonight. Demand they turn them over to you by tomorrow morning. They won't be able to comply, of course. My aide will bring you the copies we prepared for your press conference. As far as you're concerned, the copies are evidence of a murderous conspiracy and a White House coverup. You've decided to make your findings known to the American people. Just follow the script."

"Do I have a choice?"

"Not if you want to stay alive," Miner said with a laugh.

"God help me."

"God has nothing to do with helping *you*, George, he's helping *me*. And don't forget… you'll have a powerful place in the new administration, maybe vice president… as I promised. I'll talk to you tomorrow after the press conference. Get some rest, George. You sound tired. Be strong, and be convincing."

"I'll try my best."

Miner hung up and swiveled his chair around to look out the window at the trees. It was beautiful outside today. The sky was clear. The air looked clean. Thoughts of the future filled his mind. There was a new day coming for America. A day when Americans would be free of the socialists and liberals. He would have gotten rid of them already if he could have designed his drugs to only kill them, and not *everyone* who used them. He had asked, but the task was impossible, even for his experts.

For a start, he settled for the partial eradication of the cocaine addicts. America would be a better place without them. There were fewer this week, and next week there would be fewer still. After the deaths of so many users, the air was already visibly cleaner today than it had been last week, when he had to share it with them.

He hadn't made up his mind what to do with the rest of them after he became president. Maybe he would totally eradicate them. The air would be much cleaner after he became president. He liked to think about that.

"Maybe that's how I'll be remembered… The Clean Air President. My legacy," he said to himself.

He leaned back in his swivel chair and put his hands behind his head, looking up at the ceiling. He realized he needed to make a list of the order for the removal of the undesirable elements. After he got rid of the liberals and others, who should be next?

He knew there would certainly be opposition to his plan. He considered that. The logical step then was to start removing the opposition first. He might establish a committee to study the situation. Politicians loved committees. A Committee was exactly what was needed to let the American people know someone was working on a solution to the problem.

"The Committee for Societal Reform is what I'll call it. To be funded in perpetuity. Another part of my legacy," he said to himself.

He took a deep breath, savoring the feeling of cleaner air entering his lungs. He let his breath out slowly, and smiled.

Chapter 33

ICE Supervisor Ed Perez saw Stafford walk in the main entrance door, and wasn't pleased to see him, but he should have been. He knew Stafford was a better man than he was, and he didn't like that fact one bit. It gave him the feeling that Stafford was always looking down his nose at him. A more accurate assessment was that Perez was always looking up at Stafford.

Perez's dislike of Stafford was equal to the way Stafford felt about Perez. Stafford knew him to be self-serving, conniving, and manipulative. Perez was an expert at positioning himself close enough to important investigations to take credit, if any was due, and yet remaining far enough away to dodge any blame that might come if anything went wrong. Stafford thought he was a better man than Perez, in every way that mattered.

Even with the animosity Perez had for him, Stafford was the only ICE Agent to leave El Paso on reasonably good terms with Perez. Those good terms had been fostered by Stafford's ability to sidestep an excessive force lawsuit, brought by a local citizens group. Stafford's testimony during the civil trial not only exonerated him, it had the unintentional effect of making Perez look good to his superiors.

"Agent Stafford... Good to see you again. I got word this morning that you were coming. I didn't expect to see you so soon." Perez put on his happy face mask.

"Nice to see you too, sir," Stafford lied.

"I heard you shot an OPR supervisor named Turner, and the Police picked you up, yes?"

Starting right in on me, huh?

"Just taking out the trash, sir. I had to answer some questions at police headquarters afterward. It was standard procedure." Perez didn't miss a beat.

"But you've been investigated and cleared by the ICE Director, yes?"

"Of course I've been cleared in the shooting. If it was otherwise, I wouldn't have been sent here to head the Dupree murder investigation."

"Head the investigation? Well…, that's a surprise to me, because I wasn't consulted about putting you in charge of *anything*. I am also surprised to hear you were cleared of shooting a supervisor in your own apartment."

"As I said, I was cleared in that shooting, sir. After the ICE Director discovered what a dirt-ball supervisor Turner really was, he had no choice but to declare the shooting justifiable. Unfortunately, I forgot the 'two shots to the chest…, one to the head' rule, so Turner is still alive as far as I know. They made me give back my expert marksmanship medal, and I have to take remedial firearms classes."

Stafford's answer brought some grins and laughs from the other agents in the room. Perez glared at them. The brave ones glared back, but the less brave walked away out of his sight.

Perez turned back to Stafford. "That was a veiled threat against me! That's insubordination!" Small bubbles of spittle appeared at the corners of his Perez's mouth.

"I'm sorry you feel that way, sir. I didn't mean for it to sound that way."

Stafford put his carry-on bag, which he had been holding, down in an empty chair and walked toward Perez. Perez was visibly angry and prepared to meet Stafford's attack. He took a step backwards and brought his hands up. Stafford walked past him.

"I'll be right back, sir. I've got to go to the men's room." He could feel Perez's eyes on the back of his head. Another Agent followed Stafford into the men's room.

"Hey Stafford, hold up a sec," the Agent said after the door shut. Stafford had never seen the man before.

"Listen, man, we still have to work here. How about lightening up…, at least until we find out if your partner is alive or not." The words hit Stafford hard.

"Sorry. You're right. I'll straighten up."

"We'd appreciate it," the Agent said, and walked out.

Stafford went to the sink and looked in the mirror, called himself a dirty name, and splashed water in his face. He dried his face and hands with a paper towel, and went out to try to make amends. Perez was waiting for him.

"In my office, Stafford," Perez said calmly. Stafford followed Perez into his office and shut the door.

"Sir, I apologize for talking back to you out there, but I think I should tell you, I was sent here by the Secretary of ICE to conduct the investigation of Agent Dupree's murder. Of course that investigation is now secondary to the investigation into Hernandez' disappearance. I'd like you to bring me up to speed on what's been done to find Hernandez so far." Perez looked at Stafford as if he had just told him he had been made the King of Sweden.

"You think you can walk in here and just take over an investigation? And you want *me* to bring you up to speed? It's not going to happen." Stafford's cellphone vibrated on his belt. He glanced down and saw the call was from Commissioner Gomez.

"Excuse me, sir, big man on the line."

"Don't answer that phone."

"Sorry, sir." Stafford answered his phone.

"United States Department…"

"Cut that out, Stafford. This is Commissioner Gomez. How's the search for Hernandez going?"

"Hello, sir. I was just discussing the investigation with Supervisory Agent Perez. He disagrees with me about who will be in charge of what. Would you mind talking to him?" Perez got a sick look on his face.

"Oh, it's like that, is it? Is Perez in his office?"

"Yes, sir. We're in his office right now."

"Tell him to stand by for an important call."

"Will do, sir."

"By the way, Stafford…, this probably won't affect you where you are, but Agent Nelson has escaped custody. He killed one Agent, and seriously injured another. He was gone an hour before anyone knew it. We're still looking for him, so watch yourself."

"I'll be alert, sir." Gomez ended the call without saying more.

Stafford had been looking at Perez while he talked to Gomez, and could see he was trying to figure out what kind of mess he had gotten into.

"I told you not to answer that phone."

"Commissioner Gomez said to tell you to stand by for an important call."

"That was Customs Commissioner Gomez on your phone?" Stafford nodded.

"Why would Commissioner Gomez be calling you, instead of going through the proper chain of command? You don't work for him."

"We're fishing buddies with the ICE Director."

"I'm sure," Perez smirked.

"You know, sir, headquarters must have advised you that I was on my way here from D.C., and what my assignment would be after I got here. Why are you giving me such a hard time about it?" Before Perez could answer, his desk phone rang.

"Better get that, sir, it might be the phone." Perez shot Stafford a dirty look, but it lacked his usual conviction.

Perez picked up the phone, and was cut off in the middle of his greeting. After his third "yes sir" he pointed to the door, covered the mouthpiece with his hand, and said "wait outside." Stafford did as he was told, disappointed that he couldn't hear at least one side of the conversation.

After several minutes, Perez opened his door and walked out into the main office area, where most of the agents were working. He motioned Stafford to follow him. He stopped in the middle of the room.

"May I have everyone's attention please?" All the agents stopped what they were doing and looked at Perez.

"Special Agent Stafford will be in charge of the Dupree murder investigation, as well as the Hernandez disappearance. On a daily basis, I want the team leaders to report your findings to Agent Stafford. In the interim, I want the senior investigator to bring Agent Stafford up to speed on what has been done so far, and what we are in the process of doing. That's all for now. Get back to work." Perez returned to his office and slammed the door.

The agents were looking at Stafford with a mixture of indifference, amazement, and dislike. Some thought it sport to ruffle the boss's feathers every so often, but the realists knew it only made their job more difficult. Stafford got the boss riled, and their lives became a little more miserable. For that reason alone, they resented Stafford's presence.

"Which one of you can bring me up to date on Hernandez?" Stafford asked.

"That'd be me." Stafford turned towards the speaker. He didn't recognize him, and extended his hand in greeting.

"And you are?"

"Mark Tanner." He shook Stafford's hand firmly.

"Glad to meet you. Tell me what you know," Stafford said.

"We know Perez is not real happy with you."

"What else do you know, and stick to the subject, Mark."

"Right. We know the time Hernandez was last seen in the hotel. That was at 5:37 yesterday afternoon. Also, the lab called here looking for him because he wasn't answering his phone. He had called them and asked for an analysis of..."

"Tank cars of anti-freeze. I'm familiar with that. What did the lab say?" Stafford asked.

"They said the anti-freeze was about 30 percent coke. We're trying to find the tank cars now."

"They're empty and long gone by now, I'm sure. What else?" Stafford said.

"Hernandez was seen on the hotel security cameras leaving with a white male. We tracked them through the hotel, and through the parking lot. They got into Hernandez' government car, and left the area. We're trying to get city traffic camera footage to track further."

"Can't sector communications locate his vehicle with the two way radio signal?"

"We already thought of that. It only works if the radio is turned on, and it isn't on, at least that's what sector says."

"Can we track his cellphone?" Stafford's phone vibrated on his belt. He glanced down and saw it was Hernandez' number on the display.

"Whoa!" His caught his breath and his heart started to race. He snatched the phone off his belt, flipped it open and placed it to his ear.

"Frank?" There was no answer.

"FRANK!" Stafford yelled into the phone. "CAN YOU HEAR ME?"

"Agent Hernandez can't hear you at the moment, Agent Stafford," a male voice said. "He asked me to call you." Stafford pulled the phone from his ear and pressed the mute button.

"THIS CALL IS COMING FROM HERNANDEZ' PHONE. SOMEBODY GET A LOCATION FOR THE ORIGIN OF THE CALL," Stafford yelled at the office. Tanner pointed to one Agent, and he started making calls on his desk phone. Stafford un-muted the phone and walked to a quieter part of the office.

"Who is this? What do you want?" Stafford said. The man on the other end of the call laughed.

"You may call me Pedro, Agent Stafford. What do I want? As I said, Agent Hernandez asked me to give you a call."

"Where is Hernandez? Is he all right?" Stafford asked. He watched the other agents frantically making phone calls and trotting from one office to the next, spreading the news that he was talking to someone who was using Hernandez' phone. Stafford felt helpless.

"Agent Hernandez is in a safe place, and is in good condition for now."

"Let me talk to him."

"Not now. In due time."

"So Pedro, what is it you want? … ransom money?"

"Hardly." Pedro laughed again.

"What then?" Stafford said. Pedro told him what he wanted.

Stafford's stomach muscles tightened as he listened.

Chapter 34

Stafford strained to hear any sounds in the background of Pedro's end of the conversation. There was nothing.

"I'll be generous, Agent Stafford. I'll give you time to consider what I've said. I'll call again in exactly 24 hours for your answer. Nothing will happen to Agent Hernandez until you talk to me again. You will be the one to decide whether he lives or dies. Do you understand?"

"I understand. There's something you should understand, as well."

"And that is?"

"I have abilities you might not be aware of. It would not be healthy for you, or your boss, to harm Hernandez in any way."

"Well said, Señor. Agent Hernandez has a good friend in you. There is no need to worry about him, unless you make the wrong choice."

"Remember what I said," Stafford said.

"I will call you again in 24 hours… until then, Señor Stafford."

The call ended and Stafford closed his phone. Agents were standing expectantly near him. He ignored them, as he started walking towards Perez, who was standing in the open doorway of his office. Stafford was looking at the floor, with his hands on his hips as he walked. Several agents spoke at the same time.

"What was the call about?"

"Was that Hernandez?"

"Is he okay?"

Stafford stopped walking and turned around to face the others.

"It was a call from someone who said Hernandez is alive. That's all I can tell you right now." Stafford turned back and continued walking towards Perez.

"Sir, we need to talk." Perez smirked and stepped aside to allow Stafford to enter his office. He shut the door behind them.

"So what's the deal?" Perez said.

Stafford crossed his left arm in front of his chest and rested his right elbow on his left wrist, rubbing his mouth with his right hand as he considered what to say.

Was it possible Perez was in on missing coke as well as the whole conspiracy thing? The chances were pretty good that he was. It wouldn't be out of his character. On the other hand, Dupree was not too bright about covering his tracks... In fact, stupidity got him killed. For Perez not to notice the decreasing coke seizures was... well..., that was about par for Perez. But I've got to tell somebody what's going on, and I can't tell Perez.

Perez was getting impatient. This time he spoke a little louder, as if Stafford hadn't heard him.

"I said..., what's the deal?"

"They have Hernandez, and want me to back off the investigation on Dupree's murder," Stafford said.

"Dupree's murder?" Perez had a puzzled look on his face again.

"If I don't back off, they'll send Hernandez back to us in pieces."

"Dupree was killed in an armed robbery. And you haven't started to investigate his murder yet. Besides, what has Dupree's murder got to do with Hernandez?"

"It obviously has some connection, or they wouldn't be threatening to kill him if I don't back off."

"They kidnapped Hernandez before you were even here. I'm not buying it."

"So what do *you* think is going on, sir?"

"I don't know, but I'm not buying it."

"Whether you're buying it or not, we have to do something," Stafford said.

"We're doing all we can already. I have the whole office working on Hernandez' disappearance. Of course the easiest thing to do is have you step away from the Dupree investigation and see what happens."

"I suppose you're right, sir." Stafford stifled an urge to throw something at Perez.

"Will that be all, sir?"

"No. How do you know the Customs Commissioner? Why does he have your cellphone number? Why would he have the ICE Director call me personally?... and don't tell me you two are old fishing buddies." Stafford walked to the door and opened it. He turned partly to face Perez.

"He knows my dad," Stafford said, and walked out of the office.

That'll give him something to think about.

The office was still buzzing with agents trying to get information on the Hernandez call. Stafford walked over to Mark Tanner. He was leaning on his desk writing something on a pad of paper. Tanner pulled the top sheet off, and handed it to Stafford. He read the note.

"So what else is new? Hernandez is in Mexico."

"At least his phone is in Mexico," Tanner answered. Stafford didn't argue the point.

"Do we know where in Mexico the call originated?"

"We are trying to get that information. The Mexican Federal Police said they'll call us back. Don't hold your breath."

"Can you take me to the hotel where Hernandez was staying? I want to see his room, as well as check in myself."

"Sure..., but why don't you get a G-ride assigned to you, and check the hotel out yourself? There should be two agents and a forensics team there already."

"You already don't like my company, Tanner?" Tanner deflected the question.

"You think it's a good idea to stay there?" he asked.

"I doubt lightning will strike the same place twice, and besides... it's the best place in town. I may be back later... if not, I'll call you for an update. Give me your call sign and cell number," Stafford said. They traded cellphone numbers.

"I'm staying off the radio. I don't have a good call sign any more."

"I can get a call sign for you. I'll call you later with it," Tanner said.

"Take your time. I'll probably never use it." Tanner thought that was an odd thing to say, but turned his attention back to his notes.

Stafford signed for a government car, found it in the ICE parking lot, and threw his bag in the trunk, which was surprisingly clean. He opened the door and let the car air out for a half minute. It was like an oven inside. He got in and started the car.

He pulled out his cellphone and called Gomez, who answered on the second ring. He must have had the phone in his hand.

"Yes, Stafford?" Stafford was momentarily taken aback.

"Sir,…um..., Stafford here. I have something of a problem."

"Perez giving you trouble again?"

"No, sir." Stafford told Gomez about the kidnapper's call from Hernandez' phone, and what he told Perez about it. "The thing is, sir, I made all that up. What they really want is for me to come to Mexico and meet Roja. They said if I didn't come, they'd kill Hernandez."

"The same Roja who met with General Miner?"

"Undoubtedly, sir."

"What do you want to do?"

"I want to go and see what Roja wants."

"He may want you as a hood ornament."

"If he wanted me dead, he could have killed me already. You know as well as I do, if someone is willing to pay the price, anyone can be gotten to. I believe he really wants to talk to me face to face. Have you had an opportunity to talk to NSA about video chat taps on Miner?"

"I've got a call in to the FBI Director about it."

"Good luck with that. Another thing, sir..., has Hernandez' family been moved to a safe location?"

"Of course. HSI moved them to a very secure location with round the clock security."

"Provided by whom, sir?"

"You don't need to know." Gomez was getting annoyed at being questioned by a junior agent, even one he liked.

"Listen Stafford, you stay on track and let me worry about Hernandez' family, NSA, and the FBI. I don't have to tell you that you can get killed down there. Roja is in this up to his eyeballs, and Americans are dying by the thousands. Handle it the way you think best, and let me know when you're heading down. I'll officially let the right people know after you're gone."

"I'll be leaving tomorrow, sir."

"Not wasting any time are you? Okay." Gomez sighed. "Before you go, take a look at the news. Some senator called a press conference and accused the White House of involvement in a murder conspiracy. This

Senator says he has undeniable proof. I think the conspiracy he talked about is the same one the Gadsden Group is involved in. The next couple of days are going to be a three ring circus around here."

"Here too, sir."

"Remember what I said…, call for the heavy stuff if you need it. If you can get word to me, I'll give you all the help I can."

"I'll yell if I need help, sir."

"Good luck…, and God bless."

Gomez hung up, and walked around his desk once, ending up where he had started. He put his hands on his hips. He felt helpless against what was happening right in front of him. He needed to make a plan of action, just in case the story about the missing cabinet members he heard on TV turned out to be true. If they were being held against their will, the FBI would be the lead agency, but he wanted CBP to be part of any rescue attempt. He picked up the phone and called the FBI Director's office again.

Chapter 35

President Frank Forrest had been in office for two years. In that time, he had learned to count on his old friend Lou Lassiter, for his honest assessment of the political goings-on in Congress. Forrest and Lassiter had known each other since law school. As White House Chief of Staff, Lassiter saw Forrest frequently.

"Mr. President, Mr. Lassiter is here to see you," the President's secretary said on the intercom.

"Send him in, Connie."

Lassiter entered the oval office. He was calm, but knew what was coming.

"You wanted to see me, sir?" Forrest would have allowed him to call him by his given name, but Lassiter wanted to keep their relationship businesslike, even though they were old friends.

"Come in, Lou," Forrest said, as he walked behind his desk and sat down. Lassiter stood.

"What is Senator Bacster trying to accomplish with this crazy press conference?" Forrest gestured to the large screen TV on the other side of the room.

"I'd say he wants your head on a platter…, sir."

"You think? I was briefed on the tainted drug conspiracy by the Justice Department last week. Bacster couldn't honestly believe we are behind the deaths of that many of our citizens could he?"

"Apparently he does, Mr. President. He says he has proof in the form of official documents and emails, showing White House and broad government agency involvement."

"What emails? What documents? What involvement? What proof could he have? There *are* no emails or documents. It's all lies."

"Of course, Mr. President, but he's making a lot of noise, and the media is paying attention. Even if it isn't true, this is big news. He wants you and the entire cabinet to resign. No one's going to resign. I mean... it's laughable."

"Well, *I'm* not laughing." Forrest leaned back in his chair and crossed his arms over his chest. He sat that way for half a minute, biting his lower lip. Lassiter was uneasy in the silence.

"Will that be all, Mr. President?" Forrest sat up quickly in his chair and pushed the call button on his desk phone.

"Yes, sir."

"Connie, call Senator Bacster's office and arrange a meeting with him here as soon as possible."

"Right away, sir."

"Lou, I want you to contact the head of the FBI and tell him to get copies of this *proof* Bacster says he has. Start proving they're false, and find out who's pulling his strings."

"Mr. President, I imagine the FBI is already investigating, since Bacster says the FBI is part of the conspiracy. At the very least, some committee is going to be calling for an outside investigation." Forrest nodded. And leaned back in his chair again.

"What's being done about that mob across the street?"

"Nothing out of the ordinary, sir. I understand the Secret Service and Park Police have called for extra men, but..."

In the hallway just outside of the oval office, an alarm screeched loudly and then stopped. Within three seconds, two secret service men rushed into the oval office yelling orders.

The President and Lassiter did as they were told, heading for the door the Secret Service men had just entered the room by. Lassiter and Forrest were manhandled out of the room. Lassiter fell behind as Forrest was pushed down the hall.

At the end of the hall on the right, a door opened and Forrest and Secret Service men went through, and then down stairs to the White House safe room. Inside, the President would be safe from all but a direct nuclear attack.

"Your family is safe, Mr. President. They will be joining you shortly," one of the Secret Service men said.

"What was the siren we heard in my office?" President Forrest asked.

"That was an impact alarm, Mr. President. Some sort of projectile, probably from a large caliber rifle, hit one of the windows on the north side of the White House," the Agent said.

"Good Lord, someone was trying to kill me?"

"Not much chance of that happening, sir. Everyone but an idiot should know there is bullet resistant material in all the White House windows. I imagine someone was only trying to send a message."

"Well, I got the message."

"Those windows are designed to protect you from some pretty heavy ordnance," the other Agent said. "But to be on the safe side, we had to move you to a secure location until we sort out the size and strength of the attack."

"I understand," The President said.

Forrest moved further into the shelter and sat heavily on the first chair he came to. He bent forward and put his elbows on his knees, holding his head in his hands. He let out a deep sigh and rolled his head from side to side in his hands. He sat up and put his hands on his knees, his arms straight to the shoulder. He looked straight ahead, thinking about what was happening.

One of the agents flipped a switch on a console and the television monitors on the wall lit up slowly. They were the old, large, cathode ray type, and it took a while for the picture to appear. President Forrest looked in time to see someone on one of the monitors fall heavily to the ground.

"What just happened there?" The President said, pointing at the screen. On other monitors, uniformed Secret Service officers could be seen running and ducking for cover.

"What's going on?" The President said louder than the last time.

The Agent wasn't responding to the questions, because he was listening to radio transmissions in his earpiece. One finger pressed the earpiece deeper into his ear. The other Agent was listening too, but looked at the Lead Agent, waiting for instructions. Finally, the Lead Agent turned to Forrest.

"Two of our agents have been shot. One was on the roof, trying to spot whoever shot at the window earlier. The other Agent was responding to a perimeter fence alarm near the Treasury building. Someone shot him in the head."

"My God..., is there anything we can do?"

"Nothing, sir. They've got plenty of help on the way. We have to wait, and see what happens next."

*　　　*　　　*　　　*

"I have a reservation," Stafford said. He gave his name, showed his credentials, and gave his government credit card to the hotel desk clerk. The man rolled his eyes and sighed, obviously annoyed. He checked the computer, swiped the credit card through the reader, and handed it back. He typed something into his computer, and handed Stafford his room pass card.

"I suppose you want to know all about the kidnapping too?" the clerk asked, still annoyed.

"No. All I want is for you to tell me the room number of ICE Agent Hernandez."

"Room 5503. I have it memorized. You can take the elevator over there. Your room is on the same floor. That should be convenient for you. I hope your stay here is an enjoyable one." The clerk rolled his eyes again.

"Something wrong with your eyes, pal?" Stafford said.

"Excuse me?"

"Do you have a medical condition that makes your eyes roll back in your head like that?"

The clerk paused for a few seconds, looked down at his hands, and then back at Stafford.

"No, sir."

"The Agent that's missing is a close friend of mine. It's a shame our investigation is complicating your day. How would you feel right now if someone in *your* family was missing?"

"I think I'd be worried sick about it, sir."

"You might want to keep that thought in mind."

"I do apologize, sir." He smiled weakly.

Stafford successfully fought the urge to say more, and took the elevator to his floor. He dropped off a few things in his room, and then walked down the hall to Hernandez' room.

The door was open slightly, and he could hear someone moving inside. He knocked on the door with the back of his hand. He had his credentials in hand, ready to show whoever opened the door. A man wearing white coveralls opened the door, and Stafford held his credentials up so the man could see.

"I'm HSI Agent Stafford…, is it okay if I come in?"

"Sure. I'm Forensics Technician Tom Cromwell, you know... Cromwell like the Earl of Essex? Come on in... I'm almost done. Don't touch anything unless you want fingerprint powder all over yourself."

Stafford entered the room and looked around. The place was a mess. Dresser drawers were all partially open, the bed covers were pulled off, and the curtains were open as far as they would go, bathing the room in bright light and heat. Stafford had to squint when he faced the windows, which he noticed were exceptionally clean.

"How much of this mess was *your* doing, Earl?"

"Almost all of it. What *I* didn't mess up, the other two ICE agents did..., and my name's not Earl."

"Sorry, I thought you said your name was Earl. Find anything useful?"

"Not really. And I said my name was Thomas Cromwell. Thomas Cromwell like the famous English... oh never mind." Cromwell scratched his head with his latex gloved hand, leaving fingerprint powder on his forehead.

"All I've got is some smeared fingerprints that could have been anybody's from the cleaning lady to Hernandez himself. It'll take time to sort all the prints out, and figure out which prints belong to whom. From the looks of it, Hernandez wasn't here long..., he hadn't unpacked his suitcase."

"I never unpack mine either. I live out of it... saves repacking when you leave," Stafford offered.

"I found a picture on the dresser. It was of a woman and child. I suppose they are his wife and kid?" Cromwell said. He pointed to a plastic evidence bag, on the chair by the window. There was a photo inside.

Stafford picked up the evidence bag and looked at the picture closely. The picture was larger than a wallet photo, about the size you would put in an album.

"Yep... he showed me a picture of his family once... it looks like them. Okay, Cromwell... looks like you got it covered. Thanks."

Stafford walked into the hallway and toward his room. He ran through the things he had seen. A picture of Frank's family, taken from what would have been across the street from his house. Frank's bags were still packed, and he wouldn't have taken only the picture out of his bag. It was possible the picture was in his pocket, which was not likely, or someone had brought the picture to him. It was a threat that could not be ignored, or easily checked. He went willingly with whoever had come to his room.

Stafford continued to his room and sat down on the bed. He needed to make a few phone calls, and get ready for tomorrow. It was long after quitting time in Washington, so Stafford called Beth's home number. Her machine answered in its digitized male voice. Stafford was leaving a message when Beth picked up the phone.

"Hello, Ben. I'm here. I'm here. Where are you?"

"I'm in El Paso. I just got here."

"You sound tired."

"That's because I am. Frank Hernandez is missing. I suppose you heard?"

"Yes, it's all anyone is talking about..., or was until Senator Bacster held his press conference."

"I heard something about that."

"It's getting scary, Ben. The Senator says there is a huge government conspiracy to kill thousands of Americans with poisoned drugs. He said that every part of the government is involved, and the orders came directly from the White House. Just a minute ago, I heard a TV reporter say there were armed men taking members of the President's cabinet into custody. Witnesses said they looked like military men. There are angry crowds around the White House. It sounds like a revolt or something."

"That's what it sounds like to me. The military isn't supposed to go around arresting civilians, especially cabinet members. Beth, this sounds like the beginnings of a coup."

"A coup?... In America? Is that even possible?"

"It certainly looks like it's possible. What does President Forrest have to say about it?"

"He hasn't said anything yet. His press secretary says the story isn't worthy of a response. The talking heads are making a big deal out of there being no denial from the White House."

"Beth, the reason I called was to tell you I'd be out of touch awhile. I don't know when I'll talk to you again. I wanted to tell you how much you mean to me. I miss you." Stafford had just surprised himself, and Beth, by the revelation.

Beth knew there was more he couldn't say, about the way he felt, and where he was going, so she didn't ask for more. She assumed he was about to do something dangerous, and wanted to talk to her. She didn't know him well enough, but she longed to see him, and hated they were so far apart.

"Ben, I miss you too. I think about you often, and pray for you frequently. Let's take all of this one step at a time."

"Easier said than done, Hon. Keep praying for me. Pray that God will guide me every moment of every day from now on."

"You can pray that prayer yourself. In fact, we can pray together right now."

It was another in a long series of awkward moments that had recently come into Ben's Stafford's life. He didn't know how to pray. He was afraid he'd mess up and make God angry. Based on what he knew of the Bible, people who made God angry, often lived to regret it.

"Okay," he said reluctantly.

Beth began, "Lord God, we humbly approach your throne of grace, and ask for your continued guidance for your child, Ben Stafford. We ask that you place your angels around him, and keep him safe from harm. We ask these things in the precious name of your Son, amen."

"Thank you so much, Beth. I'd better let you go now. I'll call you when I can."

"Okay, Ben. I'll be here." There was the awkwardness again, of who was going to say goodbye first, then they spoke together, her goodbye merging with his. Ben hung up, his eyes began to water. But the tears never flowed.

What is wrong with me? Are you tough or not?

Ben turned on the TV news and settled down on the bed. The commentators were talking over a video of Senator Bacster at his press conference, asking various experts about what the constitution had to say about Bacster's request for the entire cabinet to resign. How would the replacements be made, and who would be president. The newsman reported there had been a shooting at the White House. A Secret Service Agent had been shot by unknown assailants.

I know the poisoned drug conspiracy that Senator Bacster is talking about is the same one that Gomez briefed me about in Washington. If Bacster was part of that conspiracy, he was going to use this opportunity to do... what? take over the government? Bacster? Not likely.

Stafford watched the video of Bacster's press conference. His observational profile training gave him insight into whether people were lying or not.

Politicians were a different breed of people. They practice lying until it's art. Some politicians had been actors, but it was usually the other way around. It was all an act wasn't it? Playing to an audience.

Stafford saw Bacster give a few of the signs that usually mean someone is lying.

So Bacster is a lying politician... nothing new there... but what was he lying about?... that was always the hard part. Still, Bacster wasn't lying about cheating on his wife or his taxes... he just accused the President of conspiracy to commit murder.

Stafford suddenly sat up on the edge of the bed.

Miner! Miner was behind Bacster. It had to be Miner! Of course. Miner is going to try to take over the government. Man that is crazy.

"Take over the government," Stafford said out loud.

Ben had a sick feeling in his stomach. It was the same feeling he got the first time he parachuted out of a C-130. Then as now, he was confident in his training and abilities, knowing he could do it. Whether his chute was going to open properly or not was the only question. Stafford grabbed his cellphone, and called Gomez.

"Sir, this is Ben Stafford. I need to…"

"Stafford, I can't talk right now. I'll call you back later."

The call died and Stafford closed the phone. He looked at the television again. The video showed several buses carrying demonstrators that had been arrested after the shootings near the White House. Stafford got the sick feeling in his stomach again. He opened his phone again, and speed dialed Hernandez' phone. He was surprised when someone answered.

"Señor Stafford, what a pleasant surprise, but I told you I would be calling you tomorrow."

"I remember, but I decided to accept your invitation to come to Mexico. Can we move the meeting up to tonight? I believe it would be in everyone's best interest."

"I don't believe my superior would have any objections. I will ask, and if he agrees, I will call you back with instructions. Good-bye"

*   *   *   *

Hernandez was laying on a hard metal bench, in a room with no windows. Daylight seeped in from the crack under the door. From the smell of car exhaust, oil, and gas, he guessed he was in a garage. He could hear men talking and laughing outside, and the sounds of vehicles coming and going.

They had removed his head-sack and handcuffs, but his wrists still hurt from where his own handcuffs had dug into his flesh, adding insult to injury. The cuffs had not been double locked during the bumpy ride in the van, and they had ratcheted down a couple of notches, cutting off the blood flow to his hands.

He sat up, rubbed his wrists, and flexed his fingers. His mind was on his family. Whether the threat to his family was real or not, he couldn't take any chances. He would risk his life only if he was sure their lives were not at risk as well.

Chapter 36

S enator Bacster's press conference had created a news firestorm. The representatives of the major networks had received copies of Miner's incriminating government emails and other forged documents. The reporters were crawling over Capitol Hill like ants, trying to verify the authenticity of the documents, and getting on-camera comments from important, and unimportant, Senators and Representatives. Many members of congress were calling for the President to resign, or be impeached.

Some government agency heads ordered their own investigations to determine whether the documents and emails were genuine. No matter the outcome of those investigations, there would be an appearance of a cover-up. In the meantime, the public relations offices of the affected agencies were either silent, or denied any knowledge of involvement in the poison drug conspiracy. The denials were enough reason for the majority of the public to believe they were being lied to.

The seizing of the three cabinet heads by unidentified, heavily armed men in civilian clothes was seen by many news commentators as a "crossing of the Rubicon" by the White House. "Constitutional crisis" were words being heard many times a day, and a crisis it certainly was.

Several state governors issued public statements calling for calm. That was good advice, but wasn't selling well in view of the number of dead Americans. Protesters filled the streets around the White House. They smelled blood. Apparently, they already had some.

The report of the dead and wounded Secret Service officers was on the news. The President issued statements of condolences to both families. The wife of the dead Agent blamed the President personally, on live television, for the death of her husband. "Why don't you just resign," she yelled tearfully into the cameras.

General Miner, like so many other Americans, was watching the news on television. Miner's news however, was displayed on an oversized monitor in the Gadsden Council Command Center.

"Perfect," General Miner said, as he watched the Secret Service Agent's wife make her appeal for the President to quit.

Miner's aides were buzzing around like flies, lighting on one phone after another. They were answering calls from the military division commanders and section chiefs, relaying the situation reports to General Miner, and then his orders back to the commanders. It wasn't very efficient, but Miner wanted it that way. He told his aides he needed distance from the emotion of the moment, to make sure he always gave good orders. One of Miner's buzzing aides interrupted Miner's news program.

"Sir, General Hallon is on the secure line. He said he needs to speak to you right away."

"I'll speak to him," Miner said. He swung his chair around to the special phone behind his desk. The main line was encrypted voice over internet protocol. He picked up the handset.

"Miner here. Go ahead, General Hallon."

"General Miner, things are not going as planned. Many of the cabinet members were located, but only three have been taken into custody. The rest of our targets, including the Vice President, were not at their scheduled locations. I assume that was because we lost the element of surprise. The other cabinet members security details changed their schedules immediately after we grabbed the first three. I thought it best not to make a broad search for the others."

"I see... continue," Miner said.

"Since my section sometimes performs security drills as a dress rehearsal of national emergencies, the FBI called and asked if our section was conducting drills. I told them it probably was an evacuation drill by some other Federal security office. They don't have a clue yet."

"Did your men encounter any resistance?" Miner asked.

"Well, several of the civilian security officers tried to physically intervene, but I sent six men to secure each member, and the guards were overwhelmed quickly. Guns were drawn, but no shots were fired. We announced as we went in that it was just a drill, and to cooperate. They were only angry about not being informed beforehand. They said somebody could have gotten hurt." Miner and Hallon both laughed at the same time.

"The plan was to take the entire cabinet and Vice President hostage. That plan has failed," Miner said. He paused, considering his options.

"Are your men prepared to execute the three we have in custody?" Miner asked.

Hallon hesitated. This was the part of the plan he had objected to when Miner first presented it, and he still didn't like it.

"Andy..., sir..., I still believe that will not be necessary. We can simply release them. We gain nothing by killing them, and gain good will by releasing them unharmed."

"You said that before..., and I heard you. If the situation changes, I won't give the order, but will your men act if I give the order?"

"I believe they will. Yes, sir." Hallon didn't believe what he was saying, but couldn't be sure his men wouldn't kill on command.

"I've heard someone was shooting at the White House..., that was not on your orders, was it?" Miner asked.

"No, sir. I gave no such order. It must have been an unhappy citizen."

"Good. Where are the President and Vice President right now?"

"Still at the White House, although I believe the White House security plan is to move them to secure locations in the basement. I'd be surprised if Forrest hasn't been moved out of the White House to Camp David. They can put a battalion of Marines around him out there." Hallon said.

"The Secret Service and Park Police still believe they can control what's happening with standard responses." Miner shook his head in disbelief. "Soon they'll know how wrong they were. Keep me informed," Miner said. He hung up as General Hallon was saying 'yes, sir.'

Miner folded his hands together in front of his face, as if he were praying, but of course he wasn't.

"They won't believe what's going to happen next," he said aloud.

*   *   *   *

Stafford paced around his hotel room, and looked out the window. He was nervous, and he wanted to make something happen. He walked over to the mirror and looked at himself, straightened his shirt, adjusted his collar, and then pulled his shirttail out. He leaned on the dresser, thinking, trying to plan his next move. It was impossible. He didn't know what his next move should be.

His cellphone chirped. He flipped it open, and recognized the number.

"Stafford."

"My boss is most anxious to meet you, Agent Stafford. Be at the New Colony Hotel in Juarez City, at eight o'clock tonight. Come alone, of course. Wait in the lobby, and someone will meet you."

"How will I know you?"

"We will find you..., don't worry."

"Okay. Colonial Hotel in Juarez at eight o'clock," Stafford repeated.

"And no tricks, Señor."

"No tricks," Stafford said.

"Very good. Until tonight then..., adios."

"Yeah, adios."

"You go with God, too. Before this is over, we may both be meeting him in person," Stafford said after he closed the phone.

He grabbed his keys, and hurried down to his government car. He quickly drove away from the hotel, and headed south. There were a couple of items he needed to pick up before his meeting tonight. He finally had a plan, but it wasn't much.

What would Beth say? It's all in God's hands. And so it is. That's what my dad would say, too.

He frowned and smiled at the same time.

Chapter 37

An hour later, Stafford returned his car to the hotel parking lot, and took one of the taxis from in front of the hotel, south to the border. The taxi dropped him off at the pedestrian lanes, and he walked through Mexican customs without being asked any questions. He found the taxi stand, and took another taxi to town. This sort of thing went on daily, and did not arouse the suspicions of the U.S. or Mexican customs officers. They simply looked at his driver license, and let him pass.

He arrived at the Colonial hotel early. Not seeing anything or anyone interesting, he made himself comfortable in a large overstuffed chair, just to one side of the hotel entrance. He wanted to see, as well as be seen.

At 8 PM exactly, a tall, well-dressed man, accompanied by three other large men, entered the hotel. They quickly spotted Stafford, and walked over to him. He got to his feet.

"Señor Stafford?" the tall man asked pleasantly.

"Yes."

"Shall we go?" The tall man gestured toward the door.

Stafford walked ahead of the men as they exited the hotel. One of the junior men placed his hand in the middle of Stafford's back and guided him towards a large delivery truck not far from the entrance to the hotel. As they neared the truck, he shoved Stafford against the side of the truck. Stafford put his hands out to stop himself, as the burly man had intended. He patted Stafford down from neck to feet, not missing much in between. He took Stafford's phone from his belt and pocketed it.

There were people around who saw what was going on. They watched, but no one seemed to care that Stafford was getting manhandled. The man finished searching, and pulled Stafford back by his shoulder. Stafford turned around and brushed the dirt from the truck off his hands. The man that searched him was standing very close, as if he wanted a confrontation. Stafford smiled at him, but kept his teeth clenched, in case the man took a swing.

Pretty good search pal, but no cigar.

"I am sorry Señor Stafford. I am sure you understand," Tall Man said.

"Completely," Stafford said. The man stepped back out of Stafford's space.

"This way, please." Tall Man pointed to an SUV sitting in front of the truck. The burly man who had patted him down walked ahead, and opened the door on the passenger side rear.

"Centro," Burly man said, pointing inside. Stafford correctly assumed that meant for him to get in and slide over to the middle.

"Naturally-amentay," Stafford made up a word, as he complied.

Nobody laughed. They others climbed into the SUV, and Stafford got sandwiched in the back seat between the two big men. Tall Man rode in the front.

"Place your hands in your lap, do not resist, and do not try to remove the head cover. Oh, and do not move around suddenly Señor, unless you want to bleed a little." Tall Man said in English, then said something in Spanish, and a dark bag went over Stafford's head. It smelled like bad breath and sweat.

They drove for 15 minutes, mainly on pot-holed roads. The road smoothed out, and a minute later the bag was removed from Stafford's head. The vehicle stopped, and all the doors opened at the same time. Stafford slid out of the car, and followed Tall Man to the front door of a very large house.

"Nice place," Stafford said.

"Naturally-amentay," Tall Man laughed. The burly men grinned.

They entered the house. The place was huge, and lavishly decorated with Romanesque statues and modern paintings. The house was a mixture of too many styles. Someone had tried too hard to impress, and made a very bad impression. Stafford kept looking around.

Eleven men inside that I can see… probably more in other parts of the house that I can't see… this guy has a small army here.

Four additional men attached themselves to Stafford's escort group as they walked to the back of the house, and into a study. Roja was sitting behind a large oak desk, in an equally large leather chair, wearing a loud short-sleeved Hawaiian shirt. The room had dark wood paneling on the walls, and a twelve foot ceiling. Bookshelves covered two of the walls. In contrast to the main entryway, this room was professionally decorated. It made Roja seem small and out of place.

"Mr. Roja, I presume," Stafford said, as he stepped toward the desk extending his hand to shake. As he expected, two of the burly men grabbed him by the shoulders and pulled him backwards, nearly off his feet.

"Have a seat, Agent Stafford," Roja said, with a hint of a smile. He pointed to the leather armchair to Stafford's right.

"No thanks, I'd rather stand. I've been sitting all day." Roja's smile left his face. He stood quickly, starting to gesture to the men behind Stafford.

"Do I scare you, Señor?" Stafford said quickly. Roja held up his hand, and the men who grabbed him, stopped.

"I fear no one, Agent Stafford, least of all you."

Roja spoke to the men holding Stafford, and they released their grip on him. Stafford could see that Roja was small, but powerfully built. His forearms were large and strong. His wrists were almost as thick as his forearms. He walked around the desk, sat on the corner nearest Stafford, and crossed his arms over his chest.

"Now, what was it you wanted to see me about, Señor Roja?" Stafford said.

Roja started laughing. The other men started to chuckle. Roja quickly stopped laughing, stared at the men, and they grew quiet. Roja was still smiling. He looked at Stafford again.

"Are you really that stupid?" Roja said.

He looked at Tall Man and said something in Spanish. Tall Man replied. Roja pointed to the door, and all the men stepped out into the large hallway. The double doors were left open.

"Please, Agent Stafford..., sit down."

Stafford decided he had played hard-head long enough. He sat down on the front edge of the leather arm chair Roja had pointed to. Roja unfolded his arms, intertwined his fingers, and placed both hands on his left thigh. He was still sitting on the corner of the desk.

"You are in a very bad position, Agent Stafford. May I call you Ben?"

"If I can call you Red."

Roja laughed so hard he began coughing. He bent slightly forward and stood up as he laughed. He walked away a couple of steps, then turned and walked behind the desk. He slowly stopped laughing. This time he sat in the chair behind the desk. He was still smiling from his laughing fit. His eyes were slightly moist from the tears that had come to his eyes. He rubbed them with his large fingers, and cleared his throat.

"Ben..., you have a lot of nerve... a *lot* of nerve."

"So do you, Red." Stafford wasn't smiling, and Roja wasn't either. Stafford decided to address Roja with respect again.

"Señor Roja, we have to trust each other. I know about your railroad tank cars filled with cocaine anti-freeze." Roja waved his hand in dismissal.

"So you know about my cocaine. What has that to do with trust? I have to trust you? You have caused a lot of trouble for me with your exams of my tank cars. That is why I brought your friend here, and why you were asked to come here, as well. Later I will kill you both. Maybe I'll drown you both in anti-freeze... that sort of thing happens from time to time." Roja smiled.

"I also know about General Miner," Stafford said. He could see Roja was surprised, and interested.

"You know about General Miner? I see, and how would you know about him? Maybe someone in my organization is providing information to you?"

If I don't watch what I say, there could be a DEA informant lying dead in a ditch tomorrow.

"Miner's men were careless when they stole the military equipment. We caught a couple of them, and they provided information about where the arms were going, to reduce their prison sentence," Stafford lied, although some of what he said was probably the truth.

"Ah yes, the same old story. At the first sign of trouble the cowards turn on their employer to protect themselves. That does not happen to me often. The price for being disloyal is very high. So you know these things, and yet here you sit..., the man who has caused me much trouble, and cost me much money," Roja said.

"I was only doing my job. You win some, and you lose some."

"You are too modest, Agent Stafford. You win more than your share, I think. But today, you have lost," Roja said seriously.

"I know. You have me and Hernandez, but I think I can help you out of your situation," Stafford said.

"*My* situation? What situation would *I* be in? *You* are in a situation." Roja laughed, and then sighed. He was smiling. "Oh, Agent Stafford, you do amuse me!"

"There are some things you don't know about General Miner. You don't know what he is doing with your cocaine," Stafford said.

At that comment, Roja sat forward in his chair. He looked directly at Stafford when he spoke.

"I don't care what the General does with my cocaine. I don't care what you know about my cocaine shipments. I have no need to trust you. You are only a single Customs Agent who wants to put me in prison. I asked you to come here simply because I wanted to talk to you before I killed you…, *and* your friend. I can kill both of you with a snap of my fingers." Roja held up his hand and put his fingers together. "I have even more reason to do that now, it seems."

"I could kill you as easily, but I won't," Stafford said quickly, before Roja could snap his fingers. Roja chuckled softly, smiling and shaking his head in disbelief.

"Thank you for having mercy on me."

"You're welcome. But I see you don't believe me. Please accept this gift as a token of my trust and good will," Stafford said smiling.

He jumped to his feet, drew the knife he had hidden inside his belt, and as quick as a wink, his right arm whipped back and snapped forward, sending the ten-inch long throwing knife an inch deep into the desktop. The knife made a loud thunk in front of Roja.

Roja's eyes went wide. He leapt to his feet and fumbled to open his desk drawer. He finally yanked the drawer open and grabbed a pistol. He pointed it at Stafford. Roja's hands were trembling, and the color had left his face. Both men held their breath.

The men outside saw, and heard the commotion. They rushed into the room. Stafford put up his hands in surrender, and stood perfectly still.

"I could have easily killed you…, but I didn't, as a gesture of my trust and good will," Stafford said.

Roja gestured at Stafford with his pistol, and yelled at his men in Spanish. Three men grabbed Stafford and spun him around to face them. One stood three feet to one side, pointing a pistol at Stafford's head. The other two searched him roughly for more weapons. If there had been more weapons to find, they would have found them.

One man grabbed and twisted at Stafford's groin during the search. Stafford wanted to yell, but didn't. He almost threw up. He kept his hands in the air, and mentally fought through the pain and nausea. The men stopped searching, satisfied that he had no weapons. They grabbed his shoulders again, forced his arms down, and spun him around to face Roja. The nausea was going away, but the ache remained. He breathed deeply and slowly through his nose. Roja had kept his eyes and pistol pointing at Stafford during the search, only afterward did he relax.

Roja looked down at the knife sticking out of the top of his expensive desk. His pistol was still aimed at Stafford. His hands were no longer shaking. Stafford knew without looking there were still guns pointing at him.

Roja grabbed the knife, and with difficulty pulled it out of the desk. He held the blade in front of his face, looking at it closely. His focus shifted from the blade to his men. He held the knife out for them to see. Roja started talking in Spanish, but Stafford caught the gist of it.

"Who searched this man?" Roja said. No one spoke. There was no need for anyone to answer. The guilty man was white with fear.

"Which one of you? You Domingo?" Roja was looking at the ashen faced man. He was still holding the knife, turning it over and over in his hand.

The light from the desk lamp glinted off the blade and raced across the paneled ceiling and down the walls. The light reflected off the pistol Domingo held in his hand. He had drawn it at the first sound of trouble. All the men, except Tall Man, were holding pistols.

"Take his gun," Roja said to the others.

The closest man pointed his pistol at Domingo, stepped closer, and pulled the weapon out of Domingo's hand. Jose', Roja's favorite gunman and Domingo's brother-in-law, watched from across the room.

"You see the trust I placed in you?" Roja said as he looked into each one of the men's faces. "I know each of you would be willing to die to protect me, and yet my trust in you was a mistake. Domingo…, you allowed a man to come into my home with a knife? He could have killed me."

"Señor Roja, I swear to you he did not have a knife when I searched him. I searched him very well. He must have found the knife in the car."

Roja's eyebrows went up. He turned his stare to the Tall Man. Tall Man knew what the next question would be.

"No, sir, he did not find the knife in the car. He was watched constantly, sitting between two men. We have always done it this way." Roja motioned with the knife for Tall Man to come closer. He handed the knife to him.

"Take Domingo far from here, and use the knife. Take two or three other men, but not Jose'."

"Yes, sir." Tall Man turned and spoke to the other men, pointing at who he wanted, and then at Domingo. The men he chose took Domingo by the arms. The group followed Tall Man out as he left the room.

Jose' wanted to intervene, but knew there was nothing he could do. Domingo made a fatal mistake. The same thing could happen to him.

Domingo and Jose' looked at each other for the last time as Domingo was escorted out of the room. Jose' nodded. Domingo hung his head. They did not make a scene, or resist in any way. Both men knew that to do so would only bring more pain to their families.

Tall Man led the small group toward the rear of the house, and the older SUV that was kept there. They all called it the Meat Car. It was filthy inside, with the byproducts of death. It was used mainly for disposing of people that offended their boss, and so it would be used again tonight.

Roja spoke in Spanish again, and all but one of the men left the room. The lone man stood behind Stafford's chair. He reached forward and pulled Stafford back by the shoulders until he had no choice but to sit or fall down. Roja spoke in Spanish again, and pointed at his own head. The lone man acknowledged his orders.

"I told him if you stood up, or did anything threatening, to shoot you in the head."

"I understood that time," Stafford said.

"So, Agent Stafford…, this is where we left off."

Roja sat down slowly, placing his elbows on the arms of the large leather executive chair. He put his hands together in front of him with the palms facing each other, but only his fingertips touched.

"I can still kill you..." Roja separated his hands and snapped his fingers, "like that…, and since you have thrown away your only weapon, you can do nothing to me, eh?"

"That is true, Señor. But I think I can still do something *for* you."

"You are very entertaining, Agent Stafford," Roja smiled. "I know what I can do for *you*. I can let you and your friend live. But tell me…, how can you do something for me?"

"Well, I already spared your life," Stafford smiled. Roja started laughing again.

"Agent Stafford, you make me laugh so much you make my stomach hurt. Maybe I should let you live for laughs… yes only for laughs." Roja chuckled.

"I don't know why you're funny. You didn't kill me that's true, but your knife is killing someone else at this very moment." Stafford showed his surprise, and dismay.

"This is dangerous business. Your man should have been more careful when he searched me," Stafford said.

"And you should not have brought the knife with you," Roja said.

"I only wanted to get your attention…, and show you I was serious," said Stafford.

"Oh, you got my attention. I see you are quite serious," Roja said.

Roja and Stafford stared at each other. Stafford was sorry he had thrown the knife. It was starting to look like he might need it later. He hadn't planned on killing anyone with it, or getting anyone killed, although he had mentally prepared himself for the possibility.

Roja looked at his watch.

"It's getting late… past your bedtime I suppose." Roja smiled.

"So tell me, Agent Stafford, what *exactly* do you think you can do for me?"

Chapter 38

Murderer and escaped Federal prisoner, Peter Nelson, took a bus from in front of his building, to a grocery store he had located months earlier. It wasn't too far to walk, but he had seen three police cars in the last ten minutes, and didn't want to chance being recognized while he was walking down the street.

He had stashed money in four banks, under four fake names. He wanted to stay away from the banks until he really needed the money. He needed to buy food, because he had to make his cash last. He thought about eating in fast food places, but he was always seeing someone he knew when he was out, and didn't want to be spotted that way either. He was wanted for the murder of a Federal Agent. If the FBI caught him, it was going to be a life sentence, if they didn't kill him during his arrest.

There was a bus stop directly in front of the grocery store. He got off the bus and walked across the parking lot. As he walked along, he looked into a car and saw a cellphone lying in the center console. The window was down. He barely stopped moving, as he reached in, grabbed the phone, and slipped it into his pocket.

After he entered the store, he pulled the phone out, opened it, and pressed the dial button. There was no security password required. He scrolled through the numbers on the quick call list as he walked around, but saw nothing of interest. He decided to make a call while he pushed an empty cart around the aisles. He knew some ICE headquarters numbers by heart.

It's amazing what people will tell you over the phone. Just give them an excuse, and they'll tell you almost anything you want to know. Now I know Stafford is on leave... I know where Beth St. James's condo is..., and from that I can figure out what train she takes to get home. Stafford will pay, even if I have to hurt his girlfriend to do it. All I have to do is be patient. I need to check in with my controller. With the FBI listening in... how am I supposed to do that?

He bought a few items, and then returned by bus to his building. It wasn't the apartment he lived in when he was working, it was his safe house, of sorts. He leased it using one of his assumed names. He had planned on using it in emergencies, and it was definitely coming in handy now. He felt pretty smart he had thought ahead.

At the same time, he felt stupid for having killed the FBI Agent. He had no choice. The man was reaching for his gun, and he reacted instinctively by punching him in the throat. He wanted to take it back. To go all the way back to the day he agreed to take money for information. After that day, he was theirs forever. He felt stupid instead of smart. They owned him.

He decided to keep the stolen phone. He was getting tired of using the bus, but he couldn't go near his car or real apartment. He made a mental note to steal an old car later in the week. Nobody looks for old cars. He would wait until things had calmed down before he did that.

He turned on the TV, and opened the bag of groceries. He found the medium sized kitchen knife he bought. He tore the packaging off, and checked the weight and balance in his hand. It would do nicely, mainly because it was quiet. He had the FBI Agent's gun, but shooting someone would draw too much attention.

He put the knife down, and surfed through the cable news channels. It was the same news on every channel. The local news was more interesting. Somebody had stolen a fully equipped ambulance.

An ambulance... let's see them sell that on the internet... HA!... and somebody took a shot at the White House... Looks like D.C. is coming apart at the seams.

Chapter 39

S tafford told Roja about General Miner's involvement with an
attempted coup in Washington. Roja interrupted him.

"I've seen the news reports from Washington. I really don't care if your
government falls or not... it will in no way affect my business," Roja said.

"That's where you would be wrong. I've heard that in Mexico, people
who try to kick their cocaine habit are sometimes murdered by the drug
gangs. I suppose that's because someone who kicks their habit cuts into the
profits. A lesson must be given. Am I correct?"

Stafford leaned forward in his chair. Roja's expression didn't change.
The man standing behind Stafford pointed his pistol at Stafford's head. His
body tensed when Stafford leaned forward. He moved his trigger finger
from below the slide, where it had been resting, to the trigger. He was
ready to fire.

"Be careful, Agent Stafford. You are making him nervous," Roja said.
He shifted his gaze between Stafford and the man standing behind him.

Stafford glanced left over his shoulder, and saw the gun pointing at his
head from less than two feet away. He leaned back in his chair. The guard
relaxed, but kept his finger on the trigger.

"And..., you are starting to bore me," Roja said, and stood up.

"Did you know that General Miner has already killed tens of thousands
of your cocaine clients in America? He's using *your* cocaine to kill them.
Have you seen that on the news? He partially refines the cocaine from the
anti-freeze you dissolve it in, and leaves enough of the toxic chemicals to
kill off the users in your American market. Killing your customers has got
to be very bad for your profits."

Roja placed his hands flat on the desk, and leaned forward on them. He was frowning, thinking about what Stafford said. He was suspicious of Miner's intentions from the beginning, not believing a man of Miner's military accomplishments and dedication to the United States could suddenly turn to drug trafficking. Roja wondered why he had heard nothing of these deaths before now.

"And how do you know this?" Roja asked slowly.

"I was invited to a top level intelligence briefing in Washington. General Miner's involvement was discussed by people from almost every agency that has anything to do with fighting drug trafficking and terrorism. You and he were mentioned quite often," Stafford said. He watched Roja think. Roja sat down in his chair and drummed his fingers on the armrests.

"You have given me much to think about, Agent Stafford. We will talk more on this matter. You may live a little longer."

Roja pressed something under his desk, and four men immediately walked into the room. He spoke to them in Spanish. Stafford understood this time. They were locking him up with Hernandez, and getting something for him to eat. Stafford rose from his chair slowly.

"If you'll give me what I need, I will stop General Miner. But you should act soon, Señor."

"And what would you need to stop General Miner?" Roja said.

"I'd need proof of his involvement in the drug smuggling…, and for you to release Agent Hernandez and myself."

Roja didn't reply. The room was quiet except for the whish of cool air coming out of the vents in the ceiling. Finally, Roja waved his hand as if he was brushing crumbs from the air.

"I'll think about it," Roja said, and looked away.

The man behind Stafford grabbed him by the arm and pulled him away. Stafford didn't resist.

Roja watched as Stafford left the room with his men. After the room was empty, he pressed another button, this one on top of his desk. In a moment, a serious looking young man wearing a business suit entered the room.

"Yes, sir?"

"Come in, Carlos…, and bring something to write on. There is some information I want you to get for me right away."

*   *   *   *

Hernandez heard the padlock on the door being undone, and sat up on the edge of his metal cot. The door opened, and Stafford walked into the room. Stafford had a wide grin on his face, and was carrying two plates of food. Stafford's escort entered and set two bottles of water down on the cot next to Hernandez.

"Hey, ole buddy. I'm glad to see you. Are you okay? Are you hungry?" Stafford said.

The guard left and shut the door. Hernandez couldn't quite believe his eyes. He stood up and listened for the door being locked again before he answered.

"What in the world are you doing here, Ben?"

"Bringing dinner. You want some something to eat, or not?" Stafford was still holding the plates of food.

"I told you I wouldn't leave you hanging, Frank."

Hernandez took the food and placed them next to the water bottles on the cot. He turned around and gave Stafford a strong hug.

"I am really glad to see you, Ben." Stafford slapped him a few times on the back, while hugging him back. It felt funny hugging another man that wasn't a family member. Stafford had never gotten used to the feeling.

"I'm glad to see you too, Frank. Your wife and daughter are fine. They're in protective custody."

"Thank you, God," Hernandez said. He looked at the ceiling, closed his eyes and lowered his head. He put his hands to his face and let out a couple of sobs. He sniffed and wiped the moisture from his eyes with the heel and back of his hands.

"Thank you, God," he said again. Hernandez' look of thanks changed as he realized his rescuer was now in the same position he was in. Panic took over.

"Ben…, what are we going to do? How are we going to get out of here? They're going to kill us aren't they? They're going to kill us." Hernandez' bottom lip quivered.

"Whoa there, Frank. Don't go soft on me. We're going to take one thing at a time. I just had a long talk with Roja, and I think he's going to let us go."

"Let us go? Why in the world would he let us go? We know way too much about his operation." Hernandez said, pacing and wringing his hands in front of him. Stafford had quickly tired of Hernandez' weakness.

"I don't think he really cares what we know…, but say you're right. He isn't going to let us go. He's going to kill us. He'll probably torture us before he kills us…, to see if we have information he can use. We're going to have to wait and see, but it's probably time to start praying," Stafford said. Hernandez was looking at him with his mouth hanging open.

"You want some of this food? It's getting cold." He sat down next to the food and picked up a plate. "I'm hungry. I didn't have any supper…, or lunch for that matter. I think it's past my bedtime too."

Hernandez took a step toward Stafford and clenched his fists. "I am in no mood to listen to any of your smart comments."

Stafford didn't look up. He knew if he did, Hernandez would take a swing at him. He picked up a burrito and took a bite. He chewed slowly, savoring the taste, and giving Hernandez time to cool off. As he chewed, he unscrewed the cap on a bottle of water and took a long drink, pouring the water in his mouth as if he were filling a glass. He swallowed, burped, sighed, and looked up at Hernandez.

"Sorry, Frank. I'm scared too, okay? If Roja won't release us, we'll have to fight our way out. That's as far as I've planned. Don't worry… we'll get out of this."

"Oh…, well I guess we have nothing to worry about then, huh? Nothing can stop a couple of determined guys like us." Hernandez sat down on the bench and put his face in his hands again.

"Will you stop whining? Get a grip. You want your wife and daughter to go to your memorial service? And eat something… you're going to need your strength no matter what happens." He took another bite of burrito.

Hernandez wanted to scream. The tears in his eyes had come and gone. He looked at Stafford. He didn't understand the courage and confidence Stafford had, but wished he had some of it.

"Eat your food," Stafford said through his food. He picked up the other burrito and held it out. Hernandez snatched the burrito out of Stafford's hand, examined it, and took a bite. It was cold, but tasted good.

*　　　*　　　*　　　*

Perez sat quietly at his desk, rocking back and forth in his oversized leather executive office chair. He rocked like an old lady sitting on her front porch. Back and forth, back and forth. His hands were on top of his head and his eyes were closed.

He was not happy. Stafford's trip to Mexico complicated things for him. He had not thought Stafford would go off half-cocked the way he had. His mind raced as he tried to think of the best way to handle the possible outcomes. He might come out looking pretty good if he handled it correctly. He imagined a newspaper headline; "Local ICE Manager Saves the Day." He imagined another headline; "Body found identified as missing ICE Supervisor."

His desk phone rang, surprising him and snapping him forward, causing his feet to make a flopping sound on the plastic carpet protector under his chair. He saw by the caller I.D. the call was from the Washington D.C. area code. He picked up the handset.

"Good morning... ICE Supervisor Perez... how may I help you?"

"Sir, the Customs Commissioner would like to speak to you. Please hold."

"Certainly." Light jazz music immediately filled the line. Perez waited about 15 seconds, and the music stopped.

"Supervisor Perez, Commissioner Gomez here... Good morning. Have you heard from Agent Stafford?"

"Good morning, sir. No, sir. I assume you know he's in Mexico?"

"Yes, I know."

"I was about to notify the Mexican authorities that he's missing and believed to be with Agent Hernandez somewhere in Mexico," Perez said.

"Notifying the Mexican authorities would be a little premature, I think," Gomez said sarcastically.

"Is there something else you think might be of more help, sir?" Perez was being sarcastic too, but unsuccessful in his attempt to not sound like it.

"Yes..., you can pry your rear out of that chair..., get out on the street..., and develop some leads on the Dupree murder investigation."

"I have several men working on that now, sir. The results aren't promising. From the witnesses, and video from the parking lot camera, it looks like an armed robbery that went bad..., that's all. And by the way, sir, you aren't in my chain of command. I really shouldn't be talking to you at all, about this investigation."

"Quite right, Supervisory Agent Perez. You'll be getting a call soon from the ICE Director. You can explain your lack of progress to him. Have a nice day."

"But Stafford took over the..." He didn't get to finish his sentence. Gomez had hung up.

Both men sat at their desks wondering what to do next. Gomez wondered what he could do to help Stafford. Perez wondered whether he was really going to get a call from the ICE Director; he was.

*   *   *   *

Sometimes waking up to a new day made everything look better. Stafford thought that was true for most people. Whatever the problem had been, sleep, time, and distance made problems seem a little smaller and easier to conquer. That was not true for Stafford and Hernandez this morning. Neither man slept well. That was a blessing for Stafford, who didn't have one of his usual bad dreams.

Hernandez was awake, sitting in the darkness, when Stafford rolled onto his side and braced himself on one elbow. His metal cot was uncomfortable, and he couldn't stay in that position for long. He pushed himself into a sitting position, pulled his knees up to his chest and leaned forward, wrapping his arms around his legs.

"Morning, Frank."

"Morn," Frank mumbled.

"Where's the john?"

"There's a bucket in the corner."

"So *that* was what I smelled all night."

"Humpf... might have been you," Frank said.

Stafford got up, did his duty and sat down on the cot again.

"Remember to tell the maid we're out of toilet paper."

"Don't you ever stop?"

"Yeah..., well..., no. Kidding around takes the edge off, I guess," Stafford said.

Stafford had just explained more than he had ever explained to anybody, about the reasons for his witty remarks. He surprised himself, and made a mental note not to let it happen again.

Hernandez tried to see Stafford in the darkness, but couldn't make out his face. He had never known anyone like Stafford. He didn't know what he was like before he went in the Army, but he was pretty sure it wasn't the way he was now. On top of being kidnapped and having his family threatened, he was locked in a drug dealer's shed with a very annoying veteran.

Even when he was a policeman, there were military combat veterans he worked with every day. None of them, as far as he remembered, were even slightly like Stafford. The most memorable of them were blowhards, who perfected the art of doing little real work, or they were extra quiet men who he thought were split seconds away from being dangerous. He stayed away from them when he could, because it seemed like the smart thing to do.

Hernandez wished he had studied them better, so he could know better how Stafford might react.

Quite possibly Stafford might be one of the last people he would see on earth. Hernandez was not pleased by the thought. He bowed his head and said a short prayer for himself and his family. He lifted his head again as the lights came on in the room. Both men blinked and squinted in the brightness. He heard the door being unlocked, and saw it pushed open. A guard stood in the doorway.

"Mr. Roja wants to see both of you... now."

"Now we'll see, said the blind carpenter, as he picked up his hammer and saw," Stafford said, as he stood and rubbed his hands together. Hernandez shook his head and stood up.

"*Venga*... let's go," the guard said while motioning them, like a father to his kids, to come out.

"Coming, dear," Stafford said, smiling. He walked through the door and caught a hard left hook to his right temple. The blow sent him face down to the ground.

"YOU CALL ME DEAR?" the guard shouted at him. He was bent at the waist over Stafford. His fists were clenched. He was waiting for a good angle to punch Stafford again.

Stafford nearly lost consciousness. He pushed himself up from the ground and steadied himself. He was on one knee. His right foot and his hands were still on the ground. His senses came back quickly. He rocked back until he was sitting on his heel, readying himself to spring at the guard. He didn't look up, but he could see the man's feet.

Hernandez stopped short at the doorway when Stafford got punched. He glanced around. There was no one else in sight. The guard looked like he was going to kick Stafford.

Hernandez caught him by surprise. He pushed down on his back and neck as he brought his knee up into the guards lowered head. When his knee hit the man's face, he let go. The guard straightened up, arched backwards and fell, landing flat on his back on the ground. His head hit the hard-packed ground with a thud, and his arms flopped limply to each side. He was out cold. Hernandez bent over the unconscious man, and looked into his half open eyes.

"There's plenty more where that came from, amigo!" Stafford saw the man lying on his back on the ground. He pushed himself to his feet and looked around.

"Now *that's* what I'm talking about, Frank. Nice move. Any more where that came from?"

"Well..., I'm not *completely* helpless you know. Good thing he didn't have a knife, huh?" Hernandez said sarcastically. He tried to brush away the spot on his pants where the man's face had met his knee. He only succeeded in adding more dirt from his hand. Stafford grinned.

"Good thing *you* didn't have a knife..., you might have gotten blood on your pants," Stafford said.

Hernandez cocked his head to one side and half grinned back at Stafford. He was pumped up from the short battle with the guard, but he still had a problem with Stafford's joking attitude.

Stafford rubbed his sore temple as he took a look around, getting a feel for their situation. He saw no other guards. He listened for footsteps, but heard nothing. He squatted and went through the unconscious man's pockets and found a fully loaded .40 caliber Glock pistol, two full magazines of ammo, and a set of car keys.

Stafford stood, tucked the magazines in his back pocket, and slipped the Glock into his belt behind his back. He looked at the car keys, noticing one key had a Ford emblem on it. He pressed the door lock button on the remote. A horn faintly sounded from next to the storage room. The car was close, but out of sight. They looked at each other.

"This is too easy," Stafford said, as he looked around again for signs of danger.

"I don't care. Let's get out of here!" Hernandez whispered, heading to where the sound of the car horn had come from.

"Hold it, Frank. I think this was planned so we would try to escape. Roja is testing us. He's testing me."

"So what? We've got a chance to get out of here. Let's go!"

"Frank, if they *are* waiting for us, we'll be dead before we make it to the car. Trust me, Frank. It's a test. If we fail, Roja's men will definitely kill us. Besides, we haven't got what I came for."

"I thought you came for me." Hernandez was looking at Stafford with his mouth hanging open again.

"I *did* come for you, but you aren't the only reason I'm here."

Standing around was starting to make Stafford nervous. He reached around and put his hand on the butt of the pistol in his belt.

"I gave Roja too much to think about last night. If he wanted us dead, he would have killed us already. No..., I'm telling you, this has got to be a test."

Stafford pulled the Glock and the magazines out of his pockets and put them behind an oil drum sitting next to the storage room wall. He tossed the car keys on the guard's chest. The guard groaned, and his eyes fluttered. Hernandez reached down and clipped the man on the chin with a right hook. The man's head snapped to one side, and his eyes went blank again. Stafford put his hands on his hips.

"You continue to surprise me, Frank. Well, come on..., time to move. This guy's going to be none too happy when he wakes up... if you let him wake up. Let's head for the house. Walk like you own the place."

Stafford started walking to the house, which was about 50 yards away. Hernandez couldn't believe Stafford was heading back into the lion's den, but he started walking that way anyway. Hernandez hung his head like a man going to the gallows. He didn't want to see what was coming.

"You're going to get us both shot," Hernandez said softly.

Stafford didn't answer. When they were about 50 feet from the house, a man appeared from around the side of the house, saw them, and stopped. Stafford and Hernandez slowed their pace, but continued walking.

"This way, gentlemen. Mr. Roja is waiting to see you," the man said.

The two agents looked at each other, shrugged and continued to the house. There was reason to be cautious, but there was not much they could do if someone wanted to make them pay for their sins.

Stafford picked up his pace again. Hernandez kept up, finally walking next to Stafford. He was gaining courage. As they turned the corner of the house, they saw a large paved brick patio, with a large vine covered arbor. Roja was sitting under the arbor in a patio chair. There was a large glass-top table in front of him. Roja was sipping from a glass of orange juice. He put his glass down and stood up as they approached.

"Good morning gentlemen. I hope you slept well. So nice of you to accept my invitation. I don't see your escort. Did you hurt him?"

"He'll get over it, but he's going to have a headache," Hernandez said. Stafford looked at Hernandez; surprised again.

"I see you share your friend's sense of humor, Agent Hernandez."

"Not very often," Hernandez said.

"Do you still have his weapon?" Roja spoke to the two men standing nearby, and they quickly searched Stafford and Hernandez for any weapons. They were very thorough this time, after hearing what had happened to the other guard last night.

"Not any more. I hid it behind an oil drum in the shed. It seemed like the right thing to do," Stafford said. The guards shook their heads, and backed away to their previous positions.

"Please gentlemen, sit down," Roja said. "Would you like some breakfast?" Hernandez and Stafford moved to the table and pulled out their chairs.

"Yes, thank you," Stafford said, and sat down.

"Nothing for me, thank you, I'm not hungry," Hernandez said, still standing.

"Nonsense," Roja answered. "Have a seat."

Roja snapped his fingers as a white jacketed servant came closer. He spoke to him in Spanish, and the man nodded and walked quickly into the house. There were still six men standing around the patio in a semi-circle. Hernandez sat down.

"So, you thought about escaping?" Roja asked.

"Of course," Stafford said.

"I'm glad you didn't try. It would have been a pity to see you both die running away like scared dogs."

"You would have had a half dozen new job openings in your guard force if we *had* tried," Stafford said.

"No doubt." Roja smiled and sipped his orange juice.

"So it *was* a trap?" Hernandez said.

Roja ignored the question. He was still looking at Stafford.

"I had to see if you were a man of your convictions, Agent Stafford. Were you just blowing smoke, as you Americans like to say, or were you willing to stay and risk your life for what you say you place so much importance on. What is it soldiers like to say... duty, honor, country?"

Roja was waiting for an answer. Stafford couldn't believe he heard the words come out of Roja's mouth. *Duty?...Honor?...Country?* They were burned into Stafford's heart and mind. They were words he lived by. Duty, honor, country were more than words. They were flesh and blood. They represented what men lived, fought, and died for. When Roja said those words, he mocked millions of men and women who served the United States with honor. He was the devil quoting scripture. Stafford fought the urge to leap over the table and choke the life out of him. He took a deep breath, and the feeling slowly passed.

"Something like that," Stafford said softly, his heart pounding.

"I can see you care quite passionately about these things, Agent Stafford. And you, Agent Hernandez..., do you care about such things, too? You are also willing to give your life for your country?"

"I am perfectly willing to lay down my life for my country, should it be necessary."

"Bravo, Agent Hernandez, Bravo!" Roja said, and clapped his hands as if he had seen an amazing performance at the opera.

"I too value bravery and loyalty." Roja was grinning like a little boy who had found his presents on Christmas morning.

"Señor Roja, have you checked out what I told you last night?" Stafford said.

"Of course, and we have much to discuss, Agent Stafford, but one thing at a time. First we eat, for tomorrow we die!" Roja laughed.

Stafford didn't see the humor, but he did smile.

Chapter 40

The morning was bright and clear, but less warm than the day before. The situation in Washington had been cooling, at least as far as demonstrations near the White House were concerned. After unknown gunmen shot at the White House and killed a Secret Service Agent, demonstrations were forbidden within a two-mile radius of the White House, except for a small area near the Washington monument.

The order came at the request of the Secret Service, and was enforced by the U.S. Park Police, and the Metropolitan D.C. Police. In areas where demonstrations were allowed, there were throngs of people, who stayed well into the night. People slept on the ground, and refused to leave. Sensing a poor climate for strong-arm tactics, the police let the demonstrators stay overnight, as long as they didn't start campfires.

The ban on demonstrations angered many politicians, Democrat and Republican alike. During press conferences, and smaller on the spot interviews with dozens of Senators and Representatives, the politicians reminded everyone that the Constitution guaranteed the people the right to peaceably assemble and air their grievances.

The most vehement opposition to the demonstration ban came from none other than Senator Bacster. As expected, he called for the resignation of President Forrest and his entire cabinet, and suggested that the missing cabinet members may have fled the country to avoid prosecution. "Rats deserting a sinking ship is common sense for rats! I invite President Forrest to join the other rats," Senator Bacster said.

During a White House press conference, a reporter asked the Press Secretary to comment on the demonstration ban.

"In view of the constitution's guarantees concerning peaceable assembly, can you explain how the ban on demonstrations would not be considered un-constitutional?" the reporter asked.

"Peaceable assembly for a redress of grievances does *not* include shooting high-powered rifles at the White House, or murdering White House Secret Service personnel," the Press Secretary said.

The press secretary's statement set off another wave of anti-government demonstrations across the country. In some cities where demonstrations were held, many citizens were seen carrying pistols and rifles. The country seemed ready to burst into flames at any moment.

General Miner was watching the reports of growing political unrest with approval. He saw it was almost time to create the spark that would ignite the fuel. He called Senator Bacster.

Bacster knew who was calling. Miner's calls had a distinctive ring of one deep 'BONG,' like a death knell. Bacster picked up the phone, but didn't have time to speak before Miner began talking.

"Bacster, this is General Miner"

"General, I think it's too risky for you to..."

"Shut up and listen, Bacster. Tomorrow there will be a major terror attack."

"What are you going to do? Or should I say... what are you going to do and blame it on al Qaida?" Bacster said. He wasn't sure he wanted to hear an answer.

"Never mind what I'm going to do. After the attack, I want you to call for the removal of President Forrest, all the cabinet heads, and the Speaker of the House. After they refuse to resign, there will be an imposition of martial law as we discussed."

"Calling for martial law would be a waste of time, General. That sort of thing is not provided for in the constitution. I would look like an idiot. As I told you the last time we talked about this, martial law can't be called for by anyone except the President."

"Have you been paying attention, Bacster? You're not driving a van full of voters to the polls on election day. This is a *coup*. I'm removing all the rotten apples at same time, and replacing them with *MY* apples. The constitution will be suspended until further notice. Congress will be adjourned until I call it back into session. When we finish correcting the problems this nation has, we will elect a new congress and president. It will happen very quickly. My men are ready to move. You just call for all loyal military officers to do what is necessary to remove Forrest and his cabinet from office. My people will take it from there."

Bacster hung his head. His chin was almost sitting on his chest.

"This will be perfect timing don't you think?" Miner continued. "The President is under investigation for his part in a mass murder conspiracy. Al Qaida takes advantage of the distraction to launch another terror attack on America. Even if Forrest is found innocent of involvement in the murder conspiracy, he will be have been negligent in protecting America from terrorists. *Everyone* will be screaming to get rid of him. Even if he resigns, I won't stop! So, you better be ready by four o'clock tomorrow."

"I'll be ready," he said. This time he didn't hear Miner hang up on him, as was Miner's habit. He put the phone down first and closed his eyes.

How did I get involved in mass murder? This is a nightmare.

He opened his desk drawer and picked up the .45 pistol he kept there. It was the gun his father carried across France and Germany during World War II. His father had simply smiled when he asked him how he managed to get it home after the war. He only said, "If there's a will, there's a way." He looked at the gun carefully, reading the manufacturer's name. The gun was made by Remington Arms.

I thought all .45's were made by Colt. Colt 45... the words go together like bread and butter. Once, America was dedicated to war. Car manufacturers and appliance makers were suddenly making bombers and walkie-talkies. Millions of men enlisted or were drafted into the military. America's fighting men were ready to kill or be killed to protect America. Such sacrifice. Facing death and destruction... to protect America... to defend liberty... to keep America free from tyrants... from people like Miner. How many lives were taken by this pistol?

He turned the gun over in his hands, looking at the worn checkering on the back of the grip. It was worn almost smooth from being in someone's hand. He ran his thumb over the letters stamped into the side; UNITED STATES PROPERTY.

He retrieved the loaded magazine from the desk drawer, and inserted it into the weapon. He remembered his father's words.

This thing has a habit of going off when you don't want it to. Leave the chamber empty until you're ready to shoot.

He pulled the slide back as far as it would go and released it. The slide stripped a bullet from the top of the magazine, and pushed it into the chamber. The hammer was back, and the thumb safety was off. The gun was ready to fire. All one had to do was squeeze the trigger. He sat looking at the gun for a minute, deciding what to do next. Bacster expertly thumbed the hammer back, which disengaged the grip safety, pulled the trigger, and slowly let the hammer move forward until it stopped. He pulled the hammer back again until it clicked into the half cocked position. The gun was now safe. He placed it in his briefcase and closed the case carefully. He pressed the intercom button for his aide.

"Yes, Senator?"

"Make an appointment for me to see President Forrest as soon as possible. Tell his secretary it's a matter of national security."

"I have the White House appointment desk on the telephone now, Senator. The President wants to see you. They want to know if you can be there in an hour."

"Tell them I'll be right over, and have my driver bring the car around."

"Right away, sir."

Bacster's hands started to sweat. He opened his briefcase and looked at the pistol. He decided to leave the briefcase in his car.

After confirming the White House appointment, and calling for the Senator's car and driver, the Senator's aide made another call. He dialed the number he had been given for times such as this. It was answered on the second ring.

"Yes?" a voice said.

"I'd like to place a take-out order," the aide said.

"He's on his way to the White House?" the voice asked.

"Yes, I can hold. Oh never mind. I'll call back later, thanks," the aide said.

"Understood." The phone went dead, and the aide hung up as Senator Bacster walked past his desk on the way out of the office.

"I won't be back today, Jeff."

"All right, sir. See you tomorrow."

"Maybe so, Jeff. Have a good night."

* * * *

FBI Director Brad Clement had his hands full. Three cabinet members had been kidnapped by armed men under the guise of a security drill. Nobody had an idea where they were at the moment. Clement had about an hour before he reported to the White House on the situation, and he probably knew less than the television reporters did.

Descriptions of the vehicles involved were sent to all law enforcement agencies, and the news outlets had broadcast them to the public as well. The vehicles were common models, and hundreds of leads were coming in.

The good leads, if there were any, had to be sifted from the bad before field agents could go out to interview people. Clement heard the knock on his office door at the same time it opened.

"Sir?" a voice from the doorway said.

"Yes?" Clement said as he looked up. In the doorway was Ellen Davies, his Executive Assistant. David Fuller, the FBI Assistant Director of Intelligence, and Agent Bonifay Schwartzchild stood nearby.

"Sorry to bother you, Brad," Fuller said. He pushed into the room past Ellen Davies, who clearly didn't like being circumnavigated. "Agent Schwartzchild has come across something I think might be very useful."

"It's okay, Ellen..., thank you. Come in, Dave..., Agent." The men walked closer to Clement's desk. Ellen Davies closed the door as she left. Clement stood and shook hands with both men.

"Have a seat, fellas," Clement said, as he sat down. The two visitors sat in the chairs in front of Clements desk. "Okay Bonnie-Faye, what have you got for me?"

"Well, Director, in a nutshell, I think I discovered video of the cabinet heads kidnapping," Schwartzchild said.

"Where would you discover something like that? Traffic or security cameras?" Clement asked.

Clement leaned forward on his elbows, crossing his forearms on the desk in front of him. Schwartzchild grinned broadly. The new Agent was quite excited about the possibility of helping the FBI on an investigation of this importance.

"Well, Director, as you may know, I am an electronic surveillance officer. I was practicing wide and narrow multi-band frequency sweeps. I was searching through the higher military frequencies for any unencrypted transmissions and I... uh..." It suddenly occurred to Schwartzchild that he had just admitted violating several FBI surveillance policy directives, and probably more than one section of the United States Code dealing with electronic surveillance authority and procedures.

"I...uh, I..." Schwartzchild repeated.

Clement leaned back in his chair, frowning. He closed his eyes for several seconds and rubbed his forehead with both hands. He took a deep breath and exhaled slowly.

"What a week," Clement said with the last of his breath.

Schwartzchild was sitting with his hands flat on top of his thighs, as if he was about to jump out of his chair. He rubbed his palms back and forth on his pants, trying to dry them. He licked his lips and opened his mouth slightly. He imagined his FBI career might be over, as it likely was.

"Bonnie-Faye," Clement said. He didn't have the heart to make fun of the young Agent any longer. He leaned forward, continuing to rub his forehead with one hand.

"*Agent* Schwartzchild," Clement said.

"Yes, sir?" The Agent smiled slightly. He stopped rubbing his palms on his pants.

"You have fumbled the ball this time, and you *will* answer for it. But, what you saw may mean life or death for somebody. So let's have it, and I mean all of it. We'll figure out how many laws you've broken later. Tell me what video you've got on the missing cabinet heads."

"Yes, sir." Schwartzchild took a deep breath. "I recorded some transmissions coming from a military drone flying over the capitol."

"A military drone over Washington? Taking video of the kidnappings? That figures," Clement said.

"I *think* it was video of the cabinet kidnappings. I can't be absolutely sure of course, because I don't know the locations of the cabinet heads when they were abducted. But there are three separate transmissions. All the videos showed armed men forcing people into large vans. The drone camera followed each of the vans for some distance when they left. The vans all headed west on Interstate 66. They were still heading in that direction when the transmissions ended."

"Interstate 66 west? What's out that way?" Clement asked.

"I-66 stops around Strasburg, Virginia. Then you could head north or south on I-81. If they kept going west, its pretty hilly; lots of back roads, sir," Schwartzchild said. Clement looked at Fuller.

"Get him the addresses where the missing cabinet heads were when they were abducted. After you've done that, report here to me." Fuller nodded.

"Agent Schwartzchild, take the addresses Assistant Director Fuller gives you, and verify the locations you saw on the video are the same locations the cabinet heads were kidnapped from. Make absolutely sure, and then report immediately to me." Clement looked at his watch, and saw it was almost nine in the morning.

"Do that now, and hurry up." The two men hurried out of Clements office.

"I'm glad I'm not you today," Fuller said. He slowed down enough to see Clement's reaction.

"Move it!" Clement said.

He grabbed a hand-full of papers and flung them at Fuller's face as it disappeared behind the closing door. The papers fluttered harmlessly to the floor.

Chapter 41

Roja pushed the food around his plate, barely eating. Hernandez only nibbled at a sweet roll. Stafford's appetite made up for them both. He was working on his third helping of scrambled eggs and ham.

Stafford finished chewing, placed his knife and fork at the five o'clock position, as his mother had taught him to do when he ate in public, and looked up. Roja and Hernandez were watching him with interest. Stafford noticed their stares.

"So what? I'm hungry. Can I have more coffee and toast please?" Stafford asked.

Roja looked at a white jacketed servant, snapped his fingers, pointed at Stafford's cup and bread plate, and said "*más pan, tostado, y café.*"

The servant immediately filled the cup to the brim, and placed a fresh plate of toast next to the coffee as he cleared away the empty plate.

Stafford picked the cup up with both hands and took a long, loud, slurp, which cooled the hot coffee passing over his lips. He put the cup down, dunked a piece of toast in the coffee, blew on it, and took a big bite. Stafford's manners weren't really this bad. He knew how to eat politely, but he was always an entertainer. They liked watching him eat that way, so he was happy to give them something to watch. Roja laughed and folded his hands over his ample stomach.

"Would you like something more to eat, Agent Stafford?" Roja asked, smiling.

"Got any pancakes with real maple syrup?"

"No." Roja stopped smiling.

"Well, then no thanks, I'm good here. Can we talk some business now?"

"Certainly," Roja said. "I found out many interesting things this morning. Last night I asked my aide to verify the things you told me about, and to do research on both of you. Just as you said, my product has been used to kill many Americans. Also as you said, General Miner is behind this."

"So what are you going to do about it? Will you help us get Miner?" Stafford said.

"I don't need to help you *get him,* as you say. I can *get him* myself," Roja said.

Stafford rubbed his chin as he thought.

"While it might be a just punishment for what he's done, killing General Miner would leave too many loose ends. He's a traitor, as well as a mass murderer. He deserves to be shot by a firing squad. That probably won't happen, but one never knows. I want him to face justice in an American courtroom, with the entire world watching. I want everyone to know exactly what he's done, and see him punished for it."

Hernandez nodded in agreement. "If he's convicted, and isn't sentenced to be executed, he'll spend the rest of his life in prison."

"Watching television and playing cards no doubt. So, you are both in agreement that he should pay for his crimes?" Roja asked.

"Of course"... "Yes," Hernandez and Stafford responded.

"So what punishment should be given to a person who has killed another person? Would you say they always deserves to die, as well?"

Roja held his hands in front of his chest, tapping his fingertips together as he toyed with both men. Stafford and Hernandez looked at each other, wondering where Roja was going with the conversation.

"Well, what do you say?" Roja asked.

"What are you getting at?" Hernandez said, frowning.

"Ah..., Agent Hernandez is most interested, eh?" Roja was still tapping his fingers together. He began to smile at Hernandez. Stafford's face was expressionless.

"Well, I'm most interested too. What *are* you getting at?" Stafford said. He dipped another half slice of toast in his coffee and stuffed it in his mouth, in contrast to his expressed interest.

"Agent Stafford, did you know that Agent Hernandez killed a 15 year-old boy when he was a police officer? The boy wasn't armed. Of course he was not charged," Rojas said, looking at Stafford. Hernandez hung his head, and bit his lower lip.

"I thought he had a gun. I thought my life was in danger," Hernandez said, still looking down.

"You don't have to talk about it Frank," Stafford said, as he put his hand on Hernandez' shoulder.

"And, Agent Hernandez, did you know Agent Stafford killed his own father?"

Stafford swallowed hard. He felt sick to his stomach as the memory of his father's death rushed back to him. Hernandez picked his head up, and saw Stafford's reaction to Roja's words.

More than anything, Stafford wanted to put his fist into Roja's grinning face. He restrained himself with difficulty. He knew Roja was toying with them like a cat playing with a mouse. There was no need to kill the mouse. The mouse could be batted around like a ball, for amusement. If the mouse lay still, a cat might lose interest. Stafford hoped he could remain still, so Roja would leave him alone. He longed for home, his mother and father, and for Beth. He wanted out of this asylum.

"Isn't that true, Agent Stafford?" Roja said.

Stafford decided he wasn't going to be Roja's mouse. He sat back in his chair and breathed deeply several times, calming himself before he spoke.

"Can I speak freely, Señor? without fear of retaliation?"

"Of course, Agent Stafford. Say what you wish. Have no fear. We are all friends here."

"I wouldn't go that far. Listen, you are a major drug dealer..., and that makes you complicit in the deaths of many thousands of people in Mexico and the United States. You're like a plague." Roja's face grew red with anger, but he remained silent.

"You ask me what I think should be done to people who kill other people? I've killed people in the Army, but none since I got out of the Army."

"Did you forget about killing your father? You shot him in the head, didn't you?" Roja said with a sneer.

"My father was killed in a hunting accident when I was a boy. I didn't kill him," Stafford said angrily.

"Saying you didn't kill him doesn't make it true. Why did you kill him? Was he sexually abusing you? No one would blame you killing him for that," Roja said with satisfaction.

"I did not kill my father! When I killed, it was to protect myself and my men, to protect the people of Afghanistan or Iraq, and to protect my country. My duty as a soldier put me in that position. Agent Hernandez killed when he believed *his* life was in danger. *You*, on the other hand, kill to protect your drug business, and for revenge, but mainly because you like it, and you especially like it because you can have someone else do it for you. You don't even get your hands dirty. So, I think for the deaths you are responsible for, no punishment could be too severe." Stafford paused, still glaring at Roja, whose eyes were unfocused, looking at nothing.

"Speaking of having people killed..., did you order the murder of Agent Dupree?" Stafford said. Roja came out of his fixed stare.

"Agent Dupree? Who is Agent Dupree?" Roja said, glad for the change of tone.

"He was murdered in a grocery store parking lot two weeks ago. Did you order him to be killed?"

"Should I have? Did he deserve to die?" Roja asked seriously.

"Not you, huh? If it wasn't you, it was probably one of Miner's minions." Roja huffed in amusement, and repeated Stafford's words.

"One of Miner's minions. I like that."

"You know what *really* amazes me about all this? The fact that Jesus loves me as much as he loves you. Part of me says that shouldn't be possible, but it's true. If you were the only person on earth, Jesus would still have died for you, because that's how much God loves you," Stafford said. Roja rolled his eyes like a teenaged girl being scolded by her mother.

"It's not too late you know. You can still turn your life around and make a positive difference. God will forgive you," Stafford said.

Stafford had been looking Roja in the eyes the entire time he was talking, and Roja had not looked away. Roja hated what he heard, but he wanted to hear more. He liked playing with Stafford, because Stafford seemed not to fear him.

Stafford removed the napkin from his lap, wiped his mouth and hands, and put it on the table. He pushed his chair back and sat forward on the seat edge with his hands on his thighs.

"I've had enough to eat, and I've had enough of you," Stafford said. "Are you going to let us out of here to get Miner or not?"

"I think not." Roja answered without hesitation. His face was a little red, but he looked calmer.

"You may want to reconsider that answer, Señor. I *know* you'll want to reconsider it after General Miner is caught. One way or another, we *will* stop him. When we do, and Miner goes on trial for his crimes, your personal involvement will be made perfectly clear. If you don't cooperate fully with us now, your picture will be on every police and military special operations bulletin board with the words 'Wanted, Dead or Alive,' written above it. The United States has done a lot more, for a lot less reason than you've already given us. I'd get my affairs in order if I were you. You'll be meeting Jesus sooner, rather than later."

Now Roja was the one who wanted to put his fist into Stafford's face, but he knew Stafford was telling the truth. Roja had no reason to think the Americans wouldn't come after him. Roja knew his only chance of staying alive was to cooperate.

Roja felt embarrassed. He knew God was watching him, but he still felt no need for God, even though he feared going to hell when he died. He had been given a lot to think about.

"It is of little consequence," Roja said with a wave of his hand. He stood up, giving orders in Spanish to one of his guards, who went into the house. Hernandez stood up, looking at Stafford.

"He told him to go get the documents and our things," Hernandez said. Stafford stood up slowly.

The guard returned with a large manila folder, and a CD. He handed both to Roja, who tossed them onto the breakfast table in front of Stafford.

"Our things?" Stafford asked.

"The proof you wanted. I give you proof, and your freedom. No need to thank me. Go before I change my mind." Roja spoke in Spanish to two guards, and then turned and walked toward the house. One of the guards started walking toward the SUV parked in the driveway.

"This way gentlemen," he said over his shoulder to Stafford and Hernandez in perfect English. They followed him. The other guard trailed behind them all. Suddenly Hernandez turned and ran back to the house, and Roja.

"STOP," yelled the trailing guard who went after Hernandez, his hand on the pistol under his coat.

"Just a minute, Señor Roja!" Hernandez yelled.

Roja stopped as Hernandez slowed to a walk as he neared him. The trailing guard grabbed Hernandez' shoulder, and the other guards crowded around him. Stafford could see he was talking to Roja.

Whatever Hernandez said made Roja very angry. Roja pointed his finger in Hernandez' face, and then pointed in Stafford's direction. One of the guards shoved Hernandez backwards, and he almost fell. He regained his balance, stood for a moment looking at Roja, and then walked back to where Stafford and the other guard were waiting. Roja and his guards went into the house.

"What was that all about, Frank?" Hernandez didn't answer.

"Come on, Frank, what did you tell him?" They resumed their walk to the SUV waiting in the driveway.

"I told him if he ever threatened my family again, I'd come back here and make him sorry he was born!"

"Whoa! Those are big words, Frank. What did he say to that?"

"He told me if I said another word, he'd gut me like a pig."

"Hmmpf." Stafford mumbled thoughtfully. "He probably would, too. You really ought to learn when to keep your mouth shut."

"Yeah, I know, but it felt good," Hernandez said.

"Famous last words," Stafford finished.

As they walked, Stafford peered into the folder Roja had given him. There were about two dozen pages of hand written notes, along with some photographs, their cell phones, wallets, and hotel keys. He fished out the personal belongings, put his own in his pockets, and gave Hernandez his things. He dropped the CD into the envelope with the papers. He wanted to read it all right away, but decided to look in greater detail when he and Hernandez were safely across the border.

They got into the SUV. Stafford looked at his watch, it was almost eleven o'clock.

My, how time flies when you're having fun.

Chapter 42

FBI Director Clement was on his way to the White House presidential briefing. The drone video transmissions were verified by Agent Schwartzchild as having come from the cabinet heads original locations. Clement asked the Assistant Director to have the videos double checked by another agent. If the Director told the President something was a fact, it had better be so. What a military drone was doing over Washington to begin with, he didn't know, but he feared it meant connections to active duty military personnel that was more widespread than anyone knew.

As his armor plated SUV stopped outside the White House, Clement was ending his cell-phone call with Eduardo Gomez, the Commissioner of Customs. Gomez had called to offer whatever help Clement needed.

"I'm telling you Director, right now I've got two agents in Mexico trying to get evidence connecting Miner to the drug death conspiracy. I have confidence the proof will be coming soon."

"You're talking about Stafford and Hernandez, right?

"Right," Gomez said.

"I know Agent Hernandez was kidnapped and probably taken to Mexico... I've seen the report from our El Paso office. But you sent Stafford to Mexico after him? That was stupid, don't you think?"

"Stupid? Listen, Clement, Stafford was the one who made the connection between Miner and the drugs, and one of Miner's men tried to kill him for getting that close!"

"Can you prove that?"

"Are you kidding me? If you'd tap the video chat lines Miner uses to communicate, *you* could prove it. NSA would help you with that, but did you ask for NSA's help? Don't tell me the answer, I already know... you never asked! The FBI *never* needs help! Well, you better learn to ask for it, in case my men don't make it back to pull our fat out of the fire!"

"Well, it's been nice talking to you, Commissioner. I've got to go now," Clement said.

"Same to you, Pal," Gomez said. "I'll call you again when I hear from Stafford."

"I can hardly wait," Clement said. He ended the call.

The FBI wasn't used to asking for help, and this time was no different. They would go it alone, mainly because they considered themselves to be America's best law enforcement agency, and the best didn't need help.

Before he left FBI headquarters, Clement instructed the Deputy Director to plan for a rescue operation. The location was to be determined later. Clement knew he was first going to have to negotiate his way through a minefield of jurisdictional issues before the rescue could begin. A word from the President would smooth the way for the FBI in that regard.

Clement hoped the kidnappers would simply give up when their hideout was discovered, but the number of dead from the poisoned drugs indicated they were not afraid to kill lots of people.

After the usual White House security checks, Clement was taken directly into the oval office. President Forrest greeted him at the door with his usual firm handshake.

"Good to see you, Director. Please make yourself comfortable." Forrest gestured for him to sit on the couch in the middle of the room.

"Thank you, Mr. President." As Clement took a seat on the sofa, he scanned the room's windows, looking for possible bullet impacts. That wasn't likely, as the office was completely shielded from public view.

"If you're looking for bullet holes, there aren't any. The bullets hit another part of the building. The Secret Service had the damaged windows replaced the next day. They are extremely efficient and serious men... I can tell you. Those agents whisked me out of here seconds after the alarms went off." Forrest sat in a wing chair across from Clement.

"The kind of excitement one never needs, Mr. President."

"To be sure. Okay, I suppose we can dispense with the chit-chat. Bring me up to speed on my missing department heads, and the poison drug conspiracy... the Gadsden Council."

"They appear to be connected, sir."

"Really? How so?" Forrest asked. Clement explained what he knew about the drone videos, the direction the vans carrying the cabinet heads had headed, and the former and current military people involved.

"This is huge, Mr. President. The people behind the kidnappings are most likely behind the drug deaths. There are many people involved. We think approximately 250, based on our communication intercepts. When their encrypted messages cross to non-encrypted lines, we get an opening for a wiretap. Unfortunately, there aren't many opportunities to tap. I have over 20 FBI agents under investigation who we suspect are involved in the conspiracy. I can't be sure the agents doing the investigating aren't involved themselves."

"What do you think these people want?" Forrest said.

"I would say they want you to resign from office. They are using the false documents and emails about the poisoned drugs to start a popular revolt. I guess they expect you to leave for the good of the country..., whether you're guilty or not. If they can't force change that way, I believe they may use military force."

"A military coup?" Forrest laughed. "In America? Impossible! The government had nothing to do with those drug deaths."

"I know, sir, but convincing the public is not easy. Your administration is under suspicion, and any proof the administration provides will be considered suspect from the outset. The network polls show the majority of Americans believe the government is involved in the murders. I would have to say a coup is possible, Mr. President."

"How can we stop them, Brad. And how do we get my kidnapped people back?"

"We can start rounding people up and charge them with conspiracy, treason, trespassing..., whatever we can think of. We can lock them up under the anti-terrorism laws, and hold them indefinitely as enemy combatants. As for getting your people back, there hasn't been a ransom demand, and I'd have been surprised if there had been. The kidnappings obviously didn't go as planned. What would be the point of kidnapping only three? They must have planned to grab all the cabinet members, and failed because our security alert went out so fast," Clement said.

"Thank God the others weren't taken too," Forrest said. He thought for a few seconds.

"Are you serious about just rounding people up and charging them as enemy combatants? Send them to Guantanamo?"

"Arrests would stop them in their tracks, sir. The Canadians did it in the 1960's."

"This isn't Canada..., and what about the constitution? Do we throw it in a drawer until we feel safe again?"

"Well..."

"That was a rhetorical question, Director."

"Of course, sir. We would not arrest anyone without a warrant. Their constitutional rights and access to due process, in most cases, would be protected," Clement said. Forrest looked at his watch.

"Director, I have another appointment, and then I want to discuss this with you further. Would you mind waiting outside?"

"Not at all, sir." As Director Clement left, he saw Senator Bacster standing by the door, briefcase in hand, waiting to enter. Clement noticed Bacster looked nervous. He was fidgeting with the lock on his case.

"Thank you for asking to see me, Mr. President. I was about to ask for an appointment when your secretary called my office," Bacster said cordially, as he entered the oval office.

"Really, Senator? Come in and have a seat. We have a lot to discuss," Forrest said.

Chapter 43

Stafford and Hernandez were sitting in the back of the SUV, with the two guards sitting up front. The drive to the U.S. border wouldn't take long. When the car was about ten minutes away, the driver pulled over and stopped in front of a small grocery store.

"Hector, I'm thirsty," the driver said to the other guard. "Go get a couple of sodas for us." Hector looked at the driver with contempt, and didn't move.

"What do I look like to you Miguel, your maid? Go buy your own soda."

"All right, Hector, I wouldn't want anyone to think you were my maid. Stay here with the car then." Hector crossed his arms over his chest and glared at the driver.

"Señor Stafford, would you like to stretch your legs?" Miguel said. Stafford got the hint.

"Sure, I could use a soda and a stretch. Frank, how about you?" Stafford made a low hand signal for Hernandez to stay put.

"No thanks, I'll stay here." Hernandez said. He was curious, but followed Stafford's lead.

The driver and Stafford got out and went in the store. They saw a drink cooler in the back of the store, and headed for it. As they walked, Miguel handed Stafford a folded piece of paper. On the paper was a local phone number, a bank name, an account number, and the words Argentina, and Dallas.

"What's this?" Stafford asked.

"A friend asked me to give that to you. If you want something to happen to my employer, you call that number. If you want him delivered to the border, you say Argentina. They will tell you where and when to meet them. If you want him to disappear forever, you say Dallas. All this for a price. You understand?"

"What price?"

"Ten million dollars would be a bargain either way. Half after you call, and the other half afterward," Miguel said.

"Why would you want to help us to get your... employer?" Stafford said. He didn't want to say Roja's name out loud. He looked left and right to see if anyone was close enough to hear. No one was near, but they were being watched by two customers and the cashier.

"This has nothing to do with you. My employer has many enemies, but their pockets are not as full of money as your uncle's." Stafford nodded, and tucked the paper into his pants pocket. The driver picked out two sodas and paid for them. They went out and climbed back into the car.

No one said anything for the rest of the drive to the Paso del Norte bridge crossing at the border. Stafford and Hernandez were dropped off at the pedestrian lanes. As soon as they had closed the doors, the car drove away.

They started walking toward the U. S. side, and Customs processing. There were about a dozen lanes open, but before they got to them, they saw a U.S. Customs officer, who was observing the arriving pedestrians for anything unusual. He was asking a few questions, and looking at border crossing cards and passports. Mainly, he was waving people into the various lanes for more processing before they were allowed to enter the United States.

Another Customs officer stood nearby with his hands on his hips. He wore the blue CBP rough duty uniform known as BDU, for battle dress uniform. The name GARRITY was stitched over his shirt pocket. He was looking directly at Stafford and Hernandez. He spotted them because they were out of place in the crowd. He waved them over to him with his left hand, and kept his right hand on his weapon.

"Come over here please, gentlemen," Officer Garrity said.

Smart... he's keeping his weapon safe in this crowd... and ready to draw if he needs to.

Stafford knew what he and Hernandez must look like. Neither had shaved in two days. They had slept in their clothes, their hair was dirty and tossled, and Stafford's face was red and swollen where he got punched.

They walked confidently over to Garrity with their credentials in their hands.

"You two have a rough night in town?" Garrity asked, smiling.

"You could say that," Stafford said. They showed him their credentials. He held each of the credentials in his left hand, reading them, but still kept one hand on his weapon. He recognized the credentials as genuine.

"We've been searching for an Agent named Hernandez. Is that you?"

"Yep, that's me. You can call your supervisor and tell him I'm here."

"And I'm gonna need access to a secure phone line and fax machine... like right now!... and no parades okay? We have time sensitive information to pass on," Stafford said.

"Roger that," Garrity said. He made a call on his radio.

Stafford immediately knew from the words he was using on the radio, that Garrity was prior military. No wasted words. Only facts, calmly, quickly, and accurately transmitted. Garrity motioned for them to follow him, as he repeated the messages Stafford and Hernandez had given him. In his radio earpiece, Garrity received authorization to escort Stafford and Hernandez to a more secure Customs area.

"Roger that..., *on* the way," Garrity said into his microphone as he walked.

"Were you in an armored unit in the service?" Stafford asked. Officer Garrity turned halfway around, but kept walking.

"Yeah..., how did you guess? Were you armor too?"

"No, just a good guess... the way you said *on the way*. I'm a former Ranger... Iraq and Afghanistan," Stafford said with a smile.

"*Hoo-ah!*" Garrity said in Army fashion. "Welcome home, sir!"

"Thanks," Stafford said. He looked at Hernandez, who was frowning slightly, shaking his head in disbelief.

"One day you'll appreciate people like Garrity and me, Frank." Hernandez stopped frowning and stuck his right hand out. Stafford took it, a little puzzled at Hernandez' gesture.

"I'm sorry, Ben. I already appreciate people like you." He slapped Stafford lightly on the chest with his left hand as they continued to shake as they walked. Frank had a mountain of gratitude rising in his chest.

"*Hoo-ah,* Frank. I told you I wouldn't leave you hanging. Here we are back in the U-S-A, with all our fingers and toes. Welcome home," Stafford said with a smile. He squeezed Hernandez' right hand tighter, and laid his left hand on top, in a gesture of sincerity. Tears welled in Hernandez' eyes.

"*Woo-wah!*" Hernandez said with a smile. "Thanks for coming after me, man."

"Nice try, Frank... and you're welcome."

Chapter 44

Director Clement was waiting outside the oval office. He heard the President's assistant call his name. He stood and looked at the woman who had called him. He thought he was about to be shown back into the oval office, but remembered Senator Bacster had not come out yet.

"Director, your Assistant, Ms. Davies, is on the phone. I'll transfer the call to the phone in the ante-room." Clement knew it had to be important for Helen Davies to call the White House to reach him. The phone on the table buzzed, and he answered it.

"Director Clement speaking. What's the emergency?"

"I'm sorry to bother you, Director. Customs Commissioner Gomez called a few minutes ago. He sounded very excited. He said he had evidence that could help close a case you two have been working on. He knew you were at the White House and thought I might have a way to contact you. When I told him you could not be reached, he got so excited I thought he was going to have a heart attack. He was quite adamant, so I thought it best to call you right away."

"You did the right thing, Helen. I'll call him as soon as I get back to the office."

"Director, I think you should call him right now," Helen said. Clement was about to remind her that she worked for him, and not the other way around, when he heard someone shout.

"CLEMENT!" The man's voice was loud enough that a Secret Service Agent, as well as Clement, spun around to make sure everything was okay. It was Commissioner Gomez, clutching a folder, thick with papers.

"I'm glad I got here in time! Hang up the phone, man. I've got something you have to see!" Gomez said, as he strode across the room to Clement. He stood next to Clement, waiting for him to hang up.

"Helen..., there's no need for me to call him; he's here. Clement hung up, and faced Gomez.

"For crying out loud, Gomez. You couldn't wait for me to finish my appointment with the President?"

"No, I'm sorry. This can't wait. Take a look at this stuff. No wait... you better sit down first."

Gomez pushed Clement, gently but firmly, into a nearby chair, and handed him the folder. Gomez pulled up another chair, and sat directly in front of Clement. As Clement read the contents of the folder, Gomez filled him in on what Stafford had told him over the secure line from El Paso. The notes, and what Stafford told him, were enough to turbocharge the Gadsden Council investigation.

Clement was amazed. Not only had Roja kept meticulous notes of his personal meetings with General Miner, he also recorded all their telephone conversations onto a disk. Stafford and Hernandez had listened to it, and summarized it to Gomez. If all that wasn't enough, Roja also had his agents in the United States track Miner and some of his lieutenants for several months. Roja's men discovered where his cocaine was being shipped to, and who Miner's major dealers were, all over the country. There was enough evidence to ask for Federal arrest warrants for everyone they could identify.

"Not so stupid letting Stafford go to Mexico, huh?" Gomez asked.

Before Clement had a chance to fully appreciate all he had read and heard, the door of the oval office opened, and President Forrest appeared in the doorway. He saw Clement and Gomez sitting together in the next room. They stood up.

"Director Clement, would you come in please? there's something you need to hear."

"Mr. President, there's some news you need to hear as well. I personally received it from Customs Commissioner Gomez just seconds ago." Clement gestured to Gomez to follow him as he walked to the President. Gomez hesitated.

"In that case Commissioner Gomez, would you come in, too?" Forrest said.

"Of course, Mr. President," Gomez said, with a lump in his throat.

President Forrest walked back into the oval office, leaving the door open. As Gomez and Clement followed him in, a Secret Service Agent reached in and shut the door behind them. President Forrest waited for Gomez and then offered his hand.

"I don't believe I've met you before, have I?"

"No, Mr. President. I was a political appointment of your predecessor. You decided to keep me on when you became president. Thank you very much for your faith in me, sir," Gomez said.

"Yes. I remember that now. I kept you on because you were doing such a good job. You still are... obviously."

"Thank you, Mr. President."

Forrest walked in front of his desk, and sat on it, keeping one foot on the floor. He crossed his arms over his chest. He wasn't wearing a suit-coat, but did have a tie on.

Senator Bacster was sitting on the couch in the middle of the room. His eyes were red. Every so often Bacster would sniff and wipe his eyes with a handkerchief.

"Gentlemen, Senator Bacster's integrity has been compromised by General Miner. He won't say how, and I don't really want to know, but the Senator's had a change of heart. He just told me about Miner's plan to take over the government. Isn't that amazing? That's what all this is about. Miner hoped to make me a villain, and himself a savior. The American people would accept a military coup to get rid of me. It's simply FANTASTIC!" he shouted. Gomez looked at the door, expecting a Secret Service Agent to come in.

"Senator Bacster said he planned on killing General Miner himself, but quickly realized he didn't know where he was. He said he thought about killing himself too, but lacked the strength." Forrest stared at the Bacster.

"Bacster, I'm glad you didn't kill yourself, but I have little tolerance for traitors," Forrest said. Bacster winced at the word traitor, but said nothing.

"The Senator also told me Miner is planning a major terror attack of some kind. He plans on making it appear it was the work of al Qaida. It's supposed to happen before four o'clock tomorrow," Forrest said.

"Well, go ahead Senator. Tell it all again, won't you?"

Forrest was visibly angry. His face had a pink flush. He unfolded his arms and placed his hands on the edge of his desk, gripping it so tightly Clement and Gomez heard his knuckles pop.

"No, better yet I'll tell it." Forrest repeated what Bacster had told him about Miner's plan of attack on the presidency, and the press conference

Bacster was supposed to give after the terror attack, calling for the removal of America's leaders.

"Did I cover everything, Senator?" Forrest let go of the desk top, and folded his arms back over his chest. Bacster simply nodded.

Clement and Gomez were waiting to see what would happen next. Neither man was as shocked as Forrest was. He noticed their calmness as he looked at their faces.

"I take it from your *lack* of reaction, that you already knew about this plot, and didn't inform me?" he asked. He was about to turn his displeasure upon both of them. Clement immediately moved to defuse the situation.

"Sir, we did not know about Senator Bacster's involvement, or the impending attack, but I do have other information to give you. May I suggest we discuss it without Senator Bacster being present?" Clement looked at Bacster.

"Quite right," Forrest said. "Senator, would you excuse us please?... unless there's another felony you'd like to confess to?"

Senator Bacster looked at the floor. Even though Forrest loathed what Bacster had done, he respected his courage to come forward and tell him about it in person.

"I'm sorry, Senator. Thank you for telling me about this. I know it was difficult for you."

"Thank you, Mr. President. This may not mean much, but I am sorry. I'll do whatever I can to help." He stood to leave.

"Senator," Clement said, "do you have any idea what the target of Miner's attack is going to be?"

"I'm sorry..., no. I have no idea."

"In the interest of our investigation, we are not going to arrest you at this time. We will still need your complete cooperation. Would you make yourself available for an interview by our agents later today?" Senator Bacster paused for a moment, weighing his choices. He had none.

"Thank you. You will have my complete cooperation of course. I'll be at home, writing my resignation. You can find me there. Good day, gentlemen." Bacster left the office without saying another word.

"All right Director, what is the new information?" Forrest asked.

"May I use your desk, sir?" Clement said.

"Certainly." Forrest said. Clement opened the folder and spread the contents out for him to see.

"Commissioner Gomez, please tell The President what you told me,"

Gomez was surprised. He expected Clement to take the ball and run with it, making it appear the FBI had been the agency coordinating the intelligence. Gomez brought the information to Clement because the FBI had the most influence with all branches of government, and he thought they were in the best position to exploit the information quickly. That influence came from the FBI's history of investigating espionage and terrorism. Today it was teamwork, because it had to be.

Gomez explained the documents, and the source of the information on them. There were many photocopies of hand-written notes. The notes listed every meeting Roja had with General Miner over a four year period. There was also a list of military equipment received from Miner, and the amount of cocaine Roja had exchanged for it.

Not only had Miner imported tons of cocaine into the country for use in his murder conspiracy, he had armed most of the drug cartels in Mexico. As a result, Mexico had been in a state of near civil war for almost as long as Miner had been shipping equipment south.

Gomez added that the source of the information was reliable, as far as HSI Agent Ben Stafford was concerned. He explained how Stafford had gone to Mexico searching for a kidnapped ICE Agent, how Stafford had made contact with Roja, and convinced Roja to cooperate.

"Did Stafford find the missing Agent?" President Forrest asked.

"Yes, sir," Gomez said proudly. "He found and gained the release of Agent Hernandez, who was his partner before this began."

"Stafford sounds like a good man."

"He is, Mr. President. And I think Director Clement will agree that there is more than enough information here to start taking Miner's organization apart." Clement nodded in agreement.

"Then please do, gentlemen, and when Agent Stafford returns, I'd like to meet him." Gomez smiled and straightened up from leaning over the desk.

"He should be back tonight, Mr. President, but I know we're all going to be pretty busy for the next few days," Gomez said.

"Then whenever this is over and we can put our schedules together, Commissioner. Also, gentlemen, I don't have to tell you how important it will be to keep the public informed about the arrests you make. We've got to calm things down, and get the truth out there. We need the public on our side again, before more people get killed."

"Absolutely, Mr. President. We will be making regular press announcements after we begin, but we have to be cautious. We don't want the suspects scattering like cockroaches when the lights come on," Clement said.

"An appropriate analogy, Director. Let's go step on some cockroaches. On that note, you have my authority to proceed with the rescue operation, when you identify the location the cabinet heads are being held."

"Thank you, sir," Clement said.

Forrest was smiling as they finished the meeting. He thanked them, and shook their hands as he walked with them to the door.

"One last thought," he said. "You've given me hope that we can get the country through this in one piece, but I don't think I need to remind you that the clock is ticking. Every day the situation grows more and more serious. I may have to call out the military to maintain order."

"You may not be able to trust the military, sir," Clement said.

"I may not have a choice."

"We'll work as quickly as we can, sir. It was an honor to meet you. I'm sorry I barged over here like I did," Gomez said.

"That's all right. The information you had was important. We'll be seeing each other again soon, I'm sure. Commissioner, Director, God be with us all," Forrest said.

Gomez and Clement left and walked quietly down the hallway together. They were thinking about what they had to do next.

"I think we should start at the top. Let's bring in Miner. If we chop the snake's head off, the rest will die," Gomez said.

"That's a good idea," Clement said, "but it's easier said than done. Nobody has seen Miner in weeks. I know we would find him eventually, but *eventually* isn't going to be fast enough. I have a bad feeling about tomorrow morning. It's likely more people are going to die." Gomez agreed.

They continued walking until they were outside the White House. They could plainly see the extra police and Secret Service officers patrolling inside the perimeter fence. There were no demonstrators. It was strangely quiet.

"Why not use Bacster to set up some kind of meeting with Miner?" Gomez asked. Clement smiled.

"That was what I was thinking. So simple. All I have to do now is talk to the U. S. Attorney, get a warrant for Miner's arrest, get a wiretap request approved, contact the Air Force to see where those drones came from, and get our Hostage Rescue Team ready to rescue the cabinet members from wherever they are," Clement said. Gomez stopped, then started walking again.

"*That* was the rescue mission Forrest was authorizing?"

"Afraid so."

"I'm glad I'm not you," Gomez said.

"Thanks. You're the second person to tell me that today. Oh, and I think I better put in a request to NSA for some help with those group internet video chat wiretaps."

"Now you're talking," Gomez said.

"We've got to find Miner," Clement said.

"*We* is an important word, Gomez said. "I don't want to deflate anyone's balloon, but I have a letter saying DHS will be the lead in the investigation of the Gadsden Council, and anything arising from that investigation belongs to DHS as well. You got a copy of that letter, I'm sure. Frankly, I was surprised you didn't make a lot of noise about it. I know being lead agency on an investigation as far reaching as this, is a big bite... a bite that's too big for one agency to chew. Let's work together and do what each of our agencies does best."

"Well said. I knew you were in over your head when I got that letter. I knew you'd need our help. This isn't a big deal for me. I'm a political appointee like you. When the political winds change direction, we'll be gone, and so what? That being said, I'm willing to share assets. Let's do the best job we can and get these guys."

"Glad to hear you say that," Gomez said.

"By the way, you wouldn't have a couple of extra Customs Blackhawks sitting around would you? Half of our choppers are down with mechanical problems, and I have a feeling we're going to be heading into the mountains of West Virginia," Clement said. Gomez grinned.

"I believe I might have one I can spare. Of course I'd need to have some of my people go along and make sure nobody puts bullet holes in it. In the meantime, why not go public with all we know about Miner and his conspiracy? It would take pressure off the White House, and could flush some of these birds out in the open," Gomez said.

"You're not concerned with scattering the cockroaches, I take it?" Clement asked.

It'll be a trade off. We may lose a few of them, but we can regain public trust," Gomez said.

Clement nodded and pulled his phone off his belt. Gomez could hear it buzzing, even in silent mode. Clement pressed a button and answered.

"Director Clement." He listened for a short time and said, "I'll be back in less than ten minutes. Notify the HRT."

"We got a break. The vans used to grab the cabinet members have been found," Clement said. "We may need your Blackhawks soon, if we get better information."

"Right," Gomez said. Clement thought for a few seconds.

"That's a good idea about going public. Some people won't believe what we say, but most will. At the least, it will take some wind out of Miner's sails. We should also alert the nation to the possibility a terrorist attack might be imminent," Clement said.

"I'll call the DHS Secretary when I get back, and brief him on what we know. He can follow up with a call to you for more information if he needs to," Gomez said. Clement nodded.

They started walking again, but at a quicker pace.

Gomez opened his phone and punched the number to the Special Situations room. The officer on duty answered.

"This is Commissioner Gomez. Have the Director of Air Operations call me. Next call HSI Intelligence Supervisor Boyer, and tell him to call me." The situation room duty officer confirmed his instructions, and Gomez hung up.

"I wasn't joking about having some of my people go with your team when you go after the kidnappers. I have two men in mind that I know we can count on," Gomez said.

"Okay, Eduardo? Your first name is Eduardo, right?"

"Right, but you can call me Ed."

"And you can call me Brad. An FBI regional tactical unit will be assigned to one of your helicopters, crewed by your people. How does that sound?"

Sounds okay to me, but they're going where I tell the helicopter to go," Gomez said.

"Naturally," Clement said. "I'm also going to send a couple of our agents to Bacster's home ASAP, if that's okay with you."

"Of course," Gomez said.

"We may be able to get more useful information from him. I really want to see if Miner will meet him somewhere. I'll be calling you later, as soon as I find out what information we have on the vans," Clement said.

"Okay, Brad. I'll be at my office. I'm going to be working on what to say at the press conference. Let's get arrest warrants for everybody we've got names for, and start bringing them in."

"I'll can take care of most of that. I'll supply you with a list of the names as soon as I can put it together," Clement said. They were at their vehicles. They shook hands.

"God help us," Gomez said.

"Amen to that, brother," Clement said.

They got in their cars and raced back to their offices. There was a lot to do before tomorrow.

Chapter 45

A government car from the ICE El Paso office picked up Stafford and Hernandez. Supervisory Agent Perez, anxious to hear the details of their activities in Mexico, drove the car himself. He peppered Stafford with questions.

"You'll have to wait and read my official report," Stafford said. "I'm tired and I don't want to talk about it now. How about taking us to our hotel so we can make some phone calls and collect our things?"

Hernandez would have nodded in agreement, but his head was lolling from side to side on the top of the back seat. He was sound asleep.

"Sorry, but all your belongings were removed from your hotel rooms and taken to the ICE office. You'll have to check in at the hotel again if you want to stay overnight."

"Great... didn't think we were coming back, huh?"

"Nothing like that. We didn't know how long you two would be gone..., so there's no reason to run up a big hotel bill," Perez lied.

Wrote us off. Checked us out of the hotel and started writing our obituaries.

They arrived at the ICE office and went inside. The agents in the office stopped what they were doing, and came over to shake Stafford's and Hernandez' hands, something that Perez hadn't bothered to do. After the agents found out there weren't going to be any war stories, they wandered back to their cubicles.

Perez showed them their personal things, which he had stored in his office. Hernandez started looking through his bags, making sure everything was there. He pulled out a change of clothes and his shaving kit.

"I suppose you'll be continuing your investigation of the Dupree murder, after you've had a chance to get your reports submitted," Perez said.

"Negative. Hernandez and I have been ordered back to Washington."

"You can't walk away from an investigation like that," Perez said. "You two were sent here to..."

"Besides," Stafford interrupted with a frown, "Roja told me plenty about Dupree's murder. I just have to build a case around what I found out. Which reminds me, I need a chain of custody form for the documents Roja gave me, are they still in the same place?"

"Well, orders are orders. We'll be perfectly okay here without you," Perez said as he stroked his face. His eyes were darting left and right, and he was blinking rapidly. Stafford watched him fidget.

I can read you like a book. You know plenty. You're going down.

Hernandez stopped what he was doing and watched Stafford, wondering what he was trying to do. Roja hadn't told him anything about the Dupree murder. Hernandez looked at Perez, saw his nervousness and realized Stafford was baiting him.

"We're only going to be gone for a week or so. We'll be coming back to wrap things up. Who's been leading the investigation while we've been gone? I want to tell them where to concentrate their efforts," Stafford said.

Perez stopped stroking his face. He didn't want to send Stafford any signs of nervousness, but it was too late.

"Agent Wellesly has been the Lead Agent while you were away," Perez said.

Hernandez dropped his things on top of his open bag. "I'll tell him you want to talk to him," he said, as he walked to Perez's desk and picked up the phone. He punched a couple of buttons. "Oh never mind, I'll tell him personally. I'll bring some chain of custody forms for you too." Hernandez walked out of the office and closed the door behind him. Perez and Stafford were alone.

"So, what did Roja tell you about Dupree's murder?" Perez asked.

"He said you did it. General Miner told him about it," Stafford said, putting his hands on his hips. "Dupree was a liability. He was weak, and talking too much. It was too risky to let him keep shooting his mouth off. Miner ordered it, and you carried it out."

"Well, why in the world would Roja tell *you* about it? For all the good it would do him! Yeah, I did it, but you'll have a hard time proving it. It would be my word against yours, and a Mexican drug dealer's," Perez said grinning.

"You know, I always knew you were an idiot. What you *should* have said was... I don't know what you're talking about. Why in the world would you admit to murder?" Stafford said, and shook his head.

"Roja didn't know anything about Dupree's murder, but I appreciate your confession," Stafford said.

"It's still my word against yours! And you can't prove anything!" Perez said.

"I'm going to make putting you away my number one priority," Stafford said.

Perez's office door flew open and banged against the wall, revealing a crowd of agents, including Hernandez. Several of the agents stepped into the office. Agent Wellesly was in front of the group.

"Sorry to interrupt, but I think we've heard enough," Wellesly said. In Wellesly's right hand, held close to his right hip, was his SIG .40 caliber pistol, which he pointed at Perez.

"Turn around and place your hands on the wall," Wellesly said. Perez, open mouthed, complied silently. Wellesly searched, disarmed, and handcuffed Perez. He turned Perez around so they were face to face, and began to read him his Miranda rights.

"You might be a little premature on that arrest," Stafford said. Hernandez walked around behind Perez's desk.

"Uh-oh, looks like I pressed the public address button by mistake. I'm afraid everybody heard what you two were talking about," Hernandez said. He reached down and punched the button, turning the public address system off. "I love the sound of handcuffs going on someone."

"You sneaky devil you," Stafford said.

"Thank you very much. I think you're starting to wear off on me," Hernandez crossed his arms over his chest and looked smug.

"That might not necessarily be a good thing. Let's clean up and get out of here."

"Roger that... on the way," Hernandez said grinning.

"Hoo-ahh!" Stafford said, grinning back. He watched Perez being escorted out of the office, and then leaned over his carry-on bag. "Honey, did you remember to pack my socks?" Stafford said. He began whistling *'Dixie.'*

Hernandez shook his head in wonder, shrugged, and began whistling *'The Yellow Rose of Texas.'* Stafford stopped whistling Dixie and began whistling 'The Yellow Rose of Texas' with Hernandez.

The other agents looked at each other, shrugged, and went to work making the notifications that their supervisor had been arrested for murder. It was not going to be a positive news day for ICE.

Chapter 46

Stafford and Hernandez cleaned up, and made airline reservations in record time. Before they left the ICE office, both men recharged their cell phones. Hernandez used the office phone and called Boyer, who gave him the phone number to where his family was in hiding. Hernandez talked to his wife and daughter for so long he almost caused them to miss their departing flight.

They had to be escorted through the security screening, and were soon on the plane heading to Dallas for the connection to D.C. They landed in Dallas on time, but had to change planes.

They found the next departure gate, and while they waited to re-board, had time to make more phone calls. Hernandez called his wife again.

Stafford called his parents, but got their answering machine. He left a message saying he was okay, and would call them later. Next he called Beth's desk phone, remembering her phone number by heart, and got her voice mail.

Stafford listened to her recording, telling everyone that she couldn't come to the phone, and to leave a number. It felt good to hear her voice again, even if it was only a recording. He smiled as he pictured her sitting at her desk, talking on the phone. He checked his watch, and left a message telling her when he would be in D.C.

I miss her. I hope she misses me too. I know she was praying for me. I wonder how it would have turned out if she hadn't prayed? The same, for all I know.

He listened to the airline employee recite the boarding instructions. She spoke too fast, and with little feeling. She had said it too many times before. Her monotone voice reminded him of the hissing sound of tires on the highway. She was a small annoyance on his way home. After

Hernandez and Stafford had boarded and were in their side by side seats, the flight attendants made more announcements about safety.

"I wonder why they bother with these announcements? Nobody pays attention. If we crash, there isn't much hope," Stafford said. Hernandez nodded.

"Did you hear about that plane that crashed in Japan a few years ago? It flew in circles while it lost altitude. It took about 45 minutes for it to crash, and the passengers had time to write letters to their families. Imagine the panic. What would you do if you knew you only had forty-five minutes left to live, Frank?" Hernandez thought about it.

"That's a good question. For all we know, this plane is going to crash on takeoff. Probability says it won't, but it's possible. I suppose what one should do, is always live as if today was your last day on earth."

"Oh, baloney, Frank. Nobody would get anything done if everybody lived that way. We'd be doing nothing but running around hugging each other and crying, or getting drunk and chasing women," Stafford chuckled. "Besides, we've been through too much already. You and I are going to die sitting in wheelchairs in some retirement home."

"What we've been through has nothing to do with what might happen later," Hernandez said.

"I don't want to get biblical on you, Frank, but I've cheated death many times. I could tell you some stories. I don't think God saved me so I could die in some plane crash. I think God still has something important he wants me to do."

"You're not getting biblical on me. In fact I'd say it isn't biblical at all. You don't have a get-out-of-a-pointless-death-free card because you didn't die in Afghanistan. On top of that, you may have already done what God wanted you to do. In that case, dying in a plane crash might be your reward."

"Getting killed in a plane crash is my reward?" Stafford couldn't believe his ears. He had never thought of going to heaven as a reward.

"I think you've said enough, Frank." And in fact, Frank *had* said enough.

They spoke little for the rest of the flight to Washington. They landed, gathered their things, deplaned, and called Boyer. He told them they were needed at work, and to come straight there. They shared a taxi to headquarters. On the way, Hernandez tried to explain his comments on the plane.

"Listen Ben, I hope you didn't misunderstand me. I heard you talk to Roja about Jesus. I figured you felt like other Christians I know; that to be absent from the body is to be in the presence of the Lord. For a Christian, dying means going to heaven, and heaven means being with Jesus. What could be better than that?"

"You're probably right, Frank. I'm new at this, and I should leave the God talk to people who know the Bible better than I do. I take it you're a Christian?"

"I was raised without much religion. I believe in God. What I know, I discovered on my own. My mom and dad never went to church. Sometimes we watched Sunday church services on television. We never discussed anything that the preacher said, unless we were making fun of him for talking in tongues or healing people. My dad said it was all fake, and all they wanted was money. Mom and Dad divorced when I was eleven. Mother told me about what right and wrong was, and that God was watching me all the time." Hernandez was quiet then, remembering the Sundays in front of the television when he was a boy.

"Sounds a little like being at my house when I was growing up," Stafford said.

"You said your dad died in a hunting accident. That must have been hard for you, Ben. After my parents divorced, my dad came to visit me once a week. But you didn't have a dad to guide you when you were growing up."

"That's about it," Stafford said.

Stafford's mind wandered to his childhood memories. He remembered his dad's funeral, and how his mother had cried so hard she couldn't stand up. He cried because he had hurt his mom, and he felt so bad about hurting his dad. He tried to comfort his mother, but he was too young to know what to say or do. He held onto her hand by the grave, and they threw dirt on the top of his father's coffin. His mind came back to the present when Hernandez spoke again.

"If you don't mind me asking, what kind of accident did your father have? Did his gun accidentally go off while he was climbing over a fence or something?"

Stafford remembered the blue of the sky, and the cool wind that was blowing the day his father died. They were hunting deer, but would have been happy with a squirrel. The bullet hit his father in the head, and he fell without making a sound. Ben stood looking at his father. His dad was lying face down in the leaves. He knew he was never going to get up again. He dropped his dad's rifle and ran as fast as he could back to the truck. A nearby hunter saw the panic and fear on Ben's face, and talked to him to find out what was wrong. Then there were police cars and an ambulance.

They took his father away in the ambulance, and the police took him home to his mother. She hugged him close and cried a long time.

"I shot my father, and I don't want to talk about it again," Stafford said.

Hernandez didn't know what to say. He wanted to know more. He assumed it was an accident, that somehow Stafford's gun had gone off and hit his father. That was the only explanation Hernandez allowed himself.

After arriving at headquarters and paying for the taxi, the two men made their way to Supervisor Boyer's office, where he was waiting for them.

"Welcome back," he said, and shook their hands.

"I'd love to hear all about your adventures, but the Commissioner is waiting for you upstairs."

"It's deja vu all over again, eh chief?" Stafford said, sounding like his old self.

"He's waiting for *both* of you," Boyer said.

"*Both* of me?" Stafford said.

"Are you okay?" Boyer said.

"I guess I am, but I do feel kind of goofy," Stafford said.

"Goofier than usual?" Hernandez asked. Stafford ignored him.

"You be sure to get something to eat later," Boyer said. It was only then that Stafford realized his body clock was messed up. He was hungry, and it wasn't time to eat. It was just as well, he didn't have time.

They walked out into the hallway and headed for the elevator. Stafford started whistling '*Jesus Loves Me*'. Hernandez and Boyer both started to say something, remembered it was Stafford, and kept quiet. After the elevator ride, and the usual security procedures to get to the Commissioner, they met a very tired Eduardo Gomez.

"Welcome back, Hernandez, Stafford, Supervisor Boyer. It's good to see you all." He shook hands with all of them.

"Sir, if you don't mind me saying so, you look like I feel," Stafford said. The Commissioner smiled.

"Is that good or bad?"

"That's not good, sir. You look tired is all," Stafford said.

"That's because I *am* tired, and that is *not* all. I've got another assignment for you two."

"Oh, Lord," Hernandez said. The conversation stopped and everyone looked at Hernandez, who realized he should have kept quiet.

"I haven't told you what it is yet, but you don't want it whatever it is, huh Hernandez? You want to go take a nap?" Gomez said.

Hernandez thought quickly, snapped to attention and said, "I'm ready to do whatever is good for America, SIR!" They all burst out laughing, including Hernandez.

"At ease, Frank," Stafford said, grinning.

"Very good, Hernandez. That's the spirit!" Gomez laughingly said as he slapped Hernandez on the back. Stafford and Boyer slapped him around too. Hernandez grinned and shuddered from the pounding.

"What did I volunteer for?" Hernandez said.

"A helicopter assault to rescue the cabinet heads from a bunch of armed kidnappers," Gomez said. Hernandez put both hands on top of his head.

"Oh, Lord," he said again.

Everyone burst out laughing again, except for Hernandez.

Chapter 47

Clement was true to his word. Arrest warrants were obtained, and a list of the wanted persons was sent to Gomez' office. Clement followed with a phone call to Gomez informing him they had just received good intelligence pinpointing the location of the missing cabinet members. As predicted, they were being held at a remote location in West Virginia. Gomez and Clement agreed they had to act immediately.

Local law enforcement agencies were notified, and a large contingent of FBI and West Virginia State Police were sent to the suspected location. The FBI Hostage Rescue Team was in route, and would coordinate with the local authorities when they arrived. The Customs Blackhawk, with Stafford, Hernandez, and the FBI tactical team aboard, would orbit the area, and land if their assistance was needed.

Hernandez and Stafford didn't have time to rest or eat before they prepared for the flight. They went to Stafford's office and were met by a crowd of curious agents, who wanted to hear about their time in Mexico. They told them a small part of what happened, but Stafford felt there was something pulling at his heart. He broke off the conversation, and he and Hernandez headed to the food court downstairs.

Hernandez left Stafford and went to get something to eat. Stafford went to the auditorium where Beth had spoken to him about Jesus. He sat in the same seat as before. He brushed God aside then, but now felt a need to pray. He prayed as he had never prayed before. Prayers of thanks for God's protection during the time he was in Mexico. Praising God for the love, mercy, and grace that was raining down on him. Prayers for safety for himself, Hernandez, and all the people involved during the coming raid.

He thought about Beth, and wanted her to be there praying with him. He smiled when he remembered they had not been on a date yet. He promised himself to correct that. After food and prayers, Hernandez and Stafford were on their way to rendezvous with the Customs Blackhawk that would take them to West Virginia.

There were special rules for flying over the District of Columbia since September 11th. A helicopter full of armed men made a few FAA people nervous. There was no emergency in this instance, just urgency. It was decided the helicopter would meet them outside Arlington, Virginia, at the police department helipad. As he and Stafford were ferried along in a government car, Hernandez thought about his family. The safe house was not far from where they were to meet the helicopter.

"Can't we take a short detour so I could see my family?" Hernandez said, as they pulled up to the helipad. He heard a helicopter flying overhead.

"Sorry, brother," Stafford said.

The helicopter landed, the door slid open, and a man stepped out and waved at them. He was making motions with his hands to stay low. Stafford and Hernandez made their way toward him.

"Do what I do!" Stafford yelled at Hernandez, as they got closer to the helicopters whirling blades.

Stafford bent over at the waist and moved to the helicopter. Hernandez, not seeing any obvious need, lowered his chin to his chest. The FBI tactical team was already waiting on board.

They climbed aboard, took their seats next to the tactical team, and were handed their gear; which included a portable radio, earplugs, and an earpiece for the tactical radio. They put on all their gear, including bullet proof vests with steel inserts, and buckled themselves in. Stafford put his radio earpiece in one ear, and his foam earplug in the other. If he had a flight helmet, he could have plugged in to talk to the crew chief, who was watching everything Stafford and Hernandez were doing. He gave Stafford and Hernandez a thumbs up after they were securely belted in, and pressed his intercom button to speak to the pilot.

"We're aboard and ready to go, sir."

"Roger that, chief." The blades spun faster, the helicopter lifted, and the nose dipped as the aircraft started to gain forward momentum and altitude. They flew off to the west. Stafford yelled so the crewman could hear him.

"HOW FAR WE GOING, CHIEF?"

The crew-chief yelled back, "WE'LL BE THERE IN ABOUT 30 MINUTES... GIVE OR TAKE A FEW. LOCAL YOKELS ARE ALREADY ON SITE WITH THE FEEBIES." Stafford nodded he understood, and leaned back to enjoy the flight, because nobody was shooting at him this time. Hernandez, who was sitting next to Stafford, motioned for Stafford to lean over so he could talk in his ear.

"Why did you duck? Those blades were too high to hit us." Stafford grinned slyly, and leaned back to speak into Hernandez' ear over the engine noise.

"I saw a guy get his head taken off by a rotor blade once. Very messy. Rotor wash from another chopper, or wind, pushed the blades down on him. Can't be too careful!" Hernandez' face went blank as he processed what Stafford had told him. He put one hand on top of his helmet. Stafford read his lips.

"Oh, Lord."

Stafford laughed, leaned back, and closed his eyes, listening to the familiar whine of the engines.

Chapter 48

The Commissioner's press briefing would be well attended. All the national networks were notified by the CBP press office of the place and time. They media was told only that an announcement of national importance was going to be made, and they were invited to hear it at the Reagan Building. The briefing would begin as soon as word was received that the kidnapped cabinet heads were safe.

Not far from Washington, General Miner sat in his command center, thinking about tomorrows attack. He was aware there had been arrests of about a dozen of his low level operatives. He knew that many of those arrested would cooperate with the government investigators. Having employees turn on you was a risk of having so many people involved, but his grand plan had demanded it. He needed foot soldiers, not generals.

Miner remembered the way Roja had dealt with disloyalty, with a bullet to the head. That sort of punishment gave people something to think about, but fear of death could not be the only way to motivate men. Patriotism, honor, glory, and the greater good was better motivation, at least Miner hoped they were.

But what Miner was using to motivate his men was a cheap imitation of patriotism and defending the constitution. Other men, in other times, were taught to think they had no right to question their orders. Everybody went along, and there was a sense of security in knowing you were not acting alone. Out of that thinking came Nazi concentration camps and Russian gulags, and the wholesale slaughter of innocent people in a dozen other countries. What Miner didn't understand, was that a man was responsible to God, his country, his family, and to himself, in that order. Right and wrong were not mysteries to be debated or discovered after the fact, by historians.

Miner's thoughts were interrupted by his aide, who entered his office without knocking.

"Sir, I got word only moments ago. The FBI hostage rescue team has been sent to the West Virginia holding point. They are probably there by now."

Miner stood up and stared at his aide. He knew that once the hostage location was known, there would be no way out for the men involved. His plan was about to come apart at the seams. He had considered the possibility the FBI might find one or two of the cabinet members if he had taken them all. When his men only managed to grab three, he knew his plan would ultimately fail. The only way for him to succeed would be for the people to be in general revolt, and that was not going to happen. Too few people had lost everything, and too many people had too much left to lose. He felt foolish for letting himself believe he could replace the executive branch of the government with himself as a benevolent military dictator. He was a proud man, and would not be disgraced in defeat.

"Get me whoever is in command at the hold point. We're not going to surrender without a fight," Miner said.

In West Virginia, the hold point Commander was watching the activity through the blinds over the living room window. His outlying guards were on the ground being handcuffed, and there appeared to be a man with a weapon behind every tree.

"What did they do, just drive up and ask them to lay down on the ground? Why did I bother to have men assigned outside if they were going to give up without firing a shot or using the radio?"

"Rich, you have a radio call from the big man himself. I guess he heard about the goings on up here."

Richard Colson was the Commander in charge of the hold point. His best friend, Davis Ball, whom he had met in the Army, held the radio out for him. Colson took the radio and made a face. Colson knew that whatever the old man had to say, it wasn't going to be good news for anybody, including the other men guarding the back of the house.

"This is the point Commander. Go ahead your message, Alpha One."

"Commander, we believe your location has been compromised. Advise your situation and if you can evacuate," Miner said. Colson keyed the radio to talk, but before he could say anything, an FBI Agent on a public address speaker answered the General's question for him. Colson kept the radio keyed so Miner could hear.

"ATTENTION IN THE HOUSE. THIS IS THE FBI. YOU ARE SURROUNDED. COME OUT WITH YOUR HANDS ON TOP OF

YOUR HEAD, AND YOU WILL NOT BE HARMED. YOU HAVE ONE MINUTE."

"Does that answer your question, sir?" Colson said into the radio.

"It does. Your new orders are to kill the hostages, inflict as many casualties as possible on the enemy, and then evade and escape," Miner said.

"Roger that, sir. Will commence now," Colson said.

"Let me speak to your second in command," Miner said.

"He wants to speak to you," Colson said, holding the radio out to Davis, who had been looking out the window at the rear of the house.

"What does he want to talk to me for?" Ball walked over to Davis.

"Probably wants you to make sure I carry out my orders," Colson replied. Ball took the radio from Davis and held it.

"What are our orders?"

"Kill the hostages. Kill the FBI. Run away," Colson said.

"Got it," Ball said. He keyed the radio.

"Alpha One, this is hold point Deputy Commander."

"Deputy Commander, this is Alpha One. Your Commander has been ordered to kill the hostages, inflict heavy casualties upon your attackers, and escape. If your Commander cannot carry out his orders, you are to assume command and see my orders are carried out. Do you understand?"

"Understood, Alpha one."

"Good luck, men. Alpha One out."

Ball looked at Colson. They had known each other for a long time, and had served in several posts together. They had never fought alongside each other in combat however, so they were not sure how the other would react.

"So what are *your* orders. Do we live or die?" Davis asked.

"Let's live, and take our medicine. We knew what we were getting into. We have it coming," Colson said.

"Okay," Ball said, looking at the floor.

"Tell the other guys we're surrendering."

The Blackhawk pilot received a radio message from the ground. He keyed the on-board speaker, so everybody could hear what he said.

"FBI reports the hostages are safe. The kidnappers have surrendered. No shots fired. Nobody hurt. No runs, no hits, no errors, and no men left on base. We're heading home."

Stafford heard one of the young tactical officers grumble in disappointment. There was a time when Stafford might have grumbled too, but not any more.

The Blackhawk stopped orbiting and headed east. The sun was low in the sky behind them, and the hills beneath them were a golden green color in the afternoon light.

Stafford was glad for everyone involved. No one had been hurt. The hostages were safe, and so was everyone else. It was the end of a very busy day. A good day. Stafford put his head back and closed his eyes.

Thank you, Lord.

Chapter 49

Commissioner Gomez addressed the audience of television and other news reporters.

"Ladies and gentlemen, thank you for coming. I am pleased to announce that moments ago, officers of the Federal Bureau of Investigation, United States Customs and Border Protection, along with state and local law enforcement officers in West Virginia, located and freed the three kidnapped members of President Forrest's cabinet. There were no shots fired during the rescue, and all the kidnappers were arrested. Those arrested have been taken to a secure location where they will be arraigned before a Federal Magistrate."

The reporters raised their hands and shouted questions at Gomez. He held up his hands for quiet. When they had quieted down sufficiently, he continued.

"And that's not all of the story ladies and gentlemen. In the coming days there will be many more arrests, but let me start at the beginning. This week has been very difficult for our country. Allegations of a government wide conspiracy of mass murder against those addicted to drugs, the poor, and minorities in America, have torn at the very heart of this country. I can tell you now, there *is* a conspiracy of murder being waged against those I just mentioned, but it is not a government conspiracy, it is a conspiracy by a group of traitorous men, bent on overthrowing the government of the United States."

The reporters were on their feet, shouting more questions. Some were in a state of disbelief. Those in disbelief had been convinced of the guilt of President Forrest and many other powerful members of his administration. They weren't sure who to believe now. Gomez continued.

"We know of this conspiracy because some of the participants were arrested for smuggling stolen U.S. military weapons to Mexico. They became informants in exchange for a reduced prison sentence. The big break occurred when an Immigration and Customs Enforcement Agent working in our intelligence section noticed a decrease in cocaine seizures along the Mexican border. He suspected the drugs were still coming in, but weren't being discovered. He also correctly theorized that the poison drug deaths, and the anti-government conspiracy were connected. His theory was confirmed by his own investigation, and also by a confidential informant."

"The informant confirmed the involvement of the alleged chief conspirator, a retired U.S. Army Major General named Andrew J. Miner. General Miner created a network of disgruntled retired and active duty military, and civilian employees of the U.S. Government. Using his government contacts, General Miner planted false emails and documents designed to give the impression that his own murderous activities were a government conspiracy directed by the White House. His plan nearly succeeded. A federal arrest warrant has been issued for General Miner, and for 84 other known conspirators. This is only the beginning."

General Miner was watching Commissioner Gomez' live news conference from the Gadsden Council command center. He was standing with his arms crossed, listening to his plan disintegrate. He unfolded his arms and let them drop to his sides. He had just heard the Commissioner of Customs use the term 'confidential informant.' Miner had a suspicion who the informant was. Commissioner Gomez made one more announcement before the questions and answers began.

"Because of a threatened attack by agents of General Miner, which is supposed to occur at an unknown location tomorrow, the National Terrorism Alert Level will be raised to ELEVATED. When we have more information to share, we will call another press conference. Thank you, ladies and gentlemen. This press conference has ended."

Miner knew who the informant was. He had only told one person something was going to happen tomorrow. Miner clenched his fists.

So that's the reason my plan fell apart so quickly... Bacster! And not one shot fired by the hold point team! Nobody knows how to follow orders anymore!

Miner picked up the phone with trembling hands. He looked on his phone pad until he found the number he wanted. He dialed the number, and a man answered.

"Yes?"

"This is Alpha One."

"Do you have a target for me?"

"Yes. Senator George Bacster."

"That will bring major heat. The price will be triple my usual rate."

"That's acceptable," said Miner.

"Location?"

"Not known."

"Special considerations?"

"None."

"Time frame?

"Today."

"*Today* will cost you an extra 300 grand."

"I don't care. Just do it."

"Consider it done."

After he hung up, Miner sent messages to all of his deputies, telling them that Operation Plow had been exposed. They were on their own. He signed off on the message and added a quote from the author, Albert Pine.

"What we do for ourselves dies with us. What we do for others and the world remains, and is immortal."

Miner had planned for this possibility. There was a safe house in Maryland. He and three of his closest aides would go there and wait until there were not so many people looking for him. After that, they would head to South America or Mexico. There were plenty of places where men with money could go to disappear.

Chapter 50

He wasn't in a hurry. He was always careful. Things done in haste usually led to mistakes, and he rarely made mistakes. He queried the appropriate internet websites and learned where the Senator lived. He was always amazed at how much information there was on the internet. He used another website to map the best route to and from the Senator's address. He used a satellite view to see what was nearby, so he could determine the best escape routes if something went wrong.

He phoned his landlord and told him he had to leave town immediately. As arranged, he left the apartment keys on the kitchen table, on top of a hundred dollar bill for the cleaning crew he had arranged to come tomorrow. The landlord said he was sorry to see him go, because he had paid on time, and in cash.

He walked through the apartment one more time, double checking for items he might have forgotten. He emptied the refrigerator and put the food into a plastic garbage bag. He turned off the lights, grabbed his suitcase and the trash bag, and went to the parking lot. On the way, he dropped his garbage in the dumpster. He placed his suitcase in the car trunk and got behind the wheel. The engine started without hesitation. A quick glance to make sure the tank was full of gas, and he drove away.

The car was the connection that was difficult to erase, but he had an arrangement with someone who would pick up or drop off his car anywhere he told him to, with no questions asked. He had never been stopped by the police, and had never gotten a parking ticket. He never knowingly broke any traffic regulation.

He never carried a gun to a job. Guns had a bad habit of turning up years afterward, after being found by some drug addict, or accidentally snagged by some fisherman. He used what was at hand at the time. Sometimes he found a handgun in a nightstand, or a knife from the kitchen. If he was lucky, there was a swimming pool, or a long flight of stairs. He used those to make the death appear accidental. If he had to, he could use his martial arts skills. A single blow to the correct spot, and the person was down for good. He always completed an assignment, and was well paid for his services. This job would be number thirteen. It was an unlucky number if one was superstitious, but he wasn't.

He mentally gauged his progress along the streets, and checked the time on the dashboard clock. He compared it to his wrist watch. The dash clock was a minute fast. With luck, he would be taxiing down an airport runway before nine that night. He often made last minute travel arrangements, and always used the same airline. He traveled regularly, even when he had no reason to. The frequent travel created a pattern, to show whoever might be checking on him, that he was a businessman traveling because of his job.

He kept his suitcase ready, and changed living locations frequently, never staying in one place for very long. He never used a credit card. He had a passport, but it wasn't issued in his real name, nor by his correct country of birth. His fingerprints were not on file with any police department or government agency anywhere. He wasn't on anyone's radar at the moment.

There was no way to track him, except by sight, or his fake documents. He changed his name and documents every six months, and made sure he was average in every way, except for the fact he killed people for a living.

He arrived at the address. The house was a large two-story with a high hedge across the front yard. The homeowner across the street had planted large bushes as a privacy screen, as well. He saw a remotely operated security gate, but it was meant to keep cars out, not people. It was perfect.

There wasn't another car or person on the street in any direction. Fifty yards farther down the road he saw a sign for a nature park. Three cars with bike racks strapped to their trunks were in the parking lot. He pulled into the lot and drove slowly past each car, seeing all were unoccupied. He stopped and backed into a space, got out, locked the car, and began walking to the Senator's house.

*   *   *   *

The two FBI agents were checking the map and looking for street names. It was a long street, with a nature park at the end. They saw the street sign at the last second and barely slowed enough to make the turn. The tires squealed as they rounded the corner, and the car wobbled a little as the driver over-corrected. They missed a car going in the opposite direction by only a foot. Sam Person laughed at the near accident.

"You want to watch where you're going, Person? I'd like to go home in the same condition I left."

"Just read the map, Nichols. And my name is *Pears-sewn*. It's Swedish, okay?"

"Yeah yeah. Turn left at the next intersection, then look for the address," Nichols said. He folded the map and put it on the seat next to the folder with Bacster's name on it. He shook his head at the idea of a Senator being involved in mass murder and sedition.

Person wasn't the best investigator to send, and hadn't done a field interview in more than two years, but he hadn't forgotten how. If there hadn't been so many agents awaiting lie detector tests, he wouldn't have been sent out at all. He and Nichols had already passed their tests, and so they were chosen to go. This was the biggest case he had ever been assigned to, and he had never interrogated a Senator before. From what he was told, Bacster would be an ex-Senator before the day was over.

"There it is. The one with the big hedge and the security gate," Nichols said.

Person turned into the driveway and pulled close to the arm holding the call button, speaker, and keypad for the gate entry code. He pressed the visitor's call button. In the speaker he could hear a phone ringing. Before anyone could answer, he heard two muffled pops.

Person and Nichols both recognized it as gunfire. Nichols un-clipped his seat belt and rolled out of the car, heading for the gate. Person grabbed the car's radio microphone and called in. Nichols was already around the security gate and running up the driveway toward the house.

"Delta Base, this is Delta 15-10. We have shots fired. Requesting back-up."

Person didn't wait for an answer. He kept talking, clearly but quickly, giving the address. The base station quickly acknowledged his transmission, and began repeating his message back to him. He dropped the hand mike on the seat, took the car keys, and went out the passenger door. He went around the security gate and started running. He saw Nichols was almost to the front walk of the house, gun drawn. He heard two more shots.

"GET THE BACK!" Person yelled.

Nichols heard Person's yell, and veered to the right. He ran further up the driveway, toward the garage and back yard. Person ran to the front of the house.

Person was almost to the front door. He drew his weapon and slowed from a sprint to a jog, deciding whether he should go to the front door, or try to look in a window. Before he could decide, the front door opened, and a man holding a pistol came outside and walked down the steps toward him. Person dropped to one knee, aiming his gun at the man, who was looking behind him, but still coming down the steps toward him.

"F-B-I! DROP THE GUN! DROP THE GUN!"

The man froze and looked at Person.

"DROP THE GUN!" Person yelled again.

The man dropped the gun. It landed on the walkway, and discharged. Person felt the bullet whiz through the cloth of his pants leg. He wasn't sure if it hit flesh or not.

At the sound of the shot, and the near miss, Person flinched and accidentally pulled the trigger. His bullet missed Senator Bacster's head by a couple of inches, and went through the beveled glass side panel next to the front door. Person knew he would be doing a lot of explaining about that bullet. Bacster dropped to his hands and knees.

"FREEZE! FREEZE!" Person yelled.

"OKAY! OKAY! DON'T SHOOT ANY MORE!" Bacster yelled back.

"FLAT ON THE GROUND! ON YOUR FACE! DO IT NOW!" Person yelled.

Bacster moved his hands forward and lay down on the grass with his hands under his shoulders. Nichols ran around the corner of the house as Person was standing up. Nichols and Person were both pointing their guns at Bacster.

"You okay, partner?" Nichols said, without taking his eyes off of Bacster.

"Yeah, I think so," Person said sheepishly.

"Would you mind not pointing your guns at me?" Bacster said.

"PUT YOUR HANDS BEHIND YOUR BACK!" Person yelled. Bacster did as he was told.

Nichols kept his gun pointing at Bacster. Person holstered his weapon, circled around behind Bacster, and placed a knee on Bacster's upper back. He applied handcuffs and rolled Bacster over from side to side, searching him for more weapons. Person stood up, leaving Bacster lying on the lawn. They could hear sirens in the distance, coming closer. Person was trembling, trying to calm himself. He looked down at his leg and felt around where he thought he had been nicked by the bullet. Nichols holstered his weapon, and stepped closer.

"Who shot at who here? Nobody got hit?" Nichols said.

"He dropped his gun when I said to, and it went off when it hit the ground. It scared a year off of me. When his shot went off, I flinched and fired into the front door somewhere. Nobody got hit, but I got a bullet hole in my pants leg. Look." Person shook his head while looking down at his pants. "Anne gave me these pants."

"What were the gunshots we heard when we drove up?" Person said to Bacster.

"I shot a man in my kitchen. I think I killed him," Bacster said.

Person and Nichols helped Bacster to his feet, as the first police cars screeched to a stop in front of the house, sirens screaming. The end of the driveway was quickly ablaze with flashing red lights, blue lights, and headlights.

"Ooooh boy," Person said, running both hands through his hair and leaving them resting on the back of his head. "What a mess, and we're in the middle of it."

The newly arrived police officers were trotting up the driveway with guns drawn. Nichols went to meet them, holding both hands in the air, with one hand holding his badge and credentials.

"FBI!"

"Stay where you are," the closest police officer said. He came closer, his gun still un-holstered, but pointing at the ground. He looked closely at Nichols badge and credentials.

"THEY'RE FEDS!" He yelled to the officers behind him, who immediately relaxed their posture.

"Officer, we have a possible dead body in the kitchen. We need the house searched for more people or victims. Try not to touch more than you have to. Follow me," Nichols said. He turned and walked to where Bacster was standing next to Person.

"Is there anybody else in the house?" Nichols asked.

"Just the man I shot," Bacster said.

Nichols drew his weapon and proceeded into the house, with two police officers behind him. Two other police officers had already gone to the back of the house.

Person retrieved the .45 Bacster dropped. He moved slowly and deliberately, making sure the gun was pointing in a safe direction. If there was going to be another shot fired by accident, he didn't want anyone hit by it. He pressed the magazine release with his thumb, caught the magazine and dropped it in his pocket. He put his hand over the slide and pushed it to the rear, rotating the gun upside down as he pushed. The ejected bullet fell into his hand. He pushed the slide lock into place with his right thumb, turned the gun right side up, and looked into the open chamber to make sure it was empty. Satisfied, he stuffed the weapon into his back pocket, and dropped the bullet in his shirt pocket.

The house was cleared by Nichols and the police. Senator Bacster was taken inside to wait for the FBI field supervisor. The police secured all the entrances to the house. The incident was reported quickly up the police and FBI chain of command. Due to the involvement of a U.S. Senator, the local Chief of Police was on the way, as well as the Deputy Director of the FBI and the FBI mobile crime lab. Person and Nichols sat waiting with Bacster in the den. Bacster was still wearing handcuffs.

"Senator, before we begin, let me advise you of your rights," Nichols said. He pulled his Miranda card from his wallet and read from it aloud.

"I know all about that stuff. I don't want an attorney," Bacster said after Nichols had finished.

"Tell us what happened," Person said.

"It happened so fast. I was sitting in my study, writing my letter of resignation. I assume you know about that, and why I was writing it?" Bacster asked. Person nodded he did.

"Well, I looked out my study window and saw a strange man walking up my driveway. He went to the back door and rang the bell. I went to the back of the house to see what he was doing. He didn't look familiar to me, so I didn't open the door. He saw me and talked to me through the glass. He said that he was Senator Winters, and wanted to talk to me about a bill he was sponsoring. I knew there was no such person, so I told him to get off my property or I'd call the police. He walked away, and I went back to my study."

"I was about to call the police anyway, when I heard glass breaking. Luckily, I had my father's old Army .45 in my briefcase, so I grabbed it and headed for the back of the house. When I went into the kitchen, he was at the other end of the room, with a knife in his hand. I keep knives in a wooden block next to the stove. He must have grabbed one from the block. He saw me and tried to hide the knife behind his leg. I pointed the gun at him and told him to drop the knife. He raised his hands like he was surrendering and then he just ran right at me. I fired, and he fell on the floor. There was a lot of blood."

"How many times did you fire?" Nichols said.

"I don't know. Until he fell down. Two or three times, I think."

"I'll be right back," Nichols said. He left the room and walked to the kitchen. The body was in the same position as when he had first seen it. The man was face down, about three feet from the kitchen door. Nichols looked around. He saw two shell casings in the hallway and two more on the kitchen floor by the refrigerator. He squatted next to the body to get a closer look. Puzzled, he stood and went back to the study. Person had stopped questioning Bacster when Nichols left the room. He wanted a witness to anything Bacster said in answer to his questions.

"And you have no idea who the man was, or why he might want to kill you?" Person asked, when he saw Nichols was back in the room.

"No. I never saw him before, but I'm sure I know who sent him," Bacster said.

"Who sent him?"

"General Andrew Jackson Miner. Now if you'll take these handcuffs off me and let me get a glass of Scotch, and I'll tell you everything I know about him."

"Maybe we'll do that," Person said.

"Can I have a word with you?" Nichols said, motioning Person to come out of the room. Person moved into the hallway, and Nichols stood near him. Nichols spoke softly.

"The D-B in the kitchen has two bullet holes in his head. From the blood splatters, I'd say he got hit in the legs with the first two shots, fell on his face and got two more in the head from close range... close enough his hair was singed around the bullet holes. This guy was not in a panic when he shot him. He put the gun to his head."

Nichols and Person were standing in the hall. Both had their arms folded across their chests. They adjusted their stance to better see Bacster. They stood for about 30 seconds, thinking, looking at each other and Bacster, who was looking at them.

"What? What are you looking at?" Bacster said.

"We're not sure yet," Person said.

Chapter 51

"Commissioner," the NSA man said, "this is actionable intelligence. The lines we checked were used moments ago. It's a rural area, so we converted the service location to grid coordinates." Gomez pressed his ear hard to the phone so he could hear the man from NSA better.

Gomez wrote as fast as he could, but had to ask the man to repeat what he said, to be sure he had copied it down correctly. He couldn't believe his luck. The FBI had gotten the NSA to rush the wiretap. Fortunately, the NSA was already at the internet service provider's main line station working a tap for another security target when they got the court order for Miner's tap. Clement told the NSA to call Gomez directly, as soon as they knew of anything that was actionable. Finding out where General Miner's calls were originating from certainly fit the definition of actionable. Gomez hung up and called the CBP situation room. He cut the man off in the middle of his greeting.

"Commissioner Gomez here. Is our Blackhawk still airborne?"

"Yes, sir. I just heard them call in. They're 20 minutes out from base."

"Re-direct the Blackhawk to these co-ordinates." Gomez gave the Agent the numbers and had him read them back to him.

"You got it. Also have local law enforcement meet them at those coordinates for back-up. Tell them to send a SWAT team if they have one. There's no telling what this might turn into. I'll be down to talk to the pilot and the tactical team leader personally."

"Understood, sir," the situation room Agent said. Gomez called Brad Clement next.

"Director Clement speaking."

"Brad, I need a search warrant for Miner's location ASAP... can you get Justice to work on it?"

"I'm way ahead of you. It just came through. I'll have it faxed to you."

"Great. Thank you... gotta go," Gomez said, and started to hang up.

"Hold it, hold it!" Clement said.

"Okay. What?"

"Thought you might like to know. Senator Bacster just killed a man in his kitchen. He said the man came at him with a knife. Maybe he did, but Bacster put two .45 slugs in the back of the guy's head. Maybe he had good reason," Clement said.

"Like what?"

"That's what we have to find out," Clement said

"Anything else?"

"That's all I've got for now."

"Thanks for the info, Brad. I'm going to be sending your FBI tactical team to Miner's last known location to serve search and arrest warrants."

"I knew you would, Ed. Good luck."

"Thanks. Bye."

Gomez sprinted out of his office to the elevator, but got impatient waiting for it to arrive. He used the stairs and started down two steps at a time until he almost tripped and fell, then went one step at a time as fast as he could. He didn't save any time, but he was too anxious to stand in one place. He burst into the situation room. The officers on duty jumped to their feet.

"Has the chopper been redirected to the coordinates I gave you?" Gomez said, puffing from his run.

"Yes, sir. The Blackhawk changed course and will be over the target coordinates in 15 minutes," the Duty Supervisor said.

"Get the pilot on the radio," said Gomez.

The supervisor pointed at one of his men and then at the radio. The man trotted to the radio, looked up the helicopter's call sign, and pressed the transmit button.

"Omaha fifteen-oh-two, this is Bravo eleven-hundred, over." The radio gave a double chirp as it encrypted the transmission.

"This is Omaha fifteen-two, go ahead." The vibrations from the rotors and whine from the engine turbines came through with the pilot's message.

"Omaha fifteen-oh-two, stand by. Bravo one-thousand has traffic for you, over."

"Omaha fifteen-oh-two, standing by," the pilot acknowledged. The Agent handed the microphone to Gomez, who was now standing next to him.

"Fifteen-oh-two, this is Bravo one-thousand, over."

"Bravo one-thousand... fifteen-oh-two, go ahead, over."

"Fifteen-oh-two, this is Bravo one-thousand. You are heading for the last known location of America's number one wanted person... General Andrew Miner. When you arrive, look for a place to immediately set down. The tactical team will be executing a search warrant there, over."

"Roger that, Bravo one-thousand. Do you want to tell the FBI team leader yourself, or shall I relay? Over."

"Fifteen-oh-two, this is Bravo one-thousand. Switch me to the team leader, over."

"Roger that, Bravo one-thousand. Switching now, over." The pilot keyed his intercom and told his crew-chief what he wanted.

"LAWSON... PLUG IN... BRAVO ONE THOUSAND... THE CUSTOMS COMMISSIONER... WANTS TO TALK TO YOU."

The crew-chief pointed to the receptacle for Lawson to plug in. Lawson held his hands out palms up, in the universal sign of 'what gives?' The crew-chief shrugged.

"GUESS WE'LL KNOW IN A MINUTE," the crew-chief yelled. Lawson nodded, unplugged his ear mike, and plugged it in where the crewman had pointed.

"Bravo one thousand this is Alpha twenty-six-ten," Lawson said.

"Alpha twenty-six-ten this is Bravo one-thousand. In about ten minutes you may be arresting America's most wanted person... General Andrew Miner. Consider him armed and dangerous. The pilot has the coordinates, and I have the arrest and search warrants. Sorry, but I don't have any other info for you. You'll have to plan your entry after you see what it looks like from the air, over."

"This is Alpha twenty-six-ten. Roger that, sir," Lawson said.

"Good luck to you and your men. Bravo one-thousand clear." Gomez tossed the mike on the table next to the radio.

"Now we wait, and pray."

Chapter 52

Lawson unplugged from the communications panel, and plugged his mike back into his portable radio. He turned in his seat to face his men. A couple of them were looking out the door of the helicopter, watching the world go by. The rest were watching him. They were waiting for some kind of explanation.

They had all worked with him a long time, and knew his habits. If the message was not a big deal, he would lean back in his seat and get comfortable again. He might give them a short smile, telling them in his way that the message was none of their business. This time they knew it was something important.

Lawson pointed to his earpiece and tapped his helmet with his hand and held up two fingers, then he reached down and turned his portable radio to another frequency. He leaned forward, rested his elbows on his knees, and began talking into his mike.

"Everybody hear me?" Most of his men nodded.

"Get those two on the net." Lawson pointed at one man he could see looking at the scenery.

The man next to the sightseer backhanded him on the shoulder and pointed at Lawson, and then to his radio and earpiece. The man turned on his radio and looked to make sure his seat mate saw what he was doing. Now everybody on the team was tuned in and waiting for Lawson's message, except for Stafford and Hernandez.

Stafford and Hernandez had been watching, but didn't know what channel to turn to. Lawson saw them looking and made a sign with his hands. He curved one hand in a crescent. The other hand held up two fingers... C-2.

"GOT IT," Stafford yelled, switching his radio to channel C-2. Hernandez switched as well.

"All right team, listen up," Lawson said. "In about five minutes we're going to be serving a search and arrest warrant on the number one wanted person in America. I don't have any other information about how many other people are there, or what kind of building it will be. We'll have to play it by ear after we arrive. In the meantime, ready your weapons."

Up until now, the team's M-4 carbines had been unloaded. A loaded M-4 was nearly always *hands on*, and therefore was considered too dangerous to be locked and loaded on board the Blackhawk, due to the likelihood of an accidental discharge. Side arms were loaded but considered safer, as they were *hands off* until needed. Stafford and Hernandez watched as the men removed their magazines, checked to make sure they were fully loaded, and re-inserted them into their weapons. They did not chamber a round. They would only do that after they were on the ground.

The crew-chief keyed his intercom and said something in return to the pilot, then looked out of the door. He looked up at Lawson and yelled, "THIS IS IT!"

Lawson leaned over to see what they were flying over. He didn't like what he saw. They were over some type of farm. There were several long, low buildings with white metal roofs. There was a house, a barn, and a large gray metal building with double sliding doors. There were also smaller buildings that looked like vehicle sheds. Three single-wide house trailers sat near the rear of a large two-story wood frame house. There were half a dozen cars parked outside the trailers. Judging by the architecture, the house was at least 60 years old. There was some sort of cash crop growing in rows on land near the house. It looked like vegetables. A long, curving drive ran for a quarter of a mile toward the main road. There was a small clearing behind the largest tractor shed, away from the house, trailers, and other buildings. The pilot saw the clearing, and descended to land in it. There were no back up law enforcement vehicles in sight.

Stafford didn't like what he saw either. The area was too big to secure with the number of people they had. They would be too spread out. They would have to stay together in a bunch. That made them one big target. There were several men outside the main house, looking up at the helicopter. Two men ran into the house. The element of surprise was gone.

Lawson slapped the crew-chief on the shoulder. The chief turned to see what he wanted. Lawson cupped his hands and yelled.

"TELL THE PILOT DO NOT LAND. WAIT FOR POLICE BACK-UP TO ARRIVE."

The crew-chief nodded and keyed his intercom, telling the pilot. The helicopter hesitated but was committed to a landing. As soon as they had touched down, the pilot turned around in his seat to look at the crew-chief and Lawson. At that moment, the windscreen of the Blackhawk shattered. Fragments of plastic showered the pilot and co-pilot.

"TAKING FIRE! TAKING FIRE," Stafford yelled, pointing out the left door.

Lawson looked where Stafford was pointing at the trailers. The doors were open and 10 to 15 men with rifles and pistols were pouring out. Some stopped to shoot, and some ran toward the helicopter. Stafford could see dirt being kicked up near the helicopter from the bullet impacts.

Lawson quickly made a decision. He slapped the crew-chief on the chest, and yelled loud enough for everyone in the aircraft to hear.

"GET US UP! GET US UP!"

The crew-chief punched his intercom switch and repeated what Lawson had yelled. Lawson turned to his men, who were busy making themselves small.

"STAY WITH THE BIRD! RETURN FIRE! RETURN FIRE!"

The agents on the left side of the helicopter immediately began firing. They fired single shots, each well-spaced and on target. Stafford saw two of the attackers get hit and fall to the ground.

After the pilot and co-pilot regained their composure, the rotor speed increased and the Blackhawk lifted off. It gained altitude and forward momentum, and began turning to the right. The pilot was using the aircraft as a shield from the incoming fire, as well as unintentionally spoiling the aim of the men in the helicopter who were shooting at the men on the ground.

"CEASE FIRE! CEASE FIRE!" Lawson yelled.

The aircraft quickly gained altitude, and straightened out from the right turn. Stafford could see the co-pilot using the radio. He knew he was calling in the incident to CBP Headquarters.

"ANYBODY HURT?" Lawson yelled, looking over his men.

They all shook their heads in the negative. He looked at Stafford, who gave him a thumbs-up. Stafford looked at Hernandez, who was pale and shaking.

"YOU OKAY, FRANK?" Stafford yelled.

Hernandez shook his head, and pointed at his left foot. There was a small, but growing, puddle of blood under his boot, which was missing a large piece of leather over the toe.

"I'M HIT!" Hernandez yelled.

Lawson knelt in front of Hernandez and began unlacing Hernandez' boot. Stafford yanked the first aid kit off the seat back and opened it. He found a compression bandage and opened it. Lawson had the boot and sock off and lifted the foot off the floor. He pushed Hernandez around on the seat until he could get the leg out straight. Stafford applied the bandage over the wound.

"HOW BAD IS IT?" Hernandez said loudly.

"YOU'LL LIVE," Stafford said.

"HARD LEFT TURN! HOLD ON!" shouted the crew-chief.

Stafford and Lawson grabbed hold of the seats with their free hands. The Blackhawk twisted in the sky and started turning left. Stafford looked out the left side door and saw nothing but ground. He felt the extra G's pressing him down. Everyone had grabbed hold of a strap or piece of aircraft to steady themselves. With the G's they were pulling in the turn, it wouldn't have been easy to fall out, but it wasn't impossible.

"WHERE ARE WE GOING?" Lawson shouted at the crew-chief, who shrugged.

The aircraft continued to turn and descend. Out the door, Lawson saw two sheriff's cruisers, lights flashing, racing down the two-lane road toward the farm the helicopter had just left. The deputies were heading into a firestorm.

The Blackhawk gained speed and passed the cruisers, still descending. When he was well in front of the speeding cruisers, the pilot turned the aircraft to the right 90 degrees to the sheriff's cars, while still moving to his left, slipping the aircraft and increasing the engine RPM's to counter the extra drag.

The sheriff's cars obviously saw the helicopter, and slowed down immediately. The pilot rotated the aircraft another 90 degrees and settled down to a hover about 10 feet over the road. The nose of the Blackhawk was pointing at the deputies, who sat open mouthed in their cars. The cruisers stopped within 30 yards of the Blackhawk. The lead deputy got out of his car and stood next to it.

Lawson and Stafford both realized why the pilot had landed. The deputies would have been cut to pieces if they had made it to the farm. Lawson hopped out of the helicopter and trotted over to the lead deputy. Stafford dismounted, but stood close by the Blackhawk, letting Lawson run the show. The helicopter blades were still turning hard. The co-pilot got out and walked around the aircraft, looking for signs of damage, and found plenty.

"GOOD CALL," Stafford yelled at him. The co-pilot gave him a thumbs up.

Lawson quickly told the deputy about the shootout at the farm. The deputy radioed his base, and road blocks were set up on all roads leading to the farm. The sheriff's SWAT team was on the way from the first call for backup from CBP headquarters.

"We were told you Federal boys were coming. You must have gotten there way ahead of us. Thanks for stopping us before it we got shot up," the deputy said.

"I'd say we *did* get ahead of ourselves a little. We didn't anticipate the reception we got. They have a small army out there. We took one casualty... a minor wound. Can you call an ambulance for him?" Lawson said.

"Sure thing," The deputy said. He called for an ambulance and turned back to Lawson. The SWAT team van, and several more sheriffs arrived and stopped behind the lead sheriff's cruisers, obviously wanting to get by.

"We want to go in with your SWAT team. I'll leave my man with you, and then we'll lift off and follow," Lawson said.

"You better talk to the SWAT Commander about that," the deputy said. He jerked his thumb over his shoulder at the van. The SWAT Commander was already out and walking to them, a puzzled look on his face. Seeing a Customs Blackhawk blocking a road was not something he saw every day. Lawson walked over to meet him.

Stafford watched, and read the situation. He got Hernandez out of the helicopter. With Hernandez leaning on him and another team member, he went hopping on one foot toward the closest sheriff's car. Lawson finished talking to the SWAT Commander, and met Stafford and Hernandez at the lead deputy's car.

"Hernandez," Lawson said. "We're going to leave you here and go back to have another run at those guys. The deputy just called for an ambulance. It'll be here in about 15 minutes."

"Okay, guys. Sorry I can't go with you," Hernandez said. Stafford and Lawson looked at Hernandez. They were trying to read whether what he said was a sarcastic comment, or if he was being sincere. Stafford could tell it was sincere.

"No problem, Frank. Get a band-aid for that foot, and we'll see you at the office tomorrow," Stafford winked. Hernandez frowned.

"The SWAT Commander says we can go in with them. He plans to drive right up to the house. I told him he better have plenty of ammo. We'll try to land in the same place we did before," Lawson said.

The SWAT van was no van at all, Stafford saw. It was an armored car that had been turned into a police SWAT vehicle. Everything about it was bulletproof.

"Well, I guess he could drive right in if he wanted to. Why don't we get out of their way," Stafford said.

Stafford and Lawson trotted back to the helicopter. The Blackhawk's rotor blades were still turning, but much slower than when they had landed. Lawson went to the right door and opened it so he could speak directly to the pilot. As Stafford was about to climb back into the helicopter, he saw the pilot shaking his head. Lawson looked at Stafford and shook his head as well. He came closer to Stafford so he wouldn't have to yell.

"The pilot says we took too many hits. He doesn't want to take the risk. He's going to lift to get off the road, and set down again right there." Lawson pointed to the open field next to the road. "Let's see if we can catch a ride with SWAT."

"We better get the okay from headquarters before we do that. You want me to call it in?" Stafford said.

"You're so right. No, I'll do it," Lawson said. He felt around in his cargo pants until he found his cellphone. He knew his field radio wouldn't work this far away from the repeater. He called the CBP situation room and informed them of what happened after the shootout, and what he wanted to do. He got his answer, closed his phone and turned to Stafford.

"Headquarters says go ahead, but we are the lead agency. I don't think that's going to go over well with the SWAT commander," Lawson said.

"That goes without saying," Stafford said.

Lawson stuck his head into the helicopter and whistled loudly through his teeth. All his men looked at him. He jerked his thumbs left and right two or three times, chest high, then made a circle with his hand held head high. His men jumped out of the helicopter and came around to him. He began walking backwards, motioning them to follow. He stopped the group where Hernandez was sitting in the deputy's car. Lawson continued by himself to the SWAT van. Stafford hung back with Hernandez, re-checking the bandage on his foot. The SWAT commander got out of the van again.

"By the way..., Major Neil Peterson." He stuck out his hand. Lawson shook it.

"Supervisory FBI Agent Robert Lawson. Got room in there for eight more? Our bird has too many bullet holes in it to fly any farther."

"Maybe. Can you move that thing out of the way so we can get by?"

"Oh yeah. We can move it. The pilot doesn't trust it enough to risk our lives on it though. He's moving it to that field to the left, and then he's going to shut it down and wait for maintenance."

"Okay. You can go in with us, but it's going to be crowded. I've got eight of my men in there already. You and your men will have to sit on the floor, and just so you know, I'll be in overall command. You'll direct your men on my orders. Can you live with that?"

"It was a Federal warrant we were trying to execute when we were attacked in force, so you and your men should be supporting *us*. We'll talk about that when we get there," Lawson said.

"Well, Mr. Lawson," in that case my first inclination is to tell you and your men to go take a hike. But, I'm not going to go with my first inclination. Get your men in the vehicle. We'll discuss this again when we get there. By now there should be about 20 deputies surrounding the place, waiting for the cavalry to arrive."

Lawson turned and motioned for his men. They trotted over, with Stafford bringing up the rear. Peterson gave the van a signal to open up, and then gave a thumbs up sign.

"All right men, we're going in with the sheriff's SWAT team," Lawson said. "Everybody get in and sit on the floor." His men trotted off to the back of the van and climbed in. Lawson and the SWAT Commander turned their attention back to each other.

"I have an idea," Lawson said. "That place had at least a dozen armed men. We knocked down two as we took off, and may have wounded more. They're armed with hand guns, AK-47's and M-16's..., some were fully automatic. I suggest we stay together and clear one building at a time, starting with the out buildings, then the trailers, and then work our way to the main house."

"That may be doable. I heard over our radio that our deputies at the road block on the east side stopped five men trying to drive out. The car they were driving had a trunk full of weapons. The deputies don't know where the men are from, but they all speak English with a foreign accent, and it's not Spanish," Peterson said. He and Lawson began walking to the van.

"English as a second language?" Lawson said. "Sure doesn't sound like the guys we're looking for, but you never know."

Lawson and Peterson climbed into the SWAT van, with Lawson in the back, and Peterson in the front with the driver. The Blackhawk moved off the road, and the van drove on toward the farm where the firefight had started. As they left the area, Stafford heard a siren and looked out the window above the firing port in the rear door of the van. He saw an ambulance arriving for Hernandez, and the sun going down.

Stafford wanted to go after the men who had shot at them, but felt naked without his M-4 carbine. He was armed only with a pistol, which was hardly a match against someone with a rifle. He brought two extra ammo magazines just in case, making five in total.

As long as you can carry it, there was no such thing as having too much ammo. I hope we won't be needing more of those ambulances. I have a bad feeling about this, especially doing something like this in the dark.

*   *   *   *

Nelson walked the block for a second time. Beth's apartment was in a nice building. There should be nobody in her apartment now. Like most people in D.C., Beth was on her way home from work. Nelson hadn't thought about work in a long time. He had to admit he missed it. He had enough money stashed away that he wouldn't have to work again for five or six years. He would have had even more money, but the organization was coming apart fast since Miner was mentioned on television. Nelson wanted to be free long enough to spend his money. There were a few things to do before he went into hiding, and one of those things would happen inside the building he was watching.

Nelson wanted to see the building from the inside. He felt brave, so he walked up to the main entrance and pulled on the door. It was locked. It was the kind of lock that required a pass card or code typed into a keypad. He tapped in several five digit numbers hoping to get lucky. None worked.

A woman came out of the elevator and turned his way. He thought about walking away, but she had already seen him. He smiled, waiting for her to come out the door. She saw him waiting, and slowed her pace. Nelson stood waiting, and smiling. The woman stopped.

"Can I help you?" she said, from several feet away through the glass.

"You sure can... open the door please..., I forgot my key."

"Show me your driver's license so I can see you live at this address," she said smartly.

"Sorry, I can't do that. I forgot my wallet too."

"What's your name? What apartment do you live in?" she asked.

"My name is Pete. I live in apartment 407. I just moved in," he said with a big smile.

"Apartment 407? What a coincidence, that's *my* apartment number." The woman took out her cellphone and pressed 9-1-1.

Nelson turned and started running. He wasn't dressed like a jogger, and people were staring at him as he ran away. He slowed his dash down to a jog, and tried to look as if he was running for the Metro, checking his watch often. It seemed to be working. People were no longer staring at him. The Metro was in sight.

The police car dispatched to the 9-1-1 call was turning the corner near the Metro a moment after Nelson went down the steps into the station. He had slipped away, but would be back.

The cautious woman who talked to Nelson would have a story to tell at work tomorrow. She would tell the building maintenance man about it too. The maintenance man said he would put a notice on the bulletin board to alert the other residents, and would also tell the building's owner about the attempted intrusion. The owner was out of town for a week, but he would tell him after he got back.

Nelson would be back before then.

Chapter 53

The drive to the farmhouse took the SWAT van five minutes. The van stopped on the far side of the road, across from the farm's driveway, and everyone got out. Lawson couldn't believe his eyes. The roadside in front of the farm was packed with marked and unmarked sheriff's cars, all with their emergency lights flashing. More than a dozen deputies were standing around the driveway, looking into the tree line. The woods were thick, and the drive curved around blocking their view. A few deputies were leaning across the trunks of their cars with shotguns and pistols at the ready. It appeared no one was in command. Peterson didn't like what he saw either, and immediately started issuing orders to move the vehicles farther away, and for the deputies to get behind cover. As the vehicles and deputies moved, he saw one sheriff's car blocking the drive to the farm.

"Whose vehicle is that?" Peterson asked the nearest deputy.

"I believe that's Deputy Johnson's car, sir. He's a new guy. He walked up the drive to see what was past the curve." Peterson cursed.

"How long has he been gone? Who went with him?"

"I don't know, sir. I think about ten minutes. Nobody went with him," the deputy said.

Peterson cursed again, and began using his radio. Lawson walked across the road and stood near Peterson to observe. Stafford walked out to the center of the road and stopped.

On the far side of the road, the sheriff's SWAT team were grabbing more equipment and weapons out of the van, and starting to move to Peterson's location. He was about to issue orders to the few men who were already near him.

"Look, sir! Johnson's coming back, and he's caught one of them," a deputy said, pointing up the drive.

Stafford strained to see. The sun was low, and it was difficult to see through the flashing emergency lights. It appeared to be a deputy escorting a prisoner down the driveway to the road. The prisoner was walking with his head up, and his hands behind his back. He was wearing a heavy jacket. Stafford could barely see the man in the deputy's uniform, because he was walking behind the prisoner. Whoever he was, he was limping. Stafford sensed something was wrong, but didn't know what.

"Lawson, this doesn't look right," Stafford said.

Lawson stared at the pair walking toward them, trying to see what Stafford was talking about. The deputy and prisoner were about 40 yards away. Lawson didn't see anything wrong.

The deputy stumbled and went down on one knee, still holding on to the back of the prisoner's jacket. The jacket looked bulky and stiff.

"Can I help please? I hurt!" the fallen deputy said loudly.

Immediately, a group of deputies, including half of the Peterson's SWAT team, ran toward the deputy to help him.

"THE DEPUTY IS WEARING SNEAKERS," Lawson yelled.

The deputies running to help, heard Lawson, but were confused by what he said. They were about 15 feet away from the deputy and his prisoner.

"IMPOSTER! EVERYBODY DOWN!" Stafford screamed. He instinctively reached for his pistol as he fell forward onto the road.

The men running toward the prisoner heard Stafford yell, and slowed to a stop, unsure of what to do. The fake deputy got to his feet, let go of his prisoner and held his arms over his head. There was something in his right hand. Stafford covered his head with his arms and opened his mouth. His warning was too late.

The deputy and his prisoner exploded. Lawson was in front of Stafford, crouching and turning when the explosion occurred. The shock wave lifted Stafford off the ground and dropped him, knocking the breath out of him. Stafford was stunned, and gasping for air. He blinked his eyes, trying to clear his vision. Lawson had been blown over and behind Stafford by the blast. He was lying on his side, bleeding from a head wound. He was barely breathing.

Lord God, please help me do the right thing.

Stafford pushed himself up onto his elbows. His head was still spinning. He looked at where the explosion had occurred. A huge cloud of dust was drifting away. Bodies, and body parts, were scattered around the area. As far as he could determine, there were ten men down. Only two of the sheriff's SWAT men were moving. They had been near vehicles, and had been spared the full force of the blast. The rest of the SWAT team was down, or missing. Stafford turned his attention to Lawson.

"MEDIC!" Stafford yelled as he knelt over Lawson.

A deputy ran over with a first-aid kit, and tore into packages of bandages. He pressed them against the wound on Lawson's head.

The men from the FBI tactical team, who had been waiting across the road behind the SWAT van, were unhurt and coming to aid Lawson and the other wounded deputies.

Prepare yourself. There is more danger.

Stafford knew what he was supposed to do.

"TACTICAL TEAM! GRAB YOUR WEAPONS AND FOLLOW ME!" Stafford yelled.

The team members looked at each other and Stafford. They knew they had to help the fallen deputies, and were reluctant to follow him anywhere. Stafford was looking at them, his eyes open wide.

"THEY'RE GONNA HIT US AGAIN! DO WHAT I SAY. GRAB YOUR WEAPONS AND FOLLOW ME!"

The men heard the confidence in Stafford's voice. Some were veterans of the wars in Iraq and Afghanistan, and knew he was right. They came running.

Stafford sprinted across the road with the tactical team close behind. Along the way, he picked up a rifle and ammunition from a fallen SWAT deputy. He turned to his men as he checked the weapon. The men were bunched around him, waiting for more orders. They all looked grim. The smell of death was all around. Stafford spoke in a normal voice.

"We'll move up this drive 50 yards. I want three men positioned perpendicular to the road on the left side in the ditch. I want the rest of you to be spread out with me, paralleling the road 10 meters away on the right. We're making an L-shaped ambush. There ought to be about a dozen men coming. Fire only on my command. Move fast, take good positions, and keep out of sight."

The Blackhawk pilot informed the CBP situation room of the suicide bombing. He got the information from a sheriff's deputy who heard it over his radio. The deputy said there were at least a dozen officers down. The CBP team had headed for the farmhouse. That was all he knew.

Stafford and his men ran up the driveway. When they had gone 50 yards, he tapped the three men closest to him and pointed to his right. He made a motion with his arm, showing them how he wanted them aligned near the road, but out of sight.

"When we start shooting," he whispered, "some will try for this side of the road. When they do, open fire, but keep your fire on your side of the road."

Stafford quickly moved to his left about ten steps, and as he moved further along the driveway he started positioning a man every five paces. He showed each man where he wanted him to be, in the brush facing the road. After he had positioned everyone, he came back and took a spot in the middle of them. They were all in place, waiting and breathing heavily.

They didn't have to wait long. Stafford heard heavy footfalls, and then saw them. A single column of a dozen armed men, running down the road toward his position. Almost all were carrying AK-47 assault rifles. They were timing their attack to kill the people who would be at the site of the bombing, trying to help the wounded and dying. Stafford knew the tactic too well. The Taliban, al Qaida, and others, had used it many times in Iraq and Afghanistan.

The jogging men were spreading out in front of Stafford's position. There would be no warning given to these men. They had already made their intentions perfectly clear. Ordering them to surrender and drop their weapons would have put Stafford and the other men's lives in danger.

Yea, tho I walk through the valley of the shadow of death...

They were spaced perfectly, not too close together, or too far apart.

I will fear no evil...

They were carrying their weapons at high port, using both hands to hold the guns high in front of their chests.

For Thou art with me...

Stafford had good concealment on the outside of the curve of the drive.

Thy rod, and Thy staff, they comfort me...

He was kneeling on one knee, next to a large tree.

Thou preparest a table before me in the presence of mine enemies...

He saw that all of the enemy were in the kill zone.

Thou annointest my head with oil...

He shouldered his weapon.

My cup runneth over...

He flipped the safety off.

Surely goodness and mercy shall follow me all the days of my life...

He took aim.

And I will dwell in the House of the Lord forever.

He yelled.

"FIRE!"

He squeezed the trigger, over, and over, and over.

The entire area was lit up with rifle fire. The muzzle flashes illuminated the men on the road, freeze framing them in a strobe-lit dance of death. They were shot to pieces. Their bodies spinning, bending, crumpling and falling, as the bullets ripped through them. Three men reacted fast enough to reach the supposed safety of the far side of the road, away from the firing, only to be shot by the other officers Stafford had positioned on that side. All the would be attackers were down. Not one was able to fire a shot. It was a perfectly executed ambush.

Stafford pressed his magazine release button, dropped his empty magazine on the ground, and inserted a full one. He released the bolt, stood up, and walked to the edge of the road, where one of the men he had shot was still moving. He aimed at him, held his finger on the trigger, and carefully walked closer. Some of the men lying on the road were moaning. He heard one of his men throw up. The sky was fully dark now, and the stars were shining.

*   *   *   *

It took the rest of the night to deal with the bombing and shootout at the farm. The search warrant was executed late the next morning, after the state police bomb squad and another sheriff's SWAT unit from a neighboring county had cleared the house and out buildings. The FBI mobile crime lab was on site. Also on site were television reporters and news helicopters overhead. Everyone had questions, but there were few answers to be had. The CBP shooting investigators were going to be working on this one for days.

Commissioner Gomez arrived before midnight, and talked to all the DHS and FBI people involved. Stafford was unusually quiet during his meeting with Gomez, who could see how shaken Stafford and the men of the tactical team were. He called for transport for the team and sent them home with orders not to talk to reporters.

"Well done, Stafford. You saved a lot of lives last night," Gomez said.

"Thank you, sir," Stafford said.

Gomez shook his hand and held it as he talked. "How did you know they were going to attack again?"

"I don't know, sir. I just knew more danger was coming. I can't explain it." Stafford shrugged.

"Hernandez is okay and already home, resting. He lost the tip of his big toe. Lawson, the FBI team leader, is going to be okay too. He's got a concussion, and a big cut on the side of his head," Gomez said.

"Glad to hear his injuries aren't life threatening. I knew Hernandez was going to be okay," Stafford said.

As Gomez was shaking Stafford's hand again, his cellphone rang. He pulled it out to answer, but paused and said, "go with the other men back to town and turn in your weapons, then take 24 hours off. I want to see you tomorrow after lunch, in my office."

"Roger that, sir. But this weapon..., the weapon I used last night, belonged to a dead sheriff's deputy. I took it from him as I went by his body... on the way to the ambush site."

"Deputy! May we speak to you for a moment?" Gomez said, as he motioned the man to come closer.

"This is a sheriff's department weapon used by HSI Agent Stafford last night. Can you take possession of it for the shooting investigation?"

"I don't see why not," the deputy said.

Gomez hadn't waited for the deputy to answer. He answered his phone as the deputy was answering him. The deputy shrugged and introduced himself to Stafford.

"Michael Clark."

"Ben Stafford." They shook hands.

"Who did you get this weapon from?"

"From a deputy who was killed in the explosion," Stafford said solemnly. He made sure the weapon was safe and handed it to Clark.

Clark looked the rifle over and saw initials painted on the stock. He looked up the road at the results of the ambush. DHS, FBI, and Sheriff's Department officers were doing the shooting investigation. The bodies of the men Stafford and his team had killed were being searched and placed into body bags. Investigators were taking photographs, and making measurements of the scene.

"You and your men responsible for that?" Clark asked, still looking at the scene.

"Yes," Stafford said, glancing at the scene in the distance.

"You're former military?" Clark asked from behind his sun glasses, his head cocked to one side.

"U.S. Army Ranger."

"They taught you well. This weapon belonged to Deputy Miller. I knew him pretty well. I knew Deputy Johnson too. They found Johnson's body up there near the house. They killed him and... the bomber wore Johnson's uniform to get close."

Clark stopped talking and sighed. Stafford knew what he was feeling. A mix of emotions. Grief, anger, remorse, hate, and thoughts of his own mortality flowed. A battle was going on inside him.

"I don't think anybody is going to say anything about you using his weapon," Clark said. "As a matter of fact, I think he'd be glad you did. I'll take care to make sure it's turned in properly." He looked again at the bodies being zipped into bags. "You sure knew what you were doing."

Stafford lowered his head, looked at the ground, and nodded. He was tired and his mind was dulled. He wanted to lay down, but knew it would be many hours before he could close his eyes.

Gomez shut his phone and cursed loudly, catching Stafford and Clark off guard. Clark heard trouble coming and walked away. Gomez put both hands on top of his head and paced away from Stafford. When he turned around, Stafford saw his face was red with anger. Gomez' lips were moving but nothing was coming out. Before Stafford could ask what was wrong, Gomez exploded in another burst of cursing. Stafford waited for the cursing to stop, prudently counted to five, and then asked the obvious question.

"What's wrong, sir?" Gomez' answer was thick with sarcasm.

"That was FBI Director Clement. It seems *this* address... the one given to us by NSA, was a diversion. *This* address was placed in the optics source code stream by Miner to misdirect us. The real source code address was discovered later by NSA and given to the FBI, who are as I speak, searching the *correct* address. There was no one at the *correct* address, so Miner has escaped. They're processing the scene for intelligence and prints right now."

"You think the FBI deliberately withheld the real address and sent us on a wild-goose chase?" Stafford asked.

"The thought occurred to me, but no... I don't think it was intentional," He was still pacing. His hands were on his hips. He stopped and looked at Stafford.

"So who in the world were *these* guys, sir? He pointed toward the farm. "They were certainly intent on killing as many of us as they could," Stafford said.

"Nobody has any idea at the moment. Can you believe it? We've got seven dead sheriff's deputies, 14 dead bad guys, one seriously wounded FBI agent, 10 wounded sheriff's deputies, and a shot-up Blackhawk, and we don't know who did it, or why. My guess is it was a domestic terror cell. Whoever it was, you still need to rest. See you tomorrow around lunch. Come to my office. Now get out of here."

"Yes, sir." Stafford walked to the ICE van waiting to take him back to D.C., and got in.

"Let's go home," Stafford said.

"Amen," someone said.

*   *   *   *

No one said much on the ride back to headquarters. After what they had been through, nothing was important, but everything was noticed. The clouds where high and gray in the sky, but the sun was trying to break through. As they rode along, car's passed them on both sides. Men in German made cars drove and talked on their cell phones. Mothers in SUV's drove with children strapped in the child seats behind them. The women were on their phones, as well.

For the men in the van, something earth-shattering had happened to them. Out of respect, the world should have stopped and taken notice, but it didn't stop, it kept turning. The grass was still growing. The trees were still standing. The birds were still flying. Even the garbage trucks were still collecting. The world didn't care. Nobody cared. Nothing changed, only the men who had been in the bombing and ambush had changed. If more people had seen what happened, they would have stopped. They would have said something. But whatever they could have said wouldn't have been enough. They would be changed too. They would be more thankful.

The rest of America would go on with their lives, without much thought about the people who would lay their lives down to protect them. That was the way it had been. That was the way it was, and always would be. Most people were only too happy to let someone else take the risks, and the pain. So spirits were singed, the world turned, and the van rolled along its surface.

After arriving at headquarters, the men shook hands with Stafford. Some thanked him for leading them. Some walked away without speaking, still in a state of disbelief. They went their separate ways, now tied together by the emotional strings of shared fear, and death.

Stafford avoided people as he changed into his street clothes. He left immediately for home. He rode the Metro to his apartment, took off his shoes, and collapsed onto his sleeping mat fully clothed. He fell asleep face down, and didn't dream.

When he awoke, the sun was going down, and his neck was stiff. He showered and let the hot water play on the back of his neck for a long time. He finished by turning off the hot water and standing in the cold. He didn't last long, but it woke him up.

He put on sweat clothes, microwaved a frozen dinner, and settled down in front of the television to eat. The cable news was giving good coverage of the arrests of the Gadsden Group members. They had found out the name of the group from a *"source close to the investigation."* Stafford thought he knew who told them, or rather what agency told them, but it wasn't a secret any more anyway.

According to the news, the number of demonstrations were decreasing nationwide. People who could think, saw the obvious connection between Miner and the drug deaths. There were some who insisted it was a cover-up. People liked believing the unbelievable.

The best news was that independent computer forensic experts verified the emails and documents attributed to government personnel were fakes. How the experts came to that conclusion was explained in some detail. So much detail was given in fact, that most people couldn't understand it, and most people included Ben Stafford.

There was also news coverage of the shootout at the farm. Aerial video taken from news helicopters that morning, showed the dead bodies on the road. There was also video showing ambulances taking the injured away from the site of the bombing. He saw himself for a moment, talking to Gomez and pointing to where he had set up the ambush. The reporter didn't mention his name. The newswoman said only that agents of the Department of Homeland Security, and FBI, were involved in the shootout. He looked at the wall with the bullet hole in it and shook his head.

Check, and double check.

Lastly on the news, the FBI had discovered the hideout of General Miner, who had so far eluded capture. There was a treasure trove of intelligence being sifted through at the moment. Nearby, in an abandoned garage, the FBI found an ambulance filled with explosives.

Sure would like to know who those guys we ambushed were, and why they wanted to kill us so badly. Where did Miner want that ambulance to explode?

Chapter 54

The next day Stafford arrived early at work from his time off, and spent the first half hour shaking hands and getting congratulated. As he shook hands, he smiled weakly. He was acutely aware he had taken several men's lives. The men he killed would have killed him if he had allowed them to, but killing always weighed heavily on him. He was skilled at killing, that much was obvious, but he never reveled in it. He hated it.

Stafford cheered up when he saw Hernandez limping toward him in the hall outside of his office. Hernandez had a white bandage showing through an oversized sandal.

"I say there, Hoppy, how does it feel to get your first purple heart?" Stafford said in a mock British accent. He and Hernandez shook hands.

"Throbbingly good, old boy. I ought to be okay in a day or two. I'm sorry I wasn't there to back you up in the shootout."

"Don't be sorry. I'm glad you didn't have to experience it. I've got to cover some bases before I go up to the Commissioner's office, so I'll check with you later, okay?"

"Yeah, okay. I heard some big shots were coming here today. Be sure you comb your hair," Hernandez said, as he limped off.

"Thanks for the warning." Stafford wondered who the big-shots might be. Stafford went back to his desk and checked his voice mail.

"You have 22 messages," the digital woman said.

He got a steno pad and pen and prepared to take notes. It was easier than he thought. Fifteen of the calls were from Beth. She called several times on each of the days he was away. She talked about how she missed him and was praying for him, and wondered what he was doing, and if he was safe, over and over again. The other calls were from well-wishers expressing their pleasure in knowing he was safe. He called Beth's number and cut her off before she could recite her greeting.

"Hey, Beth. This is Ben. I just listened to my messages. Is there something you'd like to tell me in person?"

"Ben! I'm so glad your back! I'm coming down to see you right now."

"Hold on a minute. Why don't we meet by the Wilson Center in ten minutes, and then we'll go to lunch?"

"I'll come by and get you for lunch in five minutes. Forget about the center. See ya then." She hung up before Stafford could respond. He pulled the handset away from his ear and looked at it, as if he could better make sense of what he had heard by looking at where the words had come from. Looking at it didn't help.

Women... who can figure 'em.

Stafford went to the men's room to make sure his hair was straight, washed his hands, and met Beth in the hall when he emerged.

"Beth, It's good to see you." He smiled at her.

She didn't say anything. She took him by the arm and led him into the empty conference room across the hall. She flipped on the light and closed the door. She threw herself into his arms, hugging him so hard he thought his back would crack. When she let go of him, she took his face in her hands and kissed him gently on the lips. Stafford was flummoxed, and showed it.

"It's good to see you too. I've missed you. Now pick your chin up off the floor and take me to lunch."

"Yes, ma'am," he said cheerfully.

She opened the door, and he followed her into the hallway as she led the way to the elevator. She punched the down button, and smiled at him.

"Listen, Beth, did I miss something while I was gone?"

"Did you miss something? What do you mean?" she said.

"I mean..., you're friendlier than I remember you being..., and that kiss..., what was that for?"

"Really, Ben..., I'm glad to see you. I'm glad you got Hernandez back from Mexico safely. I'm glad you didn't get hurt yesterday. It doesn't mean we're engaged. It doesn't even mean we're going steady. You still have plenty of room to mess things up before we get serious. Stop worrying."

"Oh, I'm not worried..., just a little surprised. You really took me off guard. I like being kissed by you. May I have another please?"

"Later, hungry man. You might get another kiss after our first date..., you *might*," she said with a smile.

"Might makes right," Stafford said, wagging his head left and right with each word.

"That's my old Ben. Where's he been?" Beth grinned.

"Out of town, I think." The elevator opened and Boyer stepped out.

"Glad I caught you, Stafford. The Commissioner wants to see you right away."

"Of course. Duty calls, it seems. Sorry, Beth," Stafford said.

"No problem. I'll hold off having lunch for an hour or so. Give me a call when you're ready."

Stafford watched Beth walk away. He got on the next elevator going up, and Boyer wished him well as the door closed.

This time Stafford was shown directly into Gomez' office. Two other men were in the room with Gomez, and they stood up when Stafford entered. Gomez introduced the other men.

"Secretary Romano, Director Clement, this is HSI Agent Benjamin Stafford."

"Jim Romano... I'm pleased to finally meet you, Agent Stafford. I've heard many good things about you." They shook hands.

"Thank you. It's a pleasure to meet you, sir."

The Secretary of Homeland Security himself.

"Brad Clement... pleased to meet you, Agent Stafford." Clement shook Stafford's hand.

"Pleased to meet you, Director," Stafford said.

And Mr. F-B-I too.

"Please be seated, gentlemen," Gomez said. They all sat.

"I'll get right to the point," Gomez said, looking at Stafford. "You've done a fine job the last week or so. You prevented yourself from being murdered. You got Agent Hernandez back from his kidnappers in Mexico. You solved a murder investigation in El Paso. You provided information that averted a national crisis. You led a team that took out 12 bad guys who had just killed a half dozen sheriff's deputies and were about to kill a dozen more. I'd say that's a full week's work. In recognition your accomplishments, the Secretary of Homeland Security has authorized a merit promotion of two pay grades for you. The ICE Director heartily agrees. I assume you'll want to stay in your present status, and not fill a Supervisory Agent position?"

"Thank you very much, Mr. Secretary, and yes I'd like to stay in my present status."

"Your quite welcome, Agent Stafford," Romano said. "You certainly earned it. That was quite remarkable..., ambushing that bunch at the farm."

"Since we're talking about that bunch at the farm, sir..., can you tell me who they were? They were definitely committed."

"We aren't having much success there," Romano said. "Three or four were in the visa database as Slovenians who had jumped their student visas. They were in the NCIC database as wanted persons. Another was a foreign born U.S. Citizen, and the others have not been positively identified. Most had identification from several different states, in several different names. We don't know how they formed their group, who was financing it, or how General Miner found out about them. We assume he purposely diverted us to them. Whether he did it out of malevolence, or benevolence, is anybody's guess."

"Thank you for the information, sir," Stafford said.

Probably turn out they sneaked in across the Mexican border, like a few hundred thousand Mexicans do every year.

"Agent Stafford, Director Clement also has something he'd like to say to you," Gomez said.

"Agent Stafford, I'd like to apologize for the mistake that sent you and the other men to the wrong location to begin with..., the location where the bombing and shootout occurred. NSA called FBI headquarters with the correct location later, but we didn't get the new information out to you fast enough. For our part in that mistake, I apologize. I have already called the other members of the tactical team, including the Blackhawk crew, and apologized to them personally."

"That was good of you, sir. What about Agent Lawson?"

"You'll be happy to hear that I spoke to Supervisor Lawson this morning," Clement said. "He'll be leaving the hospital this afternoon."

"I am happy to hear that, sir."

"And here's something else you'll be happy to hear. Secretary Romano and I met with President Forrest this morning. After he was briefed on the week's important events, during which your name was mentioned more than once, he decided to invite you to the White House to thank you personally. There will be a special ceremony at the White House, and then a luncheon. You can bring your parents and one friend along with you. I can tell you, being invited to the White House for lunch is quite an honor," Clement said.

"I should say so. I'll be looking forward to that, sir."

"Well, Agent..." Secretary Romano said as he stood up, causing Gomez and Clement to stand as well, "that's why I was here today..., to inform you of the lunch invitation, and to thank you for your outstanding service to our country. People like you make me proud." Romano shook Stafford's hand.

"You're a military veteran aren't you?" Romano said.

"Yes, sir. I'm a former U.S. Army Ranger."

"Ah yes, Semper Fi and all that, right?"

"Not quite, sir. Semper Fi is the Marine Corps. The Ranger motto is *Rangers lead the way*." Stafford smiled.

"Oh, of course. Well, good job anyway," Romano said.

"Thank you, sir."

"Commissioner, it was a pleasure to see you, as always. I'll be in touch," Romano said. He shook Gomez' hand, and turned to Clement.

"Director Clement..., nice to see you again. Good day to you all," Romano said. He turned to walk to the door.

"Secretary Romano, I'll walk out with you," Clement said. He shook hands with Gomez and Stafford. "Good day, Commissioner..., Agent Stafford..., good job."

"Thank you, Director," Stafford said.

Stafford started to leave with Clement and Romano, but Gomez held up his hand for him to stay where he was. Stafford returned to his chair and stood next to it. Gomez followed the other men out, and exchanged a few more comments before they got in the elevator. He returned, and looked at Stafford as he shut his office door.

"Semper Fi, huh? I'm surprised he didn't say Tempus Fugit." Gomez smirked as he walked to his desk.

"I wanted you to wait so I could show you something." He picked up a folder and handed it to Stafford. He opened it and saw the restrictive stamps on the cover sheet; FBI REPORT OF INVESTIGATION. FOR OFFICIAL USE ONLY. NOT FOR PUBLIC DISCLOSURE.

"Are you sure you want me to see this, sir?"

"Absolutely. Take your time. Have a seat," Gomez said.

Stafford sat and scanned through the document. It was a report of the interrogation of Senator Bacster, after he killed a home intruder. Stafford shifted in his chair and continued to read. He stopped when he read Bacster had put two bullets in the intruders head after he was on the kitchen floor.

"Senator Bacster executed the man who broke in to kill him?" Stafford said. "Off-hand I'd say he shouldn't have done it, but if the man was sent to kill him..."

"Keep reading," Gomez said.

Stafford went back to the report and read more slowly. During Bacster's questioning by Agent Person, Bacster revealed that the man he shot had begged for his life, and offered to tell him where Miner was if Bacster would let him go. Bacster agreed and then shot the man after he told Bacster where Miner was. According to Bacster, Miner was in Virginia at a place called Silvercents.

"So we know where Miner is? Has he been arrested?" Stafford asked.

"Yes, and no," Gomez said. "We can't find Silvercents. The FBI has been combing the entire state looking for anyplace that even sounds like Silvercents. So far they've found nothing. I think the killer told Bacster a lie, hoping he'd believe him and let him go. Trouble is, Bacster believed him and then shot him. We may never know if it was the truth or not."

"So what do we do now?" Stafford said.

"We go back to work. I believe you have more than one report to submit don't you?"

"Oh... my... gosh." Stafford put his hands on his knees and leaned forward. "I completely forgot about that. I'll get started right away."

"You do that," Gomez said. "And for your information, the luncheon at the White House is tomorrow. It is considered an official function, and your parents and one guest are invited. Travel costs can be charged to your government credit card. You better get on top of that, too."

"Right away, sir. Thank you very much." Stafford was so excited he almost ran out of Gomez' office, which amused Gomez for a few minutes after Stafford left.

As soon as Stafford got to his desk, he called home.

"Hel-lo?" Dan Stafford said in his usual way.

"Hey, Dad. I've been invited to lunch at the White House tomorrow and you and Mom are invited. Can you get the next flight here?"

"Slow down, Son. Where are you? What happened in El Paso? Is your missing man okay? And did you say lunch at the White House? What did you do, win the Medal of Honor?"

"Okay, I'm sorry. I'm in Washington. It's a long story about all the other things you asked about, but you can stop worrying..., the worst is over. And no I didn't win the Medal of Honor. The President just wants to say thanks. Oh, and I can voucher your travel as official business, so don't worry about the cost," Stafford said.

"Isn't that nice. The President wants to say thanks for what?" his father said.

"For the good work I did, I suppose. Come on, Dad. Can you and Mom come or not?"

"We'll be there of course. I can't imagine turning down an invitation to the White House. I better go tell your mom, and call the airline. We'll see you tomorrow, Son, and I want some answers then."

"Okay, Dad. I'll make hotel reservations for all of you at the Washington Hotel. It's across the street from the Treasury building. Call me in the morning on my cellphone."

"Okay, Son. We'll have rooms at the Washington Hotel. I'll call you in the morning. That will be very convenient. I better go now." Stafford hung up and called Beth. He cut her off again before she could recite her greeting.

"Beth, this is Ben, meet me in the food court in 5 minutes. I've got some news for you!"

"I'm on my way, hungry man," Beth said, and hung up.

Hungry man... ohhh boy.

Chapter 55

S tafford and Beth sat at their usual lunch table. They were both having pizza and salad. It was a well-balanced lunch, since it contained something from every food group, at least that was what Stafford told Beth after she voiced her concerns about the fat content.

Stafford was waiting for Beth to finish eating before he told her where she would be eating lunch tomorrow. He was looking intently at her chewing, with his chin in his hand, and his elbow on the table. He had really missed her, even though he had been gone less than a week.

"You know, Beth, you've got the cutest nose. The end wiggles a little when you chew." Beth smiled and was about to respond to his remark, but didn't get a chance to.

"Hey guys..., we haven't seen you for a week. Where have you been?" said Anne Dawson. Sam Person was standing next to her, holding their lunch trays.

"Hey guys yourself. I've been out of town, but Beth's been here. I don't know why you haven't seen her," Stafford said.

"Is it okay if we sit with you two?" Anne asked.

"Of course. Have a seat," Beth said. Anne and Sam sat down.

Stafford wasn't very happy with Beth's invitation. He wanted to have a nice talk with her, since he hadn't seen her in a few days. He was annoyed at the company he didn't need or want, and annoyed again because he realized his annoyance meant he was caring more for Beth. He always ended up getting hurt when he cared for someone. Today he didn't care whether he got hurt or not, he wanted to be near Beth. If she wanted to share their time with other people, he'd have to live with it.

"Ben," Anne said. "I want to thank you for mentioning my name to whomever you mentioned it to," she laughed. "The Custom's Commissioner called the CDC Director and told him I had information that was of national importance. I'm receiving a letter of commendation from the Secretary of Health and Human Services himself, and I've been asked to lead a team to study other statistical anomalies like the one I told you about."

"Well, you're welcome. Glad I could help," Stafford said. Beth smiled at him.

"Dome bet you head get choo beeg for ya boody," Person mumbled through a mouth full of food. Thus Stafford was reminded of the other reason he was annoyed when Sam and Anne sat down. He figured now was the perfect time.

"By the way, Beth," Stafford said. "I've been invited to lunch at the White House tomorrow, and I can bring a guest. Would you like to have lunch at the White House with me, the president, and my parents?"

Beth was in shock. Sam and Anne stopped chewing and looked at Stafford with amusement, and then with amazement as they realized he was serious.

"You're not kidding are you?"

"Nope, I'm not kidding. So would you like to go?"

"What a question. Of course I'd like to go with you."

"Great. Then I'll call you tomorrow morning and tell you where we'll meet, and when." Stafford stood up, picked up Beth's tray, and stacked it on top of his.

"Sam, Anne, nice seeing you again," Stafford said. He turned and went to the trash can to clean off the trays.

"Ben, wait just a minute," Beth said. He kept walking.

"I'll see you two later," she said to Anne and Sam, as she left the table. They waved at her as she walked away. She caught up with Stafford as he was stacking the trays on top of the trash bin.

"Ben, I can't believe you left me sitting there like that. Ask me to lunch at the White House, and then walk away?"

"I knew you'd follow me. I wanted to talk to you alone," Stafford said.

"Oh, you think you know me that well do you?" she said cocking her head left and right and putting her hands defiantly on her hips.

"Beth, I've missed you. I wanted to see you and tell you about the White House lunch, then Romeo and Juliet showed up. I'm sorry I sprung it on you like that. Forgive me?"

"Ben Stafford, I..." Instantly she forgot the chewing out she was going to give him. "I forgive you. I missed you too. Why don't you meet me after five, and you can escort me home." Stafford smiled and wiggled his eyebrows like Groucho Marx. Beth punched him hard on the upper arm.

"Ouch, that hurt." He jerked his arm out of range.

"I said, you can *escort* me home," Beth said again. "And don't forget, I know self-defense."

"Your honor is safe with me," Stafford said.

"You talk like I'm a judge," Beth said. They both laughed.

"We better get back to work. See you at five o'clock," Stafford said.

Back upstairs in his office, Stafford worked hard on his reports. Thoughts of Beth's smiling face and soft lips drifted through his mind. The day went quickly. There was still plenty to work on with the time-line of his activities in Mexico, El Paso, and the homicide bombing. He would need another day for the narratives.

There was something else he worked on in the back of his mind. It was from Person's report. Miner was supposed to be at a place called Silvercents.

Five o'clock arrived, and he closed down his computer and went out the door. Beth met him at the stairway.

"How about we pick up some Italian food, and then eat at my place?" Beth said.

"That sounds great, but you know if we keep doing this, we're never going to have a date," Stafford smiled.

"You're right," Beth beamed back. "In that case, why don't you buy me dinner?"

"I thought *I* was supposed to ask if I could buy you dinner," Stafford said.

"Okay, so ask me."

"Maybe some other time," Stafford said.

"Oh... you are *so* pressing your luck," Beth said. She squinted her eyes at him.

"I'm not worried, I've got plenty. Come on, the train isn't going to wait for us."

Stafford offered his arm to her. and she took it. She held on to him tightly, letting go only when the crowd, or the crosswalk, or the train doors forced her to. She didn't like letting go of him at all.

They got off at her stop and walked arm in arm to her apartment. As they were about to go in the main door, Stafford stopped. Beth turned to see why, and he took her by the hands.

"It would be better for both of us if I said good night right here," Stafford said.

"Why do you say that?"

"Because I would probably do something foolish if I came up now... something I would regret later."

"Ben, it's okay. I trust you."

"I know you do, and I'm trying to honor that. I'll see you tomorrow."

He pulled her hands and she came closer. He kissed her lightly on the lips, and she smiled.

"Tomorrow then..., *not* so hungry man."

"You kill me," he said. He let go of her and walked away.

He turned to look at her one more time, but she was gone. He got an empty feeling in his stomach, but was pleased at his own emotional distress, and good judgment.

I'm going to have to be my best for her. I guess I have to grow up sometime.

Stafford didn't pay much attention to the world around him as he went to his apartment. His thoughts were of Beth, the men he had shot at the farm, his parents, the meeting with Roja, lunch at the White House. Memories and wishes, prayers, curses and tears muddled together and rushed through his mind. It was all becoming more than he could take.

He was home, lying on his mat, rubbing his eyes and trying to remember the names of his dead friends, and not remember his father lying dead on the ground. He tried to forget it all. He fell asleep in his clothes, and didn't wake until morning. He should have been hungry when he awoke, but wasn't. He redressed in fresh clothes, and walked out the door for work.

He bought a hard sausage-biscuit and a cup of stale coffee from the convenience store on the way to the Metro. It tasted like he felt. He felt better by the time he got to the Reagan building. He saw his parents waiting for him by the entrance,.

"Dad, you were supposed to call me."

"We wanted to surprise you, the way you surprised us," Marie Stafford said.

"Well, you did. The hotel is nice and close isn't it?" He hugged his mother and father.

"It's very nice," Marie said. "We ate dinner on the terrace last night. It was a little cool, but you could see the Washington monument and the roof of the White House. I'm so excited."

"Wait until lunch. You get to shake hands with President Forrest," Ben said. Marie clapped her hands together like a little girl. Dan rolled his eyes, and Ben laughed.

"Good morning, Ben." All three turned to see who had offered the greeting. Beth was quickly at Ben's elbow, looking beautiful in the morning light. Ben's attitude was doubly improved by Beth's arrival.

"Good morning, Beth," Ben said. "I'd like to introduce you to my mom and dad. Beth will be joining us at the White House lunch." Dan Stafford and Marie were smiling broadly at Beth.

"I'm Dan Stafford, and this is my wife Marie." They shook Beth's hand.

"Beth St. James. I'm pleased to meet you."

"Oh, what an interesting name. Beth is short for Elizabeth?" Marie asked.

"Yes, it is," Beth said.

"Elizabeth means my God has sworn, in Hebrew. Elizabeth was the name of the mother of Jesus' disciple John, and James was a disciple of Jesus who was martyred by command of King Herod Agrippa. Did you know that?"

"Yes, I did," Beth said.

"You did?" Marie said. Her eyes widening.

"Marie, she said she knew it," Dan said.

"Oh, I'm sorry. That was rude of me," Marie said. Her face turning red in embarrassment.

"That's quite all right Mrs. Stafford. Not many people know the Bible that well. I must have surprised you.

"You did. And Ben surprised me too. I didn't know he knew such a lovely young Christian lady."

"Aww, Mom," Ben said. He wanted to sink into the concrete.

"Marie," Dan said. "Let's go get some breakfast. Ben can call us later with the time to meet. It was a pleasure to meet you, Miss St. James."

"Yes, it was a real pleasure meeting you," Marie said. She smiled at Beth and gave Ben a kiss on the cheek. "We'll see you two later."

Dan and Marie casually walked back to the hotel for breakfast. Marie had to look back over her shoulder at Ben and Beth. Ben could see she was still smiling.

"I think your mother approves of me."

"Oh, brother... I'm sorry, Beth. That was embarrassing."

"Why are you sorry? What was embarrassing? I think your parents are sweet. What's your problem?"

"Problem? I don't have a problem."

"That's good, because the day is early. By the way, lunch at the White House is officially going to be our first date. You asked me to lunch, and I accepted. That's called a date. We can move on from there," Beth said matter-of-factly.

"Move on to where exactly?" Ben said, a bit concerned.

"To wherever God leads us. Do you have a problem with that?"

"Nope." Ben grinned.

"What's so funny?" Beth said.

"Nothing. I can hardly wait to see where he leads us..., that's all." She looked into his eyes. She liked what she saw, warts and all.

"Shall we go to work?" He made a sweeping motion with his arm toward the building entrance, and they both walked in smiling, arm in arm again.

Chapter 56

It was quiet in Stafford's office The White House lunch was a secret that was really a secret. Nobody asked him about it or wanted to know who was going to be there. He signed on to his computer and found his email in-box jammed with official and unofficial messages. He looked at the ones marked 'urgent' first.

At the top of that list was a message from the White House. It was from the appointment secretary, reminding him of his lunch. The message told him the time to arrive, what to wear, and where to go to gain entry. He called his mom and dad and left a message, telling them to meet him in the hotel lobby at noon. The White House was close enough they could walk to the entrance gate from the hotel.

Stafford worked on his reports and made some corrections to one he thought was finished. He had more narrative to write, but was still not sure of the exact time-line. He left them unfinished.

Stafford got on the internet and pulled up a map of Virginia. He was looking for Silvercents. He made queries of town and county names, hotel names, and repeated the search for states around Virginia. He didn't find anything. He looked near the coast and read some of the names, trying to find a match.

That's an interesting name, Pomonkey, Maryland.

Next he used a satellite map and poured over small towns looking for the ones with municipal airports. As he looked for airports, he noticed several runways that appeared to be dirt or grass. There were several of those near the coast that were adjacent to large homes. He made a mental note to go back and check the ones that also had hangers.

That would be the perfect place to hide. Keeping a plane or helicopter in a hanger would make for a fast exit if you thought your location was compromised.

Stafford took a break and called Beth. She was not on her usual game this morning.

"Hello?" she said.

"Hello yourself, lady. What's up with you?"

"Ooops..., glad you're not the boss." Beth laughed.

"We walk over to the Washington Hotel at noon to meet my mom and dad."

"That's in ten minutes. I wondered if you were going to call me."

"Ten minutes?" Stafford looked at his watch and grimaced.

"Man did I get lost in time. I was looking at maps on the internet and *zoom...* the morning is gone. I'll meet you outside by the entrance."

"See you in a minute." Beth hung up.

Stafford logged off his computer, and hurried out of the building. When he was outside, he saw Beth waiting for him.

"Okay, how did you do that?" he said.

"Magic. Let's get a move on." The walked a quick pace to the hotel and went in the main entrance. Stafford's parents were waiting inside the door.

"Are we ready?" Ben asked.

"Just waiting on you, Son," Dan said.

"Let's go then."

They covered the distance to the White House in about ten minutes. After the uniformed Secret Service guards checked their names and passed then through the weapons detectors, they were escorted to the informal dining room by an aide who showed them to their seats. Each place setting had a small name tag with their name on it. Stafford was glad to see he was sitting next to Beth. In another room was a podium with a dozen chairs facing it.

"The President will be in shortly. Please make yourself comfortable," the aide said. The young woman didn't get a chance to go far. She stopped at the door and turned around.

"Ladies and gentlemen, The President of the United States."

President Forrest entered the room, with a small entourage of men and women behind him. One of the men was Commissioner Gomez.

"Welcome. Welcome to the White House," said President Forrest.

The President walked toward them with a big smile and his hand outstretched to shake, ever the politician. Ben intercepted the President as he neared his father. Before Ben could introduce himself, The President spoke as he shook each of their hands in turn.

"Agent Stafford, I've been looking forward to meeting you. Mr. and Mrs. Stafford..., I'm pleased to meet you both. Miss Saint James..., delighted. Won't you all have a seat? I have a short but important presentation to make." They all took the nearest seats. Commissioner Gomez stood quietly to one side. The President stood behind the podium.

"Ladies and gentlemen, it is with great pleasure that I address you today. I have asked you here to honor Department of Homeland Security Agent Benjamin Stafford. Agent Stafford would you come and stand next to me please?"

Stafford turned pale as he rose and went to stand next to the President.

"As you are all aware, the last two weeks have been extremely difficult for our nation. With allegations of a government conspiracy to murder it's citizens, and the threat of violent anti-government demonstrations across the country, the freedoms we have enjoyed for so long were at risk. The deaths were caused by the treasonous behavior of active and former members of the military and government. Without proof of who was behind the conspiracy, our republic might have fallen. One man..., one courageous man..., risked his life to save the lives of others..., more than once. One brave man gathered the evidence needed to expose the traitors and save our republic. That courageous man is Agent Benjamin Stafford. Agent Stafford, I would like to sing your praises to the American public and the reporters who have been clamoring for the details, but I was told that you would not like the spotlight. So instead, I have chosen to honor you in this private setting, among your family and friends. I don't normally present this type of award, but under the circumstances, I've made an exception." The President picked up a medal from a presentation box on the podium.

"Agent Stafford, for conspicuous gallantry, at the risk of your own life, to save the lives of others, I am honored to present you with the Department of Homeland Security Award for Valor."

President Forrest turned to Stafford, who had been standing at attention the entire time, and pinned the medal on his lapel, then shook Stafford's hand, and spoke softly.

"Congratulations. I couldn't be more proud of you if you were my own son."

Dan, Marie and Beth all stood and applauded. The President then stood back with the others in the room and applauded politely. Marie didn't applaud long. She began to cry, and put her hands over her face. Dan put his arm around her and patted her on the back. She buried her head in his chest, sobbing, "he risked his life..., he risked his life." Stafford nodded at the President, mouthed a thank you, and went to comfort his mother.

"Mom, it's okay. Don't cry, please." He put his hand on her shoulder. She straightened and wiped the tears from her face. Dan left his hand on her back to steady and comfort her. She looked at her son with sadness in her eyes.

"You risked your life, again and again."

"Momma, it had to be done, and I was the man to do it."

"You should have let somebody else do it," she said. Commissioner Gomez saw how upset Ben's mother was, and walked over to try to calm her.

"Mrs. Stafford, I know you're upset, but let me tell you more about what your son did to receive this award."

Ben glared at Gomez and shook his head, but Gomez held up his hand and waved him away. Ben let him go on.

"Your son's partner, Frank Hernandez, was kidnapped by a drug lord and taken to Mexico. They threatened to kill him if Ben didn't come to Mexico to talk to them. Without hesitation, he went to Mexico and negotiated the release of Hernandez, as well as gathering the evidence about the conspiracy the president just spoke about. Shortly after Ben came back to Washington from Mexico, he was at the scene of a suicide bombing that killed almost a dozen sheriff's deputies. Ben took command of a team of FBI agents whose commander had been severely wounded in the bombing. Under your son's direction, the team successfully prevented a second attack that would have been more deadly than the bombing."

Marie, and Beth looked at Ben as if they were seeing him clearly for the first time. He was made of flesh, blood, and steel. The steel was courage forged in the fire of faraway wars. His father wasn't surprised at Ben's accomplishments. He looked his son in the eyes when he returned from Iraq and Afghanistan, and saw the difference in him. It was knowledge of the horror of war that they shared. They had not talked about what they experienced in war. They feared they would unearth memories they were working to keep buried. Dan Stafford grabbed Ben and gave him a hug, as he whispered in his ear.

"Congratulations, Son. I'm proud of you. We're going to have a long talk about all this someday."

"Thanks, Dad. We'll do that."

Dan let go and Ben's mother hugged him. She didn't say anything. She held his face in her hands, as she did when he was home last, and looked in his eyes. She wondered at the man her little boy had become. She let go of his face and walked slowly to the lunch table and sat, wanting to be alone with her thoughts.

Beth took him by the hand and squeezed it, and then kissed him on the cheek. She let go and walked to the table and sat in front of her name tag.

"Well, ladies and gentlemen, let's all make ourselves at home and have some lunch," President Forrest said.

The lunch table had platters placed there after the President's presentation. There were sandwich makings, and several bowls of beans and cole slaw placed around the table.

"I hope you all don't mind having and indoor picnic. If you don't see what you need, ask the wait staff for it. Help yourself everyone," the President said.

Dan Stafford had been sitting down, but stood after the President's announcement.

"Excuse me, sir, but I would like to say grace before we begin eating."

"Of course, of course, Mr. Stafford," the President said. "Please go ahead. Everyone, please give Mr. Stafford your attention as he says grace."

Everyone stopped what they were doing. Some bowed their heads. Others folded their hands on their laps and waited patiently. Beth took Ben's hand on top of the table, and bowed her head.

"Heavenly Father, we thank you for your continuous love and faithfulness. We thank you for the angels you placed around my son when he was in danger. We thank you for the love we feel for each other, and we thank you for the sacrifice of your Son, who died for us even while we were sinners. Forgive us Father, for not doing the things you have commanded us to do. Forgive us for not loving our neighbors as we love ourselves. Forgive us for not feeding the hungry or clothing the naked. Even though we are unworthy of the love and salvation you give to us, you have told us to boldly approach your throne and bare our hearts to you. Whatever things we ask of you, the Holy Spirit interprets our requests and asks for what we need, and not what we want. We ask you now to give wisdom to our president. Help him to lead the nation so many have sacrificed so much to protect. We ask you to place angels around our servicemen and women wherever they are, and if they must fight, to give them skill in battle. And now we ask, Lord, that you bless this food for the nourishment of our bodies, and our bodies for your service. We pray these things in your Son's holy name. Amen."

The President walked over to Dan Stafford and shook his hand again. "I wish I had said that, Mr. Stafford. Thank you very much." Dan Stafford smiled and nodded.

The lunch was not what the Staffords had expected, but it was as good as Marie could have made back home in Dothan. Everyone made polite conversation. After they finished eating, there was socializing to do. Ben was getting tired of shaking hands. Gomez saw his exasperation showing, and walked over to see if he could distract him awhile.

"Stafford, have you finished those reports yet?"

"Not yet, sir, but I'm close. I've also got an idea about where Miner is." Gomez' eyebrows went up.

"Well, run him down, man..., run him down. Take as much time as you need," Gomez said. Stafford winced at Gomez' words, scrunching his mouth from right to left.

"Maybe we should talk about this in my office," Gomez said.

"That might be best, sir." President Forrest interrupted everyone's conversation. He spoke loud enough for them all to hear.

"Ladies and gentlemen, I hate to eat and run, but I have some other duties I have to attend to," he said. As he was leaving the room to light applause, he made his way past Stafford and Gomez, and stopped to shake their hands again.

"Commissioner, whatever this man wants, I want, within reason of course," the President laughed.

"Yes, sir," Gomez said, smiling broadly. The President shifted his gaze and handshake to Stafford.

"Thank you and your family for coming here today. I'm going to let the Secretary of Homeland Security know that I hold you in the highest regard. Congratulations on your award, and on your beautiful family and fiancee."

"Thank you again, sir, and actually, the lady isn't my fiancee."

"Not yet, she isn't. Anyone can see how she looks at you. Good luck to you both. Bye now," The President said. He left the room waving at the rest of the group.

Gomez chuckled, slapped Ben on the back and said, "as if you didn't have enough on your mind already..., fiancee?"

Stafford shook his head like he had taken a punch. He walked over to the table where Beth and his parents were getting to their feet. Gomez followed him.

"Let's blow this joint," Marie said. The whole group laughed at her remark like a bunch of teenagers.

"If you'll pardon my interrupting, I'd like a few words with my old friend. Dan, do you have a moment?" Gomez said. He was looking at Dan Stafford, who sat looking blankly at Gomez. Dan got up and walked off to a quiet corner with Gomez following.

"I wonder what that's about," Marie said. Ben shrugged, but gave a knowing look to Beth.

Dan stopped walking, and turned around to face Gomez. He didn't say anything. He put his hands in his pants pockets. Doing so would slow down his response time enough to give him a chance to change his mind. That might keep Gomez from getting punched in the mouth.

"It's been a long time, Dan. What? about 40 years?"

"Not long enough for me," Dan said.

"Look, Dan, I know there isn't any love lost between us, but Nam was a long time ago. I was young, and I made some mistakes."

"You got that right, pal."

"But I never got anybody killed. I messed up big time. I know that. I want to apologize for whatever you think I did wrong, and ask you to forgive me," Gomez said.

"No, you never got anybody killed. You just got them shot up. I heard from Stevens a year ago. He still walks with a limp because of you. That's pretty hard to forgive."

"I looked Stevens up six months ago. I called him and told him I knew it was my fault he got hurt. I asked him to forgive me, and he did. If he can forgive me, can't you?"

Dan was momentarily speechless. He and Stevens had talked for more than an hour about what a louse Gomez was. Now Stevens had forgiven Gomez, as Jesus had forgiven Dan, and everybody else who asked for forgiveness. Gomez offered his hand to Dan.

"I know I've done wrong. Please forgive me, Dan," Gomez said. He was still holding his hand out. It was hitting Dan hard. Forgiveness. Sweet forgiveness. Dan lowered his eyes, and took Gomez' hand.

"I forgive you," he said softly, shaking Gomez' hand.

"Thank you, Dan. You don't know what this means to me." Dan nodded, let go of Gomez' hand, and walked back to the table where they were waiting for him. Gomez followed him to the table.

"It was a pleasure meeting you Mrs. Stafford. Dan, I hope you and your wife enjoy your time here in Washington. Miss St. James, it was nice to meet you as well. Ben, I'll see you later," Gomez said. He walked away to speak to other people in attendance.

"What did Gomez want to talk to you about, Dad?"

"It was personal business," Dan said. Ben wanted to take his father aside and ask again, but he knew it would be fruitless. Dan might or might not tell him later. It depended on his mood.

"You can tell *me* can't you, honey?" Marie said.

"Some other time and place maybe. Ya'll leave me alone now." Marie knew Dan was serious, and dropped it.

The Staffords and Beth made their way out through the security gates for the walk back to the hotel. As they walked, they talked excitedly about meeting the president, and admired Ben's new medal.

"How many does that make, Ben?" Dan asked.

"I forget."

"You forget, or don't want to remember what you all did to get them? You be proud of those medals, Son. Other men helped you earn them. If you can't be proud for yourself, be proud for them," Dan said.

"You're right, and thank you for your words of wisdom. Can we talk about this some other time?"

"I've had my say," Dan said. "What have ya'll got planned for the week-end?"

Ben had lost track of the days and didn't realize it was Friday afternoon. He thought for a moment about what he wanted to do. He looked wide eyed at Beth and his folks.

"Let's all go sightseeing tomorrow, and Sunday we'll go to church. You're staying until Sunday aren't you?" Ben said.

"Don't see why not..., Uncle Sugar is paying for it," Dan said laughing.

"I didn't think you went to church, Son," Ben's mother said.

"I didn't think I did either," Ben said.

"I'm in," Beth said. "Sunday night I want you to come to my place for a light dinner and get together. You can invite your friend Frank," she said looking at Ben.

"That sounds nice. A quiet get-together before Mom and Dad go home and we go back to work," Ben said. "I'll call Frank and ask him to drop by. I'm sure he's ready for a little less excitement."

Chapter 57

Ben and Beth said goodbye to Dan and Marie at the hotel. There would be no dinner out for the Staffords tonight. They would also not be going to Ben's apartment to see how poorly he was living. Besides, it had been a rush for them to get to Washington in time for the White House lunch, and Ben wanted to give his parents time to rest before their sightseeing tomorrow.

After they got back inside the Reagan building, Ben left Beth in the elevator, after telling her he would call her later with a time to meet Saturday. He went to his office and sat at his desk. There was a sticky note on his computer screen. The note said the Commissioner wanted to see him as soon as he got back from lunch. He left immediately for the Commissioner's office. When he arrived, he found Gomez looking out the window.

"You wanted to see me, sir?"

"Yes, have a seat," Gomez said. They both sat down.

"I saw the look on your face at lunch. What don't you like about going after Miner?" Stafford sighed, and then let his feelings spill out.

"Sir, I'm tired. I know if I follow my instincts I'm going to end up knee deep in something..., I always do. This will turn into a big deal, and afterward I don't want to be interviewed on some morning news show. For crying out loud, I just had lunch at the White House and got a medal for killing a bunch of guys on Tuesday. I've had enough, *sir*."

Gomez took a moment to think about what Stafford had said. Ordinarily, he would have chewed him out for speaking to him so coarsely, but Stafford had earned the right to speak freely. He had been under tremendous pressure, and hadn't had time to calm himself and reflect, as most men would.

"Look, you have the week-end off to be with your parents. Take it easy. See the sights. Go to dinner. On Monday, I'll pair you with another agent who could use the benefit of your experience. Together you can pursue any ideas you have about Miner's location. How's that sound?" Gomez said.

"The weekend off sounds okay. The rest of it I'm not so sure. Who would I be paired with?" Stafford put his hands in his lap and intertwined his fingers.

"I haven't decided yet. By the way, where do you think Miner is?" Gomez asked. Stafford sighed again.

"There's an area on the coast of Maryland called Indian Head. Nearby is a town named Plata. I'm grasping at straws, but Agent Person's report said Miner was at a place called Silvercents. I thought about Indian head pennies being cents, and Plata is the Spanish word for silver. You put those two together and you get Silvercents."

"You're right, that *is* grasping at straws, but in case you're on to something, I'm going to have a bulletin sent to local law enforcement in the area, and also ask FBI Director Clement to send a few of his people there to question the residents about any strangers who might have arrived recently. Personally, I think Miner is in South America. He's probably sitting on a beach drinking a beer. At any rate, you're off the hook for the weekend. Take the rest of today off too, and come see me first thing Monday morning," Gomez said.

"Sounds good, sir. I'll see you Monday morning," Stafford said. He stood up slowly and walked out, feeling like he was carrying his old Army rucksack, hoping tomorrow would never come.

On the way down from the Commissioner's office, he stopped at Beth's office to let her know when to meet on Saturday. Her door was open, and he stuck his head inside to look around. He saw her sitting alone in the office, looking at her computer screen. He came the rest of the way in the office. Beth saw him and smiled.

"Hello. You still showing off?" she said.

"Showing off what?"

"You still have your medal on," Beth said. He looked down and saw the medal dangling on his lapel.

"Oh, for heaven's sake." He undid the clasp, pulled the medal off and tossed it on her desk.

"How about keeping that for me?" he said. Beth could see the weariness in his face and didn't try to argue with him.

"About tomorrow... let's meet at the hotel at 9 AM," Stafford said. "Most of the sights open at 10. That'll give us time to see one or two things that are close by, then have a quick lunch at the old post office building. I'll let my mom and dad know what's up, and I'll call Hernandez to invite him to your place for Sunday evening. I'm leaving early to get some rest."

"Sounds like a plan. You look like you could use some rest. See you tomorrow, hon." He waved wearily and left.

He went to his office and sat at his desk. He was dead tired. He called his parent's room at the hotel. They agreed to his plan, and said they would see him in the morning. Next, he called Hernandez and invited him to Beth's on Sunday evening. Hernandez agreed, although he would not be staying long.

Stafford left the building for home. He felt guilty about not wanting to stop and see his parents on the way home. He wanted to be by himself. He walked to the Metro as he always did, but had the feeling someone was watching him. He stopped several times to make sure he wasn't being followed. He didn't see anything unusual, and attributed his suspicions to his tiredness.

The ride on the Metro was uneventful, and he was home, showered, and on his mat before the sun set. It felt good to shower and go to bed early. His internal clock would sometimes get confused and make him late to wake up, but this was Friday evening. Except for a few drunks yelling at each other, and some noisy motorcycles roaring by, he slept soundly, even though his ears where still hurting from the bomb and the shooting. He was used to the ringing in his head.

Chapter 58

He was surprised when he woke up. It was fully light when he opened his eyes. He wasn't sure what day it was. He did not remember dreaming. He looked at his wristwatch, which for some reason he put back on after his shower. It was sunken into his arm, and left a deep wrinkle around his wrist. He had some time before he had to get up and get ready. He looked at the print of the rattlesnake on the wall, coiled and ready to strike. As he lay on his mat, he remembered how good it felt when he slept in his bed at his parent's house.

"One day I'm going to buy some furniture, when I've got somebody to impress." He looked at the snake print again.

Is that me? Am I a snake? Or is the snake the devil? Maybe the snake symbolizes something I should be warned about. Maybe it was supposed to tell me to be careful about which life path I went down. Too much thinking too early in the morning.

He ate a quick breakfast of cereal and water. He had been out of milk for days. Actually, he had a half gallon of milk in the refrigerator, but it had been there for several weeks past the expiration date. He knew it was spoiled, and didn't want to deal with it.

He performed his usual morning rituals, walked to the Metro, caught the train, and was at his parent's hotel with 15 minutes to spare. He walked inside and looked for a place to sit until Beth arrived. She had beaten him there, and was sitting on a long sofa under the window near the door. She stood up when she saw him.

Man, is she beautiful.

Tell her.

"Beth, you look absolutely beautiful." Stafford was smiling broadly. Beth blushed at the unexpected compliment.

"Thank you, Ben. You look nice too."

"That's all for me. I'm done for the day. You just made it for me." He laughed. She smiled.

"Good morning you two... been waiting long?" Marie said. Dan was standing next to her, yawning.

"Well, good morning, Mom..., Dad..., and what a nice surprise. I just knew we were going to have to pry you two out of bed this morning. Did you sleep well? I see Dad isn't all here yet."

"Good morning," Beth said softly.

"Good morning," Dan said, looking at Beth. He noted she looked very feminine this morning. "I'm awake. I haven't had my usual five cups of coffee to wake me up. The room only had two packs by the coffee maker. But I'm rearing to go. Let's take a slow walk to the Archives. The sun is shining and it's beautiful outside."

"The sun does that almost every morning," Ben teased.

"Smart guy, huh? How'd you like to be looking up your left pants-leg for the rest of your life?" Ben and Beth both laughed.

Marie was expressionless. She had heard Dan ask that question a few hundred times during their marriage. She didn't think it was funny the first time she heard it, much less this time.

"I wouldn't like it. Let's get a move on," Ben said, rubbing his hands together. "Maybe we can go to the Vietnam Memorial later. It's quite a walk from here, but we can see it if you want." Ben said, looking at his dad.

"I saw it yesterday. I walked down and looked up a few names."

"Why didn't you say something? I would have gone down there with you."

"Your mom went with me." Marie stood close to Dan and took hold of his arm. Ben read the body language correctly.

"Pretty emotional time for you I suppose?" Ben asked.

"A little bit. It was good to see the names up there... to know they'll never be forgotten." Dan patted Marie's hand. She let go and they all moved to the door.

As they walked to the mall, Beth took hold of Ben's arm and squeezed it, looking up at him. She smiled, imaging a life with him by her side.

"Your father was in Vietnam, and you were in Iraq and Afghanistan. Being a soldier must be in your blood," Beth said.

"He's not my real father. My biological father was killed when I was a boy."

"I'm sorry to hear that, but your step-father seems to be a good man. I bet he was a good father to you."

Ben didn't say anything. He nodded his head and thought about the father he had shot. It was an accident, but it had been so long ago he was no longer sure. Maybe he hated his father. Maybe he heard his father yelling at his mother, which he regularly did. Maybe he was unconsciously protecting his mother. The thoughts went through him like a knife. Beth could see he was troubled.

"I'm sorry I brought it up, but you know you can talk to me about anything."

"Thanks, Beth. Maybe I'll do that someday."

Marie looked over her shoulder at Ben and Beth. She liked what she saw. Beth obviously liked her son, and she was glad to see it. She considered herself a good judge of people, and she judged Beth would be good for Ben. She was beautiful, clear-headed, and didn't need a man to support her like so many of the women she knew back in Dothan. Those women were quick to latch onto a man with a good paying job. It was easy to keep a man interested if you pressed the right buttons.

"Are we going the right way?" Marie asked Ben.

"Yep. We hang a left here and go down Pennsylvania Avenue. Then look for ninth street and go right. The museum of American history is nearby at 14th street, we can go there to walk off our lunch." The group turned onto Pennsylvania Avenue. The Capitol dome was visible in the distance.

"Look at that, honey. It's the national liar's club headquarters," Dan said.

"Oh, cut it out. I want to enjoy my day," Marie said. She was looking up at him as she walked along, waiting for his acknowledgment. He tried to ignore her, but she took hold of his hand and waited, looking at him. He finally looked down at her.

"Okay, I'll try to be good," he said.

"I see where Ben gets his sense of humor," Beth said. Dan and Marie looked back at her.

"You do? Dad got his sense of humor from me," Ben said. "Before he knew me, he was as funny as a sun burn."

"Ben, you can cut it out too, please," Marie said, giving Ben a glance that meant she was serious.

"Yes, Mama."

And so went their day, walking, talking, eating, and being awed by the substance of what they saw, as well as the volume of it. At the National Archives, they saw the original Constitution, the Bill of Rights, and Declaration of Independence, all visible through thick glass. At the American History Museum they saw steam-powered farm equipment from the 1800's, and the flag that flew over Fort McHenry and inspired Francis Scott Key to write the Star Spangled Banner. There was too much to see, and after dinner they decided to come back the next day to see more.

They headed back. Their feet were aching when they reached the hotel. Ben and Beth didn't come in. They agreed to meet at the same time and place in the morning. Beth took Ben's arm as they walked slowly to the Metro.

"I really like your parents. Thanks for inviting me along," Beth said.

"You're welcome. I can tell they liked you too..., especially Mom. Hey, did we just have another date?" Stafford asked.

"I think we did, but I'm still waiting for real tablecloths."

"I may bring one with me tomorrow." They were both too tired to laugh at his joke.

After riding the Metro, Stafford insisted on walking Beth to her door. "It is the proper and gentlemanly thing to do," he said. Beth assured him it wasn't necessary, but it did no good.

They entered her building and walked past the bulletin board. Stafford glanced at the board and saw a picture of a man standing at the door they had just entered. The man looked familiar. He turned and went back for a second look. Beth came back to see what Ben was looking at.

"Oh, I saw that letter and picture today on the way out. It's some guy who tried to get in the building the other day. Management is just warning everybody about security."

"That's Pete Nelson." Stafford didn't take is eyes off the photo.

"Pete Nelson?" Beth leaned in to look more carefully.

"I don't know. It certainly looks like him, but I can't be sure. The picture is pretty grainy," Beth said. Stafford was still staring at the photo.

"Besides, what would he be doing trying to get into my building?"

Stafford finally took his eyes off the picture, and looked at Beth. He looked at her until her mind was on the same wavelength as his.

"Ben, you don't think he wants to get at *me* do you?" Ben was still looking at her, thinking. He thought he knew what kind of man Pete Nelson was now.

"I think he wants to kill me, and maybe you too for being close to me. He knows I was onto something with the coke seizures. He reported it to his superiors in the conspiracy, and they told him to kill me. He got captured before he could act, and so Turner tried to kill me instead. Now Nelson has escaped, and wants to finish his assignment."

"But you can't even be sure it's him." She pointed to the picture, and looked at it carefully again. "I mean, I went out with him, and I can't tell for sure."

"Yeah. Maybe I am making too much out of a simple burglary suspect. You're probably right."

Stafford moved away from the bulletin board a few steps and waited for her to catch up to him. He walked her to her apartment, and waited in the living room while she checked the rest of the apartment to make sure everything was the way she had left it.

"See? Nobody was hiding in the shower. It's okay," she said.

"All right, I'm gonna be leaving then. See you in the morning. I'll be by to get you and we'll go to the hotel together."

"Just meet me at the hotel. I'm a big girl, you know."

"Okay big girl..., see you at the hotel then. Don't be late."

Stafford went back downstairs, and stopped at the bulletin board to take another look at the picture. He looked at it a long time. He was sure it was Nelson, but if Beth wasn't sure, how could he be. He left the building and started for the Metro, and home.

From across the street, Pete Nelson watched Stafford leave Beth's building. Nelson was there for more reconnaissance, and was unprepared for this opportunity. He wouldn't be unprepared again. Tomorrow he would bring what he needed to deal with both of them.

When Stafford got to his apartment he was unusually cautious as he entered the building. The more he thought about it, the more positive he was that the picture he saw at Beth's was Pete Nelson. The thought of him running around loose made him nervous.

He checked his entire apartment, looking for signs that someone had been there. He checked all six of his tell marks. They were places in the apartment where an intruder would have to move something to enter a room or look in a drawer. Stafford had placed a piece of clothing, or a mail-in card from a magazine in a particular position. If any of the things he placed had been moved, he knew someone had been there. All his marks were as he had left them.

He second guessed every decision he had made for the last two days. If Nelson had wanted to sneak up on him in a crowd, he could have, and Stafford would never have known he was there until it was too late. Before he did anything else, he called Hernandez to warn him. Hernandez picked up the phone on the second ring.

"Hello?"

"Hey, Hoppy, what are you doing, sitting on the phone?"

"Hey, Ben. No, just happened to be walking by. It's good to be back in our old house again."

"Oh, yeah. You all moved back already?"

"Yes. Everybody figures the threat has been reduced, and no need for the special living conditions any longer."

"Is your foot going to be feeling good enough to come by Beth's apartment tomorrow night?"

"Yeah. I don't even miss my toe. One less toenail to clip. It's a real time saver."

"Glad to hear it. Listen, the reason I called was to give you a warning."

"About what?"

"I was at Beth's today, and on the building bulletin board was a picture of a guy that tried to lie his way into her building. I swear he looks like Pete Nelson."

"The guy who was involved in the conspiracy? The one who sat behind you in your office, and escaped FBI custody?"

"After killing an FBI Agent. He's the one."

"Are you sure it was him?"

"No. If I had to say, I'd say I wasn't sure. But anyway, I wanted to tell you about it so you wouldn't be caught flat-footed if you ran into him tomorrow."

"Why? Did you invite him over too?"

"Why didn't I think of that? I guess you've seen the picture of him that was attached to the global email? Everybody at work got one, along with pictures of General Miner and a few of his pals," Stafford said.

"Yeah, I saw his picture. To be on the safe side, you ought to call OPR so they can let the local cops know he might be in the area."

"Good idea, Frank. I'll do that after we hang up. I'll see you tomorrow about six then. Is your wife coming with you?"

"No. Can't get a baby sitter. At least that's her excuse. I don't think she wants to let our daughter out of her sight."

"I don't blame her. But you're okay with leaving them alone?"

"We're all in God's hands, buddy. I've got a Marine gunny sergeant living next door too. He knows what happened, and said he'll be keeping an eye on things around here. So I'm double covered."

"You got that right."

"Oh, should I bring anything?"

"Just yourself."

"Okay. Have a good night, Ben. See you tomorrow."

"Okay, Frank. Regards to your family. Bye."

Next, Stafford called sector communications, and told them of his suspicions about Nelson's whereabouts. Sector told him they would notify OPR. His duty done, he forgot to undress again, lay down on his mat, cleared is mind, and fell asleep.

Chapter 59

This morning he awoke at his usual workday time. He found he had slept in his clothes again, and was unhappy with himself about it. He had seen old men fall into bad habits after their wives died, or maybe they had lived alone and always had bad habits. It was easy to do. There was nobody else to maintain appearances for. Nobody to say you were acting strange, so you acted strangely most of the time.

That's what I need, a keeper.

He ate a big breakfast. It was a double serving of cereal and water. It was going to be a busy day, and he wanted to keep his strength up until lunch, whenever that was going to be. He finished his breakfast, rinsed the bowl without using soap, and put it in the drainer to dry. He would have used soap, but he didn't have any, or milk for his cereal either. It was on his shopping list, but he hadn't gone grocery shopping in a month. He took a quick inventory of his cabinets and refrigerator to see what else he was out of. He was out of everything. He put it out of his mind.

After showering and dressing, he stood looking out of the window at the sky. He heard the screeching of a hawk somewhere in the distance. He pictured the bird soaring on the air currents, looking far below for his breakfast.

Good hunting brother. It's life and death all the time out there isn't it? Sometimes here too.

If he didn't think about it too much, today felt like any other day. It didn't take much to break the spell. He saw people going to church in their Sunday clothes, and others, like him, who were going somewhere else. There was a pleasant difference in the Metro, there were almost no people riding today.

He arrived early at the hotel, and found Beth and his parents sitting in the lobby. He walked over smiling as usual.

"Good morning, all," he said. He received a chorus of good mornings in return.

"What's the plan today," he said, looking at his dad.

"Your mother has interrogated the hotel staff, and has come up with a plan."

"I want to see Ford's theater, the capitol building, the Washington monument, and the Lincoln memorial," Marie said.

"Whew. I hope you have on good walking shoes," Beth said. "It's about two miles from the capitol to the Lincoln Memorial, but the capitol is closed on Sundays. How about the Air and Space Museum instead? It's open today, and it's closer."

"Well, if you say so, but I did want to see the capitol dome from the inside. I see it all the time on the nightly news, and I always wanted to see what the inside looked like. Oh well. Dan wanted to see the space stuff anyway."

"Don't forget that you're coming over to my apartment tonight. Save some energy and time for that. It's at six o'clock. I'll have to get there and set up everything, so I'll be leaving you all about four o'clock."

"We didn't forget. Anyway, let's get going. We're wasting daylight," Dan said.

"I thought we were going to church," Ben said.

"I checked out a few churches on the internet last night," Dan said. "There aren't any nearby I wanted to go to. The interesting ones I found were in Alexandria, and I thought that was too far to go and get back in time to see the sights. So, this Sunday we're going to play hooky from church."

"I guess I'm playing hooky too. I was going to church with you all, but I guess one day away from church won't hurt me," Beth said.

"Where do you go to church, Ben?" Marie said.

"I haven't found one yet," Ben said. It wasn't a lie, but it wasn't all of the truth, and everyone knew it. Ben was grateful no-one pursued the matter further.

"Well, we better get going," Ben said cheerfully. And so off they went.

Their day was tiring, but they enjoyed walking and talking. Beth walked with Marie most of the time, and Ben and Dan walked along behind, like men following their wives around a grocery store. They talked about crooked politicians, the economy, and where the best places to eat were.

They saw where President Lincoln was shot, and looked out the tiny windows at the top of the Washington Monument. They spent the most time at the Air and Space Museum. Marie asked Beth lots of questions about her relationship with Ben. Dan did the same to Ben, wanting to know how serious he was about Beth. They shared their secrets, and discovered they didn't have many. They were still new to each other, but their feelings were on their sleeves.

The time came for Beth to head home, and Ben decided to go with her. He wasn't tired, but wanted to see she got home safely. Dan and Marie would see the Lincoln memorial by themselves.

"If you get lost, give me a call and I'll come get you," Ben said.

"I still get around pretty good, Son. We'll get there and back. Don't you worry," Dan said, and waved good bye. "See you two later."

Beth and Ben took the Metro from the nearest station, and were soon at her apartment, getting ready for guests.

"I'll get the food going. Will you make sure the table is set?" Beth said.

"Okay. You know, suddenly I feel all domesticated. My parents think we're a couple already."

"Well, aren't we?" Beth said from the kitchen. Ben thought before he answered.

How did I get in the middle of a minefield? It's make it, or break it time.

"Yeah, I suppose we are. There's nobody else I'd rather be with."

"I know what you mean. I feel the same way," Beth said from the kitchen.

Ben walked over and stood in the doorway, watching her work. She was wearing a white apron like his mother sometimes wore. She felt his presence and stopped what she was doing, but didn't turn around. Ben came to her and took her by the shoulders. He turned her around and kissed her. They held each other tightly, their hearts pounding. She broke the kiss and stood back from him.

"Thank you very much," she said. She smiled. He smiled, and moved to kiss her again.

"And now you have salad dressing all over your shirt." He looked down, and sure enough his shirt was a mess.

"You really know how to kill a mood, don't you?" he said. He looked around for paper towels. She pointed to where they were on the counter.

"There's a time and a place for everything." She laughed and went back to work, as he tried to get the mess off of his shirt.

They finished preparing the food, made sure the table looked presentable, and sat down to get off their feet. It was almost six o'clock.

Hernandez parked his car on the street near Beth's apartment. Stafford had given good directions, so he didn't have to walk far. He was glad for that, because his toe was starting to throb.

As he came up the sidewalk to the front of the building, he saw a man come out and hold the door open for a man going in, who was carrying bags of groceries. The man going in looked familiar, but Hernandez could only see his back and part of his profile. Hernandez stopped the man who had come out.

"Excuse me, did you know the man you let just in?" The man slowed a bit, but didn't stop. He was talking over his shoulder to Hernandez as he walked away.

"Who are you, security? I don't know. He looked like he knew where he was going. I let him in. No big deal, man."

Hernandez turned and walked quickly to the door. The familiar looking man was not far away inside. Hernandez banged on the door, and the man turned around.

"Excuse me. can you let me in? I forgot my keys!" Hernandez said loudly through the glass door. The man looked at Hernandez with a smile.

"Sorry, I don't know you." He turned and continued on his way. Frank saw the call box for the building and scrolled through all the tenants looking for Beth's name. He found her number and keyed it in. Her phone rang.

"It must be, Frank. The caller ID is for the call box downstairs," Beth said to Stafford, as she picked up the handset.

"Hello. Can I help you?"

"Beth, this is Frank Hernandez. Is Ben there?"

"Yes, he is, Frank. Do you want me to buzz you in?"

"Yes, hurry, and tell Ben that Nelson is in the building. I just saw him." Frank heard Beth repeating what he had said.

"BETH! BUZZ ME IN!" Hernandez yelled at the speaker.

"Oh my, yes, sorry," Beth said. The door buzzed and Frank snatched it open and ran inside. He ran to where he had seen Nelson go into a stairway.

Stafford was on his feet, thinking of his options. He could stay where he was and make Nelson come to him. Doing that would leave Hernandez to face Nelson alone. He could go out and look for Nelson. Doing that would leave Beth by herself, and he might miss Nelson. His parents might arrive at any minute. He made a decision.

"Beth, call 9-1-1 and tell them two Federal agents need assistance. I'm going out to help Frank. Don't go outside, and don't let my parents in if they buzz from downstairs. You got all that?"

"I've got it." She picked up the phone and pressed 9-1-1.

Stafford went to the door and looked through the peephole. He didn't see anybody, and opened the door. He stuck his head out and looked both ways. He didn't see or hear anyone. He went out and shut the door, making sure it was locked. He heard Beth throw the deadbolt.

He headed away from the nearest stairway, and went to the farthest stairway at the end of the hall. He figured Nelson might try an indirect approach. He heard a noise at the other end of the hall, and ducked around the corner. He heard a door slam shut. He stayed out of sight for a few seconds, and then peered carefully around the corner. He saw someone walking toward him carrying grocery bags. The man was too far away to recognize. He ducked back behind cover, unsure of who was coming. The grocery bags had misled him. He heard the stairway door open and slam shut.

"NELSON! HOLD IT RIGHT THERE!" Hernandez shouted from the doorway.

Stafford heard the shouting, then someone running, and stepped around the corner into the hall. In an instant, he sized up the situation. Nelson was at about 40 yards away, he had dropped the groceries on the floor, and was running in Stafford's direction. Hernandez was not near Nelson. He was another 20 yards behind him. Because of his injured foot, there was no way Hernandez would catch Nelson. Stafford moved into position, preparing himself for the confrontation. Nelson saw Stafford and stopped. He turned around, and ran full speed at Hernandez. Stafford started running after him, He saw Nelson reach in his waistband, and pull out something shiny.

Hernandez saw Nelson coming at him, and stopped to prepare himself. He saw Nelson take something from his waistband. It was long, thin, and shiny. It was a knife. Hernandez was about to reach for his gun, but remembered what Stafford had told him. There wouldn't be enough time to draw and fire.

"FRANK... KNIFE," Stafford yelled as he ran after Nelson, reaching for his own weapon.

The empty feeling in Stafford's hand reminded him he had left his pistol in Beth's apartment. He felt sick. Frank was going to die, because he forgotten to put his pistol on.

Nelson quickly closed the gap to Hernandez. Stafford was closing on Nelson, but wasn't going to catch up to him before he got to Hernandez. Stafford was preparing to attack like a wild animal.

When Nelson reached Hernandez, he lunged with the knife in his right hand. Hernandez stepped to his left and grabbed Nelson's right wrist as Nelson's momentum carried him past. As Nelson passed him, Hernandez turned right and planted his left shoulder into Nelson's right shoulder, pushing him into the wall. He kept pressing and wrapped his left arm over the top of Nelson's right. He leaned quickly forward, still pressing against Nelson, which forced them both to bend at the waist and go to the floor. Nelson was still struggling to control the knife. Hernandez pushed and lifted, as Stafford had told him to do, until he heard a popping sound. Nelson released the knife, and began screaming with every breath. Hernandez grabbed the knife and got to his feet as Stafford got to them.

"Are you okay? Did he cut you?" Stafford asked.

"No, I'm okay. I'm fine." Hernandez looked himself over, and felt his arms and stomach, making sure he wasn't cut or stabbed. There was no blood.

Nelson's screams turned to grunts. He tried to push off the floor with his good arm to get his legs underneath him. Hernandez put his foot on Nelson's butt, and shoved. Nelson hit the floor with his chest and face, and let go a loud string of profanity.

"Just stay down. You're under arrest," Hernandez said.

Hernandez bent over the cursing and grunting Nelson and searched him for more weapons. After he rolled Nelson over onto his back, he cuffed his wrists together in front of him, eliciting another volley of curses. Over the cursing, they heard police sirens getting louder and louder, and then stop. Stafford looked knowingly at Hernandez. He had done this part before.

"I'll go down and meet the police. You stay with him," Stafford said. "And by the way, that was an excellent take-down. I wish I had filmed it. Textbook man..., textbook."

"Thanks. A friend taught me how to do that." Hernandez grinned. His grin slowly turned into a grimace. "My toe hurts. I think he stepped on it."

Stafford nodded and was about to go knock on Beth's door, when he heard a door open. He looked around and saw her, and a half dozen other people, standing in the hallway. A couple of people were pointing cell phones at him, making videos. Stafford gave Beth a thumbs up. She nodded, but was frowning at the moaning man on the floor.

"It's okay everyone, we're Federal Agents. Everything is under control," he said. As he walked away to the stairs he said, "be good, Frank. You're on camera."

Stafford took out his credentials and went down the stairs and into the entrance hall. He saw three police officers standing outside the main entry door, with hands on their pistols. He slowly walked to them, keeping his hands in front of him, holding his credentials. He pushed the door open.

"Couldn't get in, huh? We've got great security here. Everybody gets in except the police." They all entered, and one of the officers physically pushed him back.

"Take it easy, fellas. I'm ICE Agent Ben Stafford. We called for back-up. My partner has captured a wanted person upstairs. The perp's hurt, and will be needing an ambulance," he said. One of the officers looked at his credentials.

"Show us," the closest police officer said. Stafford led them upstairs, as one of the officers called for an ambulance on his radio.

After verifying the identity of everyone involved, the police officers and EMT's took Nelson to the ambulance, just as Stafford's parents arrived at the entrance door. Beth buzzed them in, and Dan and Marie came to Beth's floor. They couldn't get through the crowd of police officers and tenants.

Hernandez reported the incident to the DHS communications center, and within 20 minutes, he was leaving with other HSI agents, who were also going to the hospital to take custody of Nelson.

"Well, I enjoyed it, "Hernandez said to Beth and Stafford as he left. "We need to do this again real soon."

As Stafford stepped into the hall to see Hernandez off, he saw his parents coming down the hall, and went to meet them.

"Son, what in tarnation has been going on here? What's with all the cops?" Dan asked. Ben hung his head.

"Mom, Dad, as you can see, we've had a little excitement here. Anyway, I'd like to introduce you to Agent Frank Hernandez. Frank, these are my parents, Marie and Dan Stafford. Frank is not going to be able to stay."

"Nice to meet you both. Ben has told me a lot about you." Hernandez shook both of their hands. "I'm sorry, but I really have to go. It was a pleasure to meet you. Talk to you later, Ben, Beth." Frank hurried out, limping to catch up with the other agents.

"Son, what were all the police doing here? Did somebody try to kill you again?" Marie said.

"Frank captured a bad guy before he had a chance to do anything to anyone. Come inside and I'll tell ya'll about it."

Ben didn't leave Beth's apartment until after 11 PM. It took him that long to get his mother calmed down. His dad was okay with what had happened. Beth seemed okay too, except she knew what might have happened if Nelson had gotten inside her apartment. As Ben and his parents were leaving, she gave him a long hug in front of his parents. They were happy to see he had a woman to soften his roughness. Ben was glad too, but tried not to let it show. He didn't fool his parents.

Ben escorted them back to their hotel to say good bye. After seeing them to their room, he splurged and took a taxi to his apartment, reminding himself he could afford it now with his new promotion.

*   *   *   *

The Chevy pulled into the garage and stopped. A man with short hair got out carrying bags of groceries. He slammed the car door, pressed the remote control to close the garage door, and went in to the house. He dropped the bags on the table and went into the living room, where two other men were waiting for him.

"General, you're not going to like what I saw at the grocery store. A sheriff's deputy was putting up a poster with your picture on it. The cashier told me the FBI thinks you're in the vicinity. This might be a good time to go to the safe house in Missouri. I don't think the authorities will be expecting you to turn up there." General Miner sat tapping his fingers on the arms of the chair.

"You may be right. More distance may be needed," Miner said. "We have obviously stayed too long already. Call and arrange for the plane to pick us up here tomorrow. Tell the pilot to arrange his arrival and departure so we'll arrive in Missouri at peak air traffic time. We'll blend in with the other private aircraft arrivals."

"Yes, sir. I'll call right now." The driver took out his cellphone.

Miner was about to slip away again.

Chapter 60

Stafford awoke at his usual time, but could have used more sleep. He sat up on his mat, wrapped his arms around his knees, and blinked away the fog of sleep. He thought about yesterday's capture of Nelson. He felt good about Hernandez using the disarming technique he taught him. Hernandez probably saved his own life. He felt stupid for leaving his pistol in Beth's apartment when he went out to help, and made a promise to never be that stupid again. He glanced at the floor, making sure the pistol was still where he had put it last night; it was. He chuckled to himself.

"Okay hero, time to earn your money." He struggled to his feet and stumbled into the kitchen. Remembering yesterday's breakfast of cereal and water, he decided to eat at the fast food place near the Metro station again.

He showered, dressed, and headed to the Metro. It was misting rain, and he didn't have an umbrella. He thought umbrellas were for sissies, unless it was pouring and he had a long way to go. He got to the breakfast place before he was too wet. He ordered, got his breakfast sandwich and coffee, and sat down.

As he ate, he thought about all he had done in the previous week. He had done quite a lot, and wondered when his life would ever return to normal, although his normal would have forced the average person into psychotherapy.

He thought about Beth, and Frank, and his parents. He knew that there was nothing more important than relationships. He longed for a loving one with a good woman, and he hoped Beth was the woman. He remembered her words to him, about them being a couple, and he was happy in the memory.

He finished eating, rinsed his mouth out by swishing hot coffee around in it, and tossed his trash in the receptacle. He was full, satisfied, and immediately wished he hadn't eaten the sausage and egg biscuits with gravy. He knew he had gotten a day's serving of sodium, fat, and cholesterol, but it tasted good.

Nobody lives forever. Might as well die fat and happy.

He found his seat on the Metro, and closed his eyes to ignore the other worker bees on the train. He counted the stops and listened to the station announcements. He opened his eyes again as the train arrived at his stop. When he stood up to leave, he was looking in Frank Hernandez' face.

"Morning, boss. Long night?" Hernandez said.

"Oh, hey man. Yeah, kind of late." They left the station, and walked out into the morning grayness.

"My mom was freaked out by all the goings on yesterday. All the excitement, on top of what she learned about me at the White House. She worries about me. I guess if there are any regrets in my life, it would be what I've put my mother through. How'd your wife take the news that you captured Nelson?"

"She realizes it's part of the job, but she sort of freaked out too. I know she would prefer me to be a paper shuffler in a quiet office somewhere. She thought that was what I was doing here, until you roped me into going to El Paso so I could get kidnapped."

"I'm sorry about that, but I'm telling you Frank, you're on the fast track from now on. People in the right places know your name. If there's a job you really want, go for it. You can't miss."

"One could say the same about you, hot shot. Lunch with the president, no less. Everyone will be talking about it. What's on your agenda today? Meeting the Secretary of State? Addressing the United Nations? Finding a cure for cancer?" Hernandez laughed like he was joking, but there was enough truth behind his words that Stafford felt the cut.

"How's the foot, Frank? A little sore from yesterday?" Hernandez looked at Stafford as they walked. He read Ben's words correctly, and changed the subject.

"My foot's fine. It hurt like crazy last night, but I took a pain pill. It doesn't hurt much unless I spend too much time on my feet. How are you? Are you dealing with the shootout and the bombing?"

"I'm doing okay. I try not to think about it. I know it happened, but I pretend it didn't."

"That can't be good for you, Ben."

"Probably not, but it works."

Stafford immediately thought about the death of his father in the woods. It bubbled up, and he swallowed it down again. Hernandez was thinking about the same thing, but didn't mention it.

"I'm going on a little field trip to Maryland today. The Commissioner wants me to follow up on some ideas I gave him on Friday. He's sending me and another agent out to hunt for Miner. Want to come along?"

Hernandez knew it meant trouble, because he knew Stafford was going to find something. He wanted no part of it, and yet he did.

"Sure, I'll tag along. Beats sitting in the office all day."

"That a boy, Frank. That's the spirit. You know, when I become Emperor of the World, I'm going to make you my personal assistant."

"What will my job be, carrying your scepter?"

"No, your job will be to go ahead of me and make sure all the doorways are big enough for my head to get through." Stafford laughed.

"Oh, I see, so I'll also be carrying the imperial chain saw." Hernandez was smiling, and Stafford was laughing again.

They calmed down and made it into the Reagan building, riding the elevator up together. Stafford got off on his floor.

"I'll call you later and let you know if you can come with us," Stafford said.

"Okay, your highness." Hernandez was smiling again. Stafford waved him off and smirked as the doors closed.

Stafford was not surprised to see another note taped to his computer monitor, telling him the Commissioner wanted to see him. He checked in with Boyer, letting him know where he would be, and headed upstairs.

Stafford was shown directly into the Commissioner's office. He was a familiar face on that floor now. As he entered, he saw a man sitting in front of Gomez' desk. He recognized him.

"Good morning, Agent Stafford," Sam Person said, extending his hand. Stafford shook his hand.

"Good morning, Sam..., Sir."

"I take it you two know each other. How is that?" Gomez said.

"He eats lunch downstairs sometimes, and sits at my table occasionally," Stafford said, trying not to give too much information.

"Is that right? Well, then you two don't need the usual coddling to be able to work together. Hit the road and go find Miner."

"Sir, I'd like to invite Agent Hernandez to come with us. He has a dog in this fight, so to speak," Stafford said.

Gomez thought about it for a few seconds, rubbing his chin. He looked at Person.

"It's okay with me, sir. We might need an extra hand if we get lucky."

"Okay. Tell him to notify his supervisor. Be sure you have body armor. *Now* go find that guy," Gomez said.

"Yes, sir," Stafford and Person said together.

They walked out and Stafford called Hernandez' cellphone to tell him where to meet them, and what to bring. Person went to the garage to wait for them, and Stafford stopped at his office to get his body armor. When Stafford got off the elevator in the garage, Hernandez and Person were sitting in the front seats of Person's FBI sedan.

Person's vehicle didn't look like a government issued car, unless you saw the microphone hanging under the dash over the transmission hump. Stafford walked to the rear of the car and Person popped the trunk, allowing him to toss in his body armor. He wanted to claim the passenger seat, but didn't say anything. He opened the rear door, got in, and buckled his seatbelt.

"Off to Maryland, my good man, and don't spare the horses," Stafford said. Person and Hernandez exchanged looks. Stafford saw it, but didn't care.

"Where are we going *exactly*? I've got a GPS. I'll plug it in and we won't have to guess," Person said.

Stafford unbuckled and sat forward, looking sideways at Person.

"We're going to Indian Head, Maryland, and then to La Plata, Maryland. Some of your FBI brothers should have been looking around there already. I assume they were not successful. Did they make a record of where they went and who they talked to? Are you aware of anything unusual they might have found?"

"Of course they made a record," Person said, tapping his lap top. I have all their contacts down there. They didn't find anything unusual."

"If you've got all that on your laptop, why did you ask me where we were going?" Stafford said. Person looked in the mirror and shrugged.

"If we're going to be playing games trying to figure out which one of us is smarter, I'll get out of the car right now. We don't have time to let you figure out how much I know about what Senator Bacster told you. You should have been willing to share the information anyway. Don't forget we're on the same team. If we find Miner you can have all the glory. Now, can we get moving?" Person didn't say a word. He punched in the destination and left the garage, heading east toward Maryland.

Chapter 61

It was an hour long drive into Maryland. Hernandez made small talk with Person, and Stafford fumed in the backseat. He closed his eyes and catnapped for 20 minutes, tuning out the conversation from the front seat.

Was there ever a time when people weren't self-serving? Did it take a life or death situation to snap people out of it?

Stafford thought about the people who were missionaries to Africa. They lived a Spartan existence, some for their entire lives. They were unselfish, God fearing people who gave their all, every day. He felt they were better than he could ever be, and wondered how a person gets to that point in their life.

"Hey, wake up back there," Person said.

"Are we there yet, daddy?" Stafford said.

Stafford opened his eyes and looked around. His eyes had been shut for so long the sunlight made them water. He unbuckled his seat-belt, moved to the middle of the back seat, and let his chest rest on the back of the front seats as he stuck his face between Person and Hernandez.

"Why don't you crack open that lap-top and take a look at where your agents have already been, and who they've already talked to, so we can plan where to start."

"I've already done that. I've personally talked to several of the agents who were assigned to canvas there. They said it was a wild goose chase," Person said.

"Who did they talk to down there, the sheriff?" Stafford said. Person didn't answer immediately. Stafford read the silence correctly.

"Great. So they asked the sheriff if he had seen anyone suspicious, and he said no, so they had lunch, drove around for a couple of hours expecting Miner to leap out from behind a tree, and went home.., right?"

"They talked to sheriffs from two different counties. Neither had anything pertinent to report," Person said.

Stafford hung his head. He wanted to scream. He calmed himself by reminding himself why he was there; to find Miner.

"All right," Stafford said. "We'll do this on our own. Punch Pomonkey, Maryland into your GPS, and head there. There's an airport nearby. It can handle small twin engine turbo-prop aircraft. I'm betting Miner's safe house is somewhere close by, and that airport is his way out if anyone comes snooping around."

Person punched in the destination and settled back in his seat. He only wanted to get this day over with, so he could report it as a waste of time.

They arrived in Pomonkey, and Person slowed the car to 30 miles per hour. The place was so small they would be leaving the area if they didn't stop soon.

Stafford spotted a convenience store. "Stop at that store right there." Stafford pointed on Person's left. Person pulled in and parked.

Stafford got out and started for the door. Hernandez and Person showed no signs of getting out. He stopped at the driver's side of the car, and bent to look inside.

"You coming in?"

Person smiled at him. Hernandez shook his head. Hernandez saw Stafford nod at him to come. He made a face and got out of the car.

They went inside the store and spoke to the clerk, who was also the manager, about any unusual people that might have come in over the last week. The manager said no one unusual had come in. They got back in the car and drove on.

Stafford asked Person to stop at small stores and gas stations three more times. Each time they stopped, Person stayed in the car, while Hernandez and Stafford went inside to ask questions. After the third stop, Person started sighing and fidgeting when they got back in the car.

"How much time are we going to waste doing this? What is it you two are looking for anyway?" Person said.

Stafford calmly answered, speaking carefully. He tried not to let the sarcasm come out. "I expected your agents to canvas the area and talk to the people who live here. Since they didn't do that, and we don't have the time to canvas the entire area on our own, I think our best bet is to concentrate on common traits. They have vehicles, so they need gas. They have to eat, so they need food. People in small towns see the same people all the time, and they're more apt to notice something out of the ordinary. That's why we're stopping at these gas and grub stores. Now let's go find another one. The manager said there was one more place that sells food around here. It's not far ahead on the right."

Person made a face and started the car. Hernandez looked resigned as well. They drove about a mile farther, and Person pulled into the parking lot without being directed. He turned off the ignition and put his elbow on the door, resting his head on his hand. Hernandez crossed his arms over his chest.

Stafford got out and walked to the door. He stopped at the entrance and looked at a poster in the window. It was printed on regular white copy paper and taped to the inside. The poster was a picture of General Miner. Beneath the photo it said 'Have You Seen This Man?' and had the name of the sheriff and a phone number. Stafford walked inside and went to the counter. There was a middle aged man behind the cash register. His name tag said 'Ernie.' There was no one else in the store.

"Excuse me, Ernie. I'm Agent Stafford... Department of Homeland Security." He showed Ernie his credentials. Ernie took them and studied them like he might be tested on it later. He gave the credentials back to Stafford.

"How'd you know my name?" He squinted his eyes, looking at Stafford suspiciously.

"Your name tag," Stafford said, pointing at the tag.

"So?"

Stafford took a breath. "So, I'd like to ask you some questions, if you don't mind."

"I do mind, but go ahead and ask your questions, mister tax man."

"I'm not with the Internal Revenue Service. I'm an Agent with the Department of Homeland Security."

"It's all the same. Tax man came around here asking a lot of questions. Said I wasn't reporting all my income. Said he'd take my store away if I didn't pay back taxes."

"I'm not with the IRS, Ernie. I want to ask you about that poster in the window. Did you know there's a cash reward for information leading to the arrest of the man on the poster?"

"A cash reward? How big a cash reward?"

"Big enough you wouldn't have to worry about any more questions from the IRS," Stafford said. Ernie rubbed his stubbly chin whiskers.

"What do you want to know?"

"When did you put that poster up?"

"Yesterday. A sheriff's deputy came by and asked me to stick it up. Said some FBI agents had come by and told them that Miner fellow might be in the area."

Stafford nodded. "And you haven't seen anyone that looks like him come in here for groceries or gas?"

"Course not. If I had a seen them, I'd have called the Sheriff."

"Have you noticed anybody coming in to buy groceries that had a military haircut? They would have been someone you hadn't seen before last week. They probably bought enough food for three or four people. You see anybody like that come in?" Stafford said.

Ernie rubbed his stubble again, thinking. "Now that you put it that way, there's this guy that started coming in last week. Looks like he's in the Marines. Got his hair all cut off. Comes in every day. Always comes in the morning and buys food for three or four people. Mostly coffee, sandwiches, french fries, and stuff like that. Ain't been in this morning yet. He's late. Drives a big dark blue Chevy SUV. Thing's as big as a bus." Ernie chuckled.

"You wouldn't happen to know where he lives, do you?"

"Don't know for sure, but he always comes out from that road right there." Ernie pointed past the gas pumps. Stafford followed Ernie's finger and saw a stop sign across the highway from the store.

"There ain't but four or five houses down that way. Shouldn't be hard to find," Ernie said.

"Thanks for the information, Ernie. Here's my card. Write your phone number down on the back, and I'll let you know if we find him."

Ernie took the card, wrote his number carefully, and handed it back to Stafford, who tucked it in his wallet.

"You take care now. You go find that fella and make me rich." Ernie said, grinning from ear to ear. He picked up the telephone and started to dial.

"I'll try..., and Ernie, don't tell anyone about our conversation. I wouldn't want someone talking out of turn and messing up you getting that reward." Ernie stopped smiling and put the phone down.

"Okay.., okay..., not a soul." He pressed his finger to his lips and shushed himself. Stafford smiled, and waved as he left the store.

Stafford went to the car and climbed in the back seat. Person and Hernandez were listening to music on the radio.

"Bingo, boys. I've got us a lead." Hernandez and Person turned around to look at him.

"You've got what?" Person asked.

"The guy in there just told me about someone he hadn't seen before last week. He comes into the store everyday, and buys enough food for three or four people. He has a military haircut and drives a big, blue, Chevy SUV. Comes out of that road across the highway there. He says there are only four or five houses down that way, so it shouldn't be..."

"A big, blue, Chevy SUV like that one?" Hernandez said, pointing.

Person and Stafford craned their necks to see where he was pointing. A blue Chevy SUV turned left and headed south, in the direction of the airport Stafford had seen on the satellite map.

"Follow him. Follow him," Stafford said, slapping Person on the shoulder.

Person had thought this was a waste of time, but it was hard not to get caught up in the excitement.

"Okay. Okay." Person started the car and pulled out onto the road. He was a quarter mile behind the Chevy.

"Not too close. If he turns into the airfield, go past and come back," Stafford said.

"I've done this before you know. Besides, this guy's probably on his way to work at the potato chip factory," Person chuckled. "What would be the odds of stumbling onto Miner by accident?"

"It might be an accident if *you* found him, but not if *I* found him," Stafford said sarcastically.

"I'll bet you a hundred dollars it isn't him," Person said.

"I'll take that bet," Hernandez said. He found he had new-found faith in Stafford.

"You have enough cash to cover both of us?" Stafford said.

"Sure do," Person said. "But I won't be having to part with any of it."

"Well, look at that, he's turning into the airfield. He must have missed the turn for the chip factory" Stafford said. "Go past. Go past."

As they drove past the airfield, a twin engine turbo-prop plane flew over. The plane was landing at the airfield.

"Turn around and go back. Drive in and park behind the main building. See it there to the right of the taxiway?" Stafford asked.

"I see it." Person made a U-turn and drove to the entrance to the airfield. He entered and headed for the office.

The blue Chevy SUV had driven onto the tarmac and stopped in front of other private planes. The plane that landed had gone to the end of the runway, turned around, and was taxiing back toward the Chevy. Person pulled into a parking spot and stopped.

"Did you bring binoculars?" Hernandez asked.

"I've got a pair in the trunk," Person said. He popped the trunk, and they all got out of the car. He found the binoculars and handed them to Hernandez.

The three moved to the corner of the building and watched as the plane taxied to the blue Chevy and stopped. The pilot killed the engines and the doors of the Chevy opened. Three men got out.

Hernandez put the binoculars to his eyes and adjusted the focus. Stafford was anxious to know if his hunch was panning out. He was standing next to Hernandez, holding his hand next to the binoculars, only inches away. He wanted to snatch them away the way a spoiled child would. Hernandez took the binoculars from his eyes, looked at Stafford and smiled. He handed them to Stafford and stepped back.

"It's him," Hernandez said. "How do you want to play it, boss?"

"Are you kidding me?" Person said. Stafford was looking through the binoculars, grinning.

"Read 'em and weep," Stafford said, handing the binoculars to Person.

Person looked through the binoculars, focused, and cursed.

Stafford saw one of the men unlock the door to the aircraft, and lower it. On the inside of the door were steps. A man climbed out and shook hands with the three men waiting on the ground. He was obviously the pilot. He pointed to the main building, and then at the airplane. The pilot and one of the men started walking toward the main building.

"Come on, everybody inside," Stafford said.

"What about vests?" Person asked.

"No time for that," Stafford said.

They went in the back door of the building and made their way to the front. In the waiting area there were two men behind a counter, helping two pilots. Stafford took out his credentials and stepped in front of the men being helped.

"Sorry to butt in, gentlemen. I'm Agent Stafford of the Department of Homeland Security. The men with me are Federal officers. In a moment, two men are going to enter this building. They're wanted for murder, and are probably armed. I need you all to do exactly as I say." Stafford looked out the window and saw the men were almost to the building. In another minute, they would be inside.

"Everyone move to the back of this building..., NOW! Don't go outside. Agent Person, go with them. Make sure they do what I said."

Stafford waited. Nobody moved. Stafford drew his pistol and pointed it at the counter in front of them.

"I said, MOVE!"

A couple of the men put their hands in the air, surrendering, as they hustled toward the back. Person followed them.

"Good luck," Person said to Stafford and Hernandez, as he left the room. Stafford holstered his weapon and went behind the counter.

"Sit down there by the door. Read a magazine or something, but be ready," Stafford said.

Hernandez moved to the couch and sat down on the edge. He picked up a magazine and opened it, his elbows on top of his knees. Ten seconds later the door opened and the two men came in.

"Can I help you, sir?" Stafford said. The pilot had a puzzled look on his face. Stafford didn't look like counter help.

"Where's Jimmy?" the pilot asked. Stafford suspected he was being tested.

"I'm sorry, but this is my first week. What does Jimmy look like?" Stafford said.

The pilot and his escort came closer to Stafford, giving Hernandez a stare as they passed by. Hernandez saw the bulge of handguns under their jackets. They were armed.

Stafford had passed the test.

"Never mind. I need to be topped off on the inboard tanks, and I need catering for four people," the pilot said.

Stafford smiled and looked down at the clipboard on the counter. There was a piece of paper attached to it for pilots to request service. He made eye contact with Hernandez, who rose from his seat and walked to the counter behind the two men. Stafford slid the clipboard over to the pilot. He glanced down at it.

"Where's the men's room, bud?" Hernandez said from behind the two men. They glanced over their shoulders at him, but largely ignored him.

"It's over there past the soda machine," Stafford said pointing. Both men instinctively looked away from Hernandez and followed Stafford's finger pointing at the soda machine.

The pilot looked back at the clipboard. He was reaching for his pen when Stafford struck him hard on the forehead with his open palm. The strike sounded like a wet slap. Hernandez followed Stafford's lead, and before the other man could react, punched him in the back between his shoulder blade and the top of his spine, striking a bundle of nerves under the muscle. Both men dropped like sacks of potatoes. Stafford came around the counter and took the pistol off the pilot, while Hernandez disarmed the other man.

"PERSON, COME OUT HERE AND BRING THE OTHER MEN WITH YOU," Stafford yelled down the hallway.

Stafford looked out the window at the plane. Miner and the other man were carrying bags onto the plane. Person and the others came out to where Stafford was.

One of the employees saw the men lying on the floor. "What happened?" he said, his mouth hanging open.

"Are they dead?" Person asked.

"Nope. Just taking a nap. Cuff them together," Stafford said.

"Do you have any catering trays ready to go out?" Stafford asked, looking at the man he had threatened with his pistol. The man pointed to the food cart near the ice machine. Stafford moved quickly to the cart, grabbed a tray of sandwiches, and headed for the door.

"Grab another one, Frank," Stafford said.

"Person, stay here and call for backup. Don't let anybody leave, especially those two on the floor. If this goes wrong, ram the plane with the car so it can't take off."

Person's mouth fell open. Hernandez grabbed a tray of sandwiches and followed Stafford out the door.

"Oh, Lord," Hernandez said.

Yes, Lord. Protect us. Guide us. Help us.

"Get next to me and walk normally," Stafford said. Hernandez came next to him, matching his step.

"When we get there, follow my lead again. I'll cover Miner, and you watch the other guy. If we have to board the plane, I'll board and you stay outside. Only come on board if I call you by name. Understood?"

"Understood," Hernandez said.

They were now only about 15 steps from the plane. The Chevy had been moved off of the flight line. No one was in sight. Miner and the other man were on the plane. In the distance the faint sound of a siren could be heard. It was the backup Person had called for.

"That was too fast. Here goes nothing," Stafford said.

They had reached the left side of the airplane, where the entry steps were still extended. Through the small windows Stafford could see someone moving inside the plane, coming to the rear door. He stepped on the first step and stopped, holding the tray of sandwiches in front of him.

"Catering is here. Permission to come aboard, sir?" Stafford asked. Hernandez waited a few feet away, holding another tray.

"I'll take it," the man at the door said.

Due to the restricted space inside the plane, he was bent over at the waist. He reached out of the door with both hands, for the tray Stafford was offering. As he reached, Stafford dropped the tray, grabbed him by the wrists, jerked and jumped backward off the step. As the man lurched out of the doorway, Stafford let go of his wrists and turned to one side. The man landed headfirst on the ground in front of Hernandez. Hernandez tossed his food tray away, and dropped one knee onto the back of the man's neck. He pulled the stunned man's arms behind him one at a time, and handcuffed his wrists together.

Miner heard the commotion behind him, and turned around in time to see his assistant falling out of the plane. He looked out of the window and saw him land on the pavement. He saw Hernandez handcuffing him.

Stafford had already entered the plane in a crouch. His pistol was in his right hand, and he was ready to meet any threat. Miner jumped out of his seat and turned back toward the doorway. He saw Stafford's gun pointing at him and froze. They were only five feet apart. Stafford was baring his teeth, ready for a fight. Miner stood perfectly still, waiting for what was going to happen next. Stafford's heart pounded in his chest, the blood rushed to his muscles. He breathed slowly and carefully, waiting for Miner to make a move. Miner stood still.

Stafford's eyes narrowed, and he squeezed the grip of the pistol harder. He thought about Rennie's dead daughter, and the tens of thousands of other sons and daughters who were dead because of Miner. He could hardly believe he was a man at all, in his mind, Miner was a rabid dog.

"Are you going to arrest me?" Miner asked.

Miner still dared not move. Miner didn't like what he saw in Stafford's eyes. He hadn't feared death as a young man, but now he did. He didn't know what death would bring for him. He saw Stafford trying to make up his mind. He knew he was one twitch away from being shot. He didn't want to go to prison, and he didn't want to be executed by lethal injection in front of 50 witnesses. A quick death by the hand of a fellow warrior was preferable.

Miner lunged, reaching for Stafford's gun. Stafford wanted to shoot, but when Miner made his move, he helped make the decision for Stafford. In his heart, Stafford couldn't kill without just cause. In his previous life he could have, but not as the new creation he was. He had been born again, and was of a new heart and mind. But born again or not, he was angry that Miner was responsible for so many deaths.

"Oh, no you don't," Stafford said.

He pulled his pistol back out of Miner's reach. With his left hand, he grabbed Miner by his ear. Miner let out a yell as Stafford yanked and pulled him to the door of the plane. Miner grabbed at Stafford with both hands, yelling in pain as his ear was nearly pulled from his head.

Keeping a grip on Miner's ear, Stafford kept backing up until he had passed the open door. He looked and saw Hernandez, pistol at the ready. Stafford stepped back another foot. Miner was still yelling and grabbing at his arm. He pulled Miner to his right and then pushed back hard to his left, sending Miner backwards out the open door as he let go of his ear.

Miner reached back to break his fall. He was still yelling when his back hit the steps. His feet flew up in the air and he did a backward somersault. He rolled and landed on his side, catching himself with one arm before he hit his head. Stafford rocketed down the steps after him, pistol at the ready.

Two sheriff's cars were coming fast across the tarmac, with emergency lights flashing and sirens screaming. A third sheriff's car stopped at the main building, where Person was still with the two prisoners.

"YES! YES! KILL ME! KILL ME!" Miner yelled, holding his arms out to Stafford, pleading.

Stafford holstered his weapon and looked down at him. "Not a chance, General. Not a chance."

The sheriff's cars came to a stop and two deputies, one from each car, emerged. Hernandez holstered his weapon too, and he and Stafford took out their credentials and held them for the deputies to see.

"FEDERAL OFFICERS," Stafford yelled.

Miner saw the deputies approaching. He scrambled to all fours, and then sprang to his feet, running toward one of them. Stafford went after him.

Seeing the sudden move, the deputy drew something from his holster, pointing it at Miner.

"I'LL KILL YOU. I'LL KILL YOU!" Miner screamed, arms straight out in front of him, reaching for him.

"DON'T SHOOT!" Stafford yelled.

He could see the deputy was about to fire. Stafford slanted to the right, out of the deputy's line of fire, and stopped. The deputy fired.

Stafford saw two darts trailing thin wire hit Miner in the upper torso. Miner immediately fell to the ground, yelling and shaking as the deputy adjusted the voltage.

"STAY DOWN. DON'T RESIST!" The deputy yelled. Miner was on the ground, rolling slowly left and right, grunting loudly.

"But that will work. Thank you, deputy," Stafford said.

"No problem. Glad I could help." He reached down and searched Miner as he pulled the wire darts out and threw them aside.

FBI Agent Sam Person ran full speed across the tarmac from the main building. He arrived at plane-side and looked down at the still moaning Miner, then at Stafford and Hernandez. Person's mouth was hanging open.

"What do you think, Frank? Should we throw him a bone?" Stafford asked.

"He doesn't deserve it, but yeah, why not. I think we've had enough glory and excitement." Hernandez said, smiling and nodding.

"Agent Person, this is General Andrew Jackson Miner. Would you like to officially place him under arrest?" Stafford asked. He held out his handcuffs to Person, since Person's handcuffs were already in use.

Person took the handcuffs and placed them on Miner. As the cuffs were tightened they made a distinctive clicking sound, as they tightened onto Miner's wrists.

"Now *that* is a sweet sound," Stafford said.

Chapter 62

Tuesday morning came sooner than Stafford liked, but he was glad he was on time for this. He and Beth were in the empty conference room again. She was holding his face in her hands. She kissed him lightly on the lips.

"Congratulations. I'm proud of you. For capturing Nelson, and for capturing Miner," she said. Stafford thought he could grow accustomed to being babied by her.

"Frank captured Nelson, and Person captured Miner," Stafford protested.

"We all know the score, Ben. When the dust settles, you're going to have your choice of jobs and locations. Have you thought about where you want to go? What you want to do?"

"Not yet. But wherever I go, and whatever I'm doing, I want *you* there."

Beth's eyes went wide and she stepped back, her mouth in a smile of disbelief. Stafford saw the look of surprise, and did some verbal backpedaling.

"That wasn't a proposal, it was only an invitation. I'd like to have you around. I want to get to know you better. Wherever I go, will you go with me?"

"Oh..., well." Beth was blushing. "Not a proposal, huh? Well, as long as they've got real tablecloths where you're going. I guess I'd like to get to know you better too." She smacked his chest hard with her open hand.

"Now get upstairs and see the Commissioner!" She marched out and down the hallway, away from the elevator. He knew she had to use the elevator to go back to her office. He wondered where she was going.

Apparently, anywhere he wasn't was good enough for her at the moment. He shook his head.

"I'll take that as a yes. You want to come along..., right?"

"Right," she said over her shoulder, waving good bye as she continued walking.

Women.

He rode the elevator to the Commissioner's office scratching his head, and rubbing his chest where she had smacked him. He thought about what she said. He knew where he wanted to be, what he wanted to be, and who he wanted to be with. He wanted to be far away from headquarters. Gomez was waiting for him when the elevator doors opened.

"I'm sorry I'm late, sir. I was unavoidably detained downstairs." Gomez shook his hand.

"I'll bet. How many hands did you shake this morning?"

"I've lost count, sir. Hundreds maybe."

"Now it's a hundred and one. Come into my office." Stafford followed Gomez into his office and sat down after Gomez did.

"Needless to say, after capturing Miner yesterday, DHS looks pretty good. We're mentioned on the front page of every newspaper in the country, and the DHS Secretary is doing interviews all morning with the major television networks. Too bad we didn't get Roja too."

"Sir, we can get Roja anytime we want. All it takes is ten million dollars. Didn't you read my report?"

"I must have missed that little tidbit. We may do that, as soon as we figure out whose budget to take it out of." He laughed. "So we have him too if we want him. That's amazing. Well, anyway, Secretary Romano called me this morning and said the president had called him to ask if you had anything to do with Miner's capture, which begs me to ask... why, oh why..., did you let Person arrest Miner?"

"It seemed like the thing to do, sir. You put me with him. I thought you wanted it that way, to let them have some of the glory. Besides, the FBI knows who got him there."

"Yeah, well, it was only a little inter-agency cooperation I had in mind, but that's water under the bridge now," Gomez said.

"Sorry, sir," Stafford said. Gomez waved his hand, as he tossed the apology to the side.

"May I ask, sir, what's going to happen to Senator Bacster?"

"He's going to be prosecuted of course. He's cooperating with the investigation, but he's going to serve a lot of time anyway. He was in it pretty deep," Gomez said.

"What about the man he killed in his kitchen?"

"Bacster did the taxpayers a favor on that one. The guy was a contract killer. The FBI has been looking for him for five years. He responsible for over a dozen murders. Bacster shouldn't have killed him in cold blood. Murder is murder," Gomez said.

"What was supposed to happen that caused our terror alert level to be raised? Nothing happened?" Stafford asked.

"I'm glad we dodged that bullet. Remember the ambulance full of explosives the FBI found at Miner's hideout?"

"Yes, sir."

"One of Miner's people told us it was supposed to be detonated during lunchtime on 10th street, between the IRS and Justice Department buildings. I hate to think of what could have have happened. When we made the public announcement exposing the existence of Miner's group, the men assigned to do it, didn't go through with it... probably left town."

"They were going to blame the bombing on Al Qaida?" Stafford asked.

"Evidently. To show the people the incompetency of their government, and to strike a blow at the heart of the great Satan, no doubt. I suppose Miner thought because nobody likes the IRS anyway, blowing them up wouldn't upset too many Americans, and blowing up the Justice building might slow down the people who were looking for him. Personally I think the opposite would have happened. No American could stomach someone setting of bombs in Washington," Gomez said.

"Back to what I was telling you about before..., the Secretary also told me the President called and reminded him that he liked you, and wanted him to be sure to take good care of you. So before I put my head together with the Director of ICE, I want to know what you want." Gomez let the words hang in the air for a few seconds. "You can take some time, and get back to me."

"I don't have to think about it, sir. I want some peace and quiet. I want to be somewhere beautiful, where nothing much happens, and no one is trying to kill me."

"I think we can arrange that. Anything else?" Gomez smiled.

"Yes, sir. Wherever I go, I want Beth St. James and Frank Hernandez to come with me..., if they want to."

"I think that could be arranged too. Have you heard of the Container Security Initiative? There are some pretty nice places to go... Gothenburg, Sweden for example."

"Sweden sounds good, sir. I'll take it, but I don't speak a word of Swedish."

"Consider it done. And don't worry, the Swedes speak better English than you do. St. James is already in CSI. If she wants to follow you to Gothenburg, it would be pretty simple. Transferring Hernandez to Sweden is another matter. Gothenburg is a small port, and there's no need for two agents there. I'll see if I can pull a few more strings in that regard."

"Thank you very much, sir. When can I leave?"

"Probably after Miner's trial. You may have to testify. I imagine the government is going to ask for the death penalty. Considering all he's done, I think the trial will be over quickly. I bet you'll be out of here in less than six months." Gomez stood up, and Stafford stood as well.

"Stafford..., Ben..., I can't tell you how glad I am that I chose you for the investigation in El Paso. You were the right man, in the right place, at the right time. You exceeded all my expectations, and made us all look good in the process. Thank God for men like you." Gomez stuck out his hand. Stafford shook it, and turned to go.

"Maybe I'll come see you in Sweden," Gomez said. "For now, take the rest of today off... you deserve it."

"You can come see me anytime, sir. Thanks again."

Stafford didn't want any more attention today. He went by Boyer's office to tell him he was leaving, and left without talking to anyone else, not even Beth. He walked outside and looked at the sky. He squinted. Thin clouds softened the sun's rays.

As he headed for the Metro, and home, his cellphone rang. He flipped it open and looked at the number calling. He recognized the area code, but not the number.

"Stafford."

"Ben, this is Rennie. How ya doing, buddy?"

"Hey, Rennie. I'm fine. It's good to hear your voice. How did you get my number?"

"From your dad. I heard that General Miner has been captured, and I had to talk to you. The national news said the FBI captured him, but it was you, wasn't it?"

"Well, I don't want to contradict what the national news said. Let's just say I was there, okay?"

"I knew it was you. I want to thank you for catching the man responsible... responsible for poisoning my baby." Rennie's voice changed, and Stafford knew he was crying.

"You're welcome, Rennie. I'm glad I was able to do it."

"You're the man, Ben. God bless you. Just like you used to tell me when we were young, you're the Emperor of the World."